The Grit and the Grind

The Grit and the Grind

Building High-Performing Education Systems in an Era of Polarization

JOSHUA L. GLAZER, CORI EGAN,
WILLIAM R. BERRY, AND AMAR FATTAL

THE UNIVERSITY OF CHICAGO PRESS   CHICAGO AND LONDON

The University of Chicago Press, Chicago 60637
The University of Chicago Press, Ltd., London

Published 2026
Printed in the United States of America

35 34 33 32 31 30 29 28 27 26   1 2 3 4 5

ISBN-13: 978-0-226-85261-4 (cloth)
ISBN-13: 978-0-226-85263-8 (paper)
ISBN-13: 978-0-226-85262-1 (ebook)
DOI: https://doi.org/10.7208/chicago/9780226852621.001.0001

Library of Congress Cataloging-in-Publication Data

Names: Glazer, Joshua L., author. | Egan, Cori, author. | Berry, William (Educational policy expert), author. | Fattal, Amar, author.
Title: The grit and the grind : building high-performing education systems in an era of polarization / Joshua L. Glazer, Cori Egan, William Berry, and Amar Fattal.
Other titles: Building high-performing education systems in an era of polarization
Description: Chicago ; London : The University of Chicago Press, 2026. | Includes bibliographical references and index.
Identifiers: LCCN 2026010574 | ISBN 9780226852614 (cloth) | ISBN 9780226852638 (paperback) | ISBN 9780226852621 (ebook)
Subjects: LCSH: School improvement programs—Tennessee—Memphis. | School improvement programs—United States—Case studies. | School management and organization—United States—Case studies. | School management and organization—Tennessee—Memphis. | Urban schools—Tennessee—Memphis. | Educational change—United States.
Classification: LCC LB2822.83.T2 G53 2026
LC record available at https://lccn.loc.gov/2026010574

♾ This paper meets the requirements of ANSI/NISO Z39.48-1992 (Permanence of Paper).

Authorized Representative for EU General Product Safety Regulation (GPSR) queries: **Easy Access System Europe**—Mustamäe tee 50, 10621 Tallinn, Estonia, gpsr.requests@easproject.com
Any other queries: https://press.uchicago.edu/press/contact.html

Contents

Abbreviations

AP	Advanced Placement
ASD	Achievement School District
CCSS	Common Core State Standards
CMO	charter management organization
CSR	Comprehensive School Reform
ELA	English language arts
IB	International Baccalaureate
ILD	Instructional Leadership Director
ILT	Instructional Leadership Team
IPG	iZone's classroom observation rubric
IST	Instructional Support Team
iZone	Innovation Zone
MCS	Memphis City Schools
MLK	Martin Luther King Jr. College Preparatory High School
NAACP	National Association for the Advancement of Colored People
NCLB	No Child Left Behind
NEA	National Education Association
PARCC	Partnership for Assessment of Readiness for College and Careers
PD	professional development (used in the context of teacher training)
RSD	Recovery School District
RTTT	Race to the Top
SCS	Shelby County Schools
SIG	School Improvement Grant

SPED	special education
TCAP	Tennessee Comprehensive Assessment Program
TDoE	Tennessee Department of Education
TEA	Tennessee Education Association
TFA	Teach for America

Preface

On a winter day in late 2014, I (Joshua Glazer) sat in a modern office suite overlooking South Main Street in downtown Memphis, along with several educational officials who had assembled to discuss an initiative to improve more than twenty of Tennessee's lowest-performing schools. The initiative was actually a newly formed state agency called the Achievement School District or, as most people referred to it, the ASD. The ASD's core strategy was to remove the state's most struggling schools from their home districts and convert them into charter schools that would then be managed by independent operators, most of which were charter management organizations (CMOs). The state's chief research and strategy officer, Nate Schwartz, had contacted me eighteen months earlier to discuss a possible evaluation of the ASD. He was intrigued by the ASD's underlying strategy and hoped that, beyond the typical "Did it work?" questions, my team could address more complex issues about the ways in which the ASD was both working and not working, why, and what might be learned from the experience.

As Nate told me about the ASD during our first phone call, my initial thought was that it resembled the Louisiana Recovery School District, which had become famous (or infamous, depending on your perspective) in education circles for its role in the transformation of public education in New Orleans after Hurricane Katrina. Like the Recovery School District, the ASD was a state entity with the authority to remove schools from their local districts and, in doing so, establish a new state-operated system. Also similar to the Recovery School District, the improvement strategy relied heavily on a "market-based logic" with a central role for charter schools. While the state was assuming responsibility for the schools that it took over, the actual work of hiring principals and teachers, selecting curriculum, and running the schools would be delegated to charter organizations.

But the more I listened, the more it became clear that the ASD differed in several ways from its New Orleans counterpart. One was that the ASD was not a substitute for the traditional district but a new entity that would operate alongside it. In Memphis, where most ASD schools were located, the district was not only alive and well but also the primary operator of local schools. A second important difference was that, unlike in New Orleans, the vast majority of ASD students would continue to attend their neighborhood schools. This was crucial because while ASD schools would be run by nonprofit organizations (mainly charters) that would bring new principals, new teachers, and a new philosophy, one thing that would not change was the students. Unlike typical charter schools, students would attend an ASD school not because they had made a deliberate choice or were attracted to its particular brand of schooling but because it was their neighborhood school. Reflecting on those early conversations, it is clear why Nate envisioned an intriguing research opportunity.

But sitting in that downtown office on that winter day, my questions were largely motivated by my background in the design of instructional systems and the challenge of engineering change in schools. We had already spent a year interviewing the top staff of six organizations that were running ASD schools, querying them about their vision for teaching and learning, approach to curriculum, ideas about the organization of schools, and strategies for building professional capacity. These are important topics for anyone interested in school improvement, and much of this book is informed by what we learned from those conversations. But so intense was our focus on system design that we failed to register the significance of other events transpiring in the city that seemingly had little connection to issues of teaching and learning. We were aware that the ASD had become increasingly unpopular in Memphis and that there were determined protests against its takeover of local schools. But we thought of our study as more about instructional design than politics, so these issues appeared peripheral to the system we thought we were studying.

We were mistaken. What soon became evident was not only that the protests were rooted in the political and educational history of the region but also that this history and the dynamics it spawned were inextricably tied to the work of building high-performing instructional systems. The political dynamics surrounding the ASD, in other words, turned out to be as central to its improvement agenda as the curricular and pedagogical issues that had been the focus of our inquiry.

Over the next year, Cori and Josh interviewed dozens of leaders of local organizations, school board members, local politicians, parent groups, and members of the local district. We also attended a slew of community meetings and information sessions, querying residents about their ties to local schools and their feelings about the ASD. We complemented that work with an in-depth study of Memphis's history, both as it relates to education and more generally. As many readers surely know, it is a history marred by one of the country's most pernicious systems of Jim Crow, prolonged legal battles over desegregation, wide-scale White flight, and staggering levels of poverty. While this is not the full story of Memphis, it is a part that profoundly shapes any effort to improve its schools.

It was during this time that we became increasingly curious about Shelby County's effort to use newly available federal funds to counter the ASD with its own reform program. The Innovation Zone, or iZone, as it was called, was an enclave within the larger district that would eventually encompass twenty-five schools that, like those in the ASD, had been ranked in the bottom 5 percent of the state (what the state called *priority schools*). At first blush, the iZone lacked many of the bells and whistles that had attracted so much attention to the ASD. There was no change in governance, no charters or other organizations bringing in new ideas, and no influx of private money. The big bet behind the iZone was that the same people working within the same district under the authority of the same school board could somehow chart a new course forward.

As unremarkable as the iZone looked from the outside, a conversation with Bradley Leon and Dr. Sharon Griffin, the district officials in charge of the iZone, left us wondering whether in these drab, cluttered district offices there was another educational story unfolding, no less noteworthy than that of the ASD. Leon and Griffin pointed out that the district had deep connections to the local community, and despite what some people thought, it had many experienced and talented educators. A year later, Brad and I would meet over coffee to plan what would turn out to be a three-year study of the Shelby County iZone.

The studies of the ASD and iZone seemingly encompassed the themes of system design and politics. In some publications, we talked about politics, and in others, we considered system design, each with its own questions, theories, and outcomes. Yet the end result was incomplete because what the articles on system design and the articles on politics did not address is how the two intersect. That is, what is the relationship between the professional work of constructing high-performing instructional systems and the political process of assembling a broad coalition of supporters in a context where divisiveness has often had the upper hand over collective action? Put somewhat differently, how can education reform be at once professionally sound and politically viable? These are the questions that the studies of the ASD and iZone raised but didn't answer, and which this book attempts to tackle.

A project of this duration and scope rests on the contributions of a great many individuals—more than we can name here. The scale of data collection, the volumes of transcripts coded, the endless drafting of memos, the reports to funders, and the numerous presentations and publications were the collective work of two talented research teams. Diane Massell was an instrumental partner from day one whose experience, insight, and intelligence shaped the project in countless ways. Her skill in crafting interview protocols is second to none. Laura Groth, Matthew Malone, and Blair Beuche joined the ASD study as inexperienced graduate students and left as seasoned researchers. Their individual case studies of ASD operators formed the empirical core of that study.

The iZone study was supported by an equally talented team. Sarah Lenhoff and Adrian Larbi-Cherif, along with Massell, provided additional expertise and experience. Ashley Ison and Joelle Deleveaux brought a potent combination of intellect, humor, and youth. James Taylor contributed expertise in survey design, and Zachary Millington offered a little bit of everything. Two enterprising and talented high school students, Sabina Chatterji-Len and Daniel Lee, scoured the internet for relevant articles, blogs, and reports. They are all contributors to this book.

None of this research would have happened without the generosity of the Spencer Foundation, the Walton Family Foundation, and the Memphis Education Fund. Michael McPherson, then president of Spencer, provided initial seed funding, and Marc Holley and Drew Jacobs of Walton helped us secure two multiyear grants to fund the ASD and iZone studies. The Memphis Education Fund provided a grant to support the writing of the book. We offer them our sincere thanks.

We are indebted to the countless teachers, principals, and administrators in Shelby County and the ASD who volunteered their time, insights, and collaboration. Chris Barbic opened the doors to the ASD for us, embraced the importance of study, and spoke with remarkable candor. The same is true for Malika Anderson and Margo Roen, both of whom played instrumental roles in the ASD. Stewart Brevard was a scheduling wizard without whom we'd still be waiting for our first meeting. The leaders of ASD operators, despite their long days, always found time to sit for interviews that were uniformly engaging and candid. We offer sincere thanks to Allison Leslie, Katie Kling, and Dr. Nickalous Manning of Aspire; Dr. Bobby White and Kim Clark of Martin Luther King Jr. College Preparatory High School (MLK); and Megan Quaile and Chrystie Edwards of Green Dot. Ash Solar, Marcy Singer-Gabella, Drew Sippel, and Lisa Settle also offered valuable insights.

Numerous officials at the Tennessee Department of Education (TDoE), including Commissioners Kevin Huffman and Dr. Candice McQueen, were generous with their time and support. Erin O'Hara was a trusted ally at the Tennessee Education Research Alliance. Without the initiative and support of Nate Schwartz, there would have been no study and no book.

The countless people we spoke with in the Shelby County School District were equally generous with their time. Superintendent Dorsey Hopson welcomed us with his usual aplomb; Bradley Leon supported the research every step of the way while speaking with unflinching candor and insight. Dr. Sharon Griffin and Dr. Antonio Burt, both extraordinary leaders, carved out time from running the iZone to speak with us on multiple occasions. Other iZone teachers, leaders, coaches, and administrators were equally forthcoming. We thank Dr. Alethea Henry, Raven Hawes, Thelma Perry, Pamela Giles, Lionel Cable, Tonye Smith-McBride, Kymberli Chandler, Dr. Angela Brown, Thomas Rogers, Latasha Harris, Rodney Rowan, Jaron Carson, John Bush, and Mark Neal. Their insights and observations are reflected throughout the pages of this book.

Many colleagues have provided valuable insights and critiques over the course of these studies, helping us to sharpen our analysis and refine our arguments. Gary Henry, Ronald Zimmer, and Lam Pham conducted valuable research into the impact of the ASD and iZone on student learning outcomes, as well as several other salient analyses. Their findings can be found throughout this book and help to inform its argument. Rip Correnti and Mary K. Stein developed the instructional survey that allowed us to identify patterns of instruction across the iZone and helped us interpret the results. Clarence Stone read drafts of our political analysis, helped us grasp the notion of civic capacity, and challenged us to see the potential for common ground among the seemingly divided people of Memphis. Chapter 4 owes a heavy debt to Clarence. Several colleagues provided thoughtful feedback on parts of the manuscript, including Andrea Pitman,

David Houston, Matthew Shirrell, Esther Enright, and Simona Goldin. Donald Peurach and Adam Lefstein, friends and colleagues since the very beginning, contributed to the ideas that inform this book through their own scholarship and countless conversations. Elizabeth Branch Dyson, editor extraordinaire, has an uncanny ability to deliver tough feedback wrapped and delivered in an encouraging tone. Her steady hand has guided us across numerous revisions. Two anonymous reviewers provided an array of helpful suggestions.

David Cohen (z"l) did not live to see the publication of this book, but his impact on it could hardly be overstated. His intellectual creativity, extraordinary breadth of knowledge, and uncanny ability to turn a phrase set a standard we could not possibly meet—but one that inspired us to try. This book is a humble effort to carry forward his legacy.

These expressions of gratitude would not be complete without mention of family. My father, Mickey Glazer (z"l), passed away just as this book was getting underway, but it is still a tribute to his love of public education, his life as a researcher, and his commitment to a more equitable world. A battle-hardened author himself, few people had a greater appreciation for what it takes to produce a book from beginning to end; he didn't live to see the final outcome, but there is little doubt that he would've been very proud. Penina Glazer has been editing her children's written work for the last fifty years, and this book is no exception. These pages reflect her formidable talent for distilling clear points from meandering thoughts, delivering unflinching feedback, and engaging in countless early-morning conversations about Memphis. In a family of academics, she has long set the highest bar. Haim (z"l) and Esther Noam, more second parents than in-laws, provided unwavering support, love, and much-needed respite.

Einav, Natan, and Idan—children when this project began, young adults as it nears completion—have been a source of joy, pride, and inspiration, even in the most difficult moments. Einav, a spectacular kindergarten teacher, has deduced insights about schools, children, and classroom practice that reflect her dedication to the practice of teaching and the communities she serves. She does what I can only write about. Her wisdom, intelligence, and pedagogical skill point to a hopeful future for the teaching profession. Natan inherited his grandmothers' love of history, his uncles' love of travel, and his aunt's love of sports. He is among a select group that speaks about the Habsburg Empire, the architectural history of DC, and the Boston Celtics backcourt with equal knowledge and passion. He pushes us to learn more, to do more, and to have more fun. Idan, the youngest, has a moral sophistication beyond his eighteen years. A proud graduate of DC Public Schools, he has shown us, in ways both ordinary and profound, the strength of friendships that cross lines of difference. This book's themes of pluralism and reciprocity are the values he inhabits in his daily life.

Tamar, to whom I owe this book and so much more, has supported this work in more ways than can possibly be counted—patiently listening to updates on daily walks, offering encouragement when progress stalled, and sharing in the joy of its completion. A life partner in the deepest and most profound sense of that phrase, this book could not have come into being without her; it is hers as well.—*Josh*

* * *

Brendan, after so many conversations about teaching and living in the South, thank you. Your perspective as a Northern transplant has offered new ways of seeing diversity and our own biases. I am so lucky to be yours. Charlie, Paul, and Maggie, you make me optimistic about the future of our country—I'm proud to be your mom. Mom and Dad, thank you for nurturing my dreams, for supporting my move to Eastern North Carolina, for telling me I would be a good English teacher, and for always showing me what decency and citizenship look like. For twelve years, I attended Shelby County Schools. Thank you to my teachers who taught me to see Memphis and the world through a lens of equity, tolerance, and resilience.—*Cori*

* * *

Dorothy Berry, herself born as a Black child in the Deep South in the year of the *Brown v. Board of Education* decision, was the first teacher to all her children and made sure they understood the tremendous sacrifices required for Black children to gain access to opportunity. Douglas Berry carries forward that Black culture and legacy through music, nurturing a love of gospel and jazz among churchgoers across Mississippi. Shree Berry and Dedrick Berry have offered steady guidance, love, and perspective throughout their younger brother's zany adventures. Also, it would be remiss not to mention the late Professor William J. Berry, elementary school principal, and the late Glenneth Berry, master piano teacher and Title I coordinator. Each was described together as "the father and mother of Black education in Jasper County, Mississippi." This book channels their lifelong dedication to enriching the lives of Black children in the South and draws strength from their enduring example. On a more practical level, both Ronald and Camille Dortonne provided unwavering support and encouragement (not to mention childcare) in the final few months of polishing the book's manuscript. Two companions have sustained this project in profound ways from the very beginning. Isabelle, perhaps the world's most patient person, endured countless stream-of-consciousness musings about Black educational history, offering love and support that shaped the writing at every turn. And Madeleine, born just as chapter 1 was being drafted, has been a guiding light from the beginning. Everything here, and everything that follows, is for her and for children like her: so that they may inherit schools and communities where no limits or barriers stand in the way of their dreams.—*William*

* * *

Josh, thank you for the opportunity to work on this project. Despite joining the team later in the process, you, Cori, and William welcomed me with open arms. I've learned so much working alongside the three of you while seeing this book take shape. And to my mom, Rana Fattal: I wouldn't be where I am without you; as always, thank you for all that you do for us.—*Amar*

INTRODUCTION

Of Politics and Systems

On the evening of September 17, 2014, two separate meetings took place in Memphis. They both involved new educational enterprises that had recently emerged in the city and that were generating considerable controversy. The events were remarkable, though, for different reasons. The first was a community meeting that had been organized by a parent group to discuss the local district's new school turnaround initiative, the Innovation Zone (iZone). Parents, teachers, and other concerned citizens gathered on that crisp fall evening in a clean and bright middle school lunchroom in South Memphis. Some held hand-written signs expressing their discontent while unconcerned police were parked outside. Virtually all the attendees were African American.

Nothing about the Shelby County iZone seemed particularly extraordinary or worthy of protest. Districts have long been searching for ways to improve their most underperforming schools, and Shelby County was no different. In fact, district leaders had cycled through decades of initiatives, including high-profile reforms supported by massive private investment, national school improvement projects, and scores of other interventions. By contrast, the iZone, a small subset of district schools under the authority of the superintendent and school board, seemed relatively pedestrian. An expanded budget, increased autonomy, and an additional hour to the school day were among the main features; unlike more attention-grabbing reforms, there was no influx of philanthropic money, no charter schools, and no parental choice. Still, the iZone mission was a tough one; it had to reverse the academic fortunes of schools identified as among the lowest performing in the state in an environment beset by intergenerational poverty and neglect. Moreover, the iZone existed within the same district and was managed by the same people under whose watch the schools' performance had precipitously declined.

But it was not the extra hour, greater flexibility, or pedagogical approach that brought parents out that evening. It was the fact that once a school entered the iZone, it would be assigned a new principal who, in turn, had the authority to replace the school's teachers with other district teachers deemed more qualified. In short, once a school entered the iZone, the majority of its professional staff would be replaced. The attendees at the community meeting had come to save the positions of teachers whom they had known for years and who, in some cases, had been *their* teachers when they were in school. The protest was also one of principle; these were neighborhood schools, and the community felt it should have direct input into these types of decisions. District leaders' efforts to explain the rationale behind placing the most accomplished teachers in the neediest schools did little to lower the temperature in the room.

Then something extraordinary happened. The representative for the local branch of the National Education Association (NEA), the largest teachers' union in the country, walked up to the mic. One need not be an expert in labor relations to anticipate that the NEA rep would be among the loudest voices protesting the displacement of local teachers from the schools they had worked in for years. Indeed, protection from administrative decrees of this nature has long been at the center of union efforts, and the district's decision to replace the entire faculty of iZone schools seemed particularly egregious.

But to the surprise of all in attendance, the union representative urged the community members to drop their demands. Although seemingly incongruous with a traditional union stance, her argument was not without logic. The primary threat to teachers' job security and the main issue concerning the public, she explained, was not the iZone but the Achievement School District, or the ASD, as it was more popularly known. And from a union perspective, she was right. Unlike the iZone, which was a local, district-run initiative, the ASD was a new state agency that operated entirely outside the control of the locally elected school board (see fig. 1). Even worse, the majority of ASD schools were operated by charter organizations that typically shut out unions altogether.

The ASD, however, was not a typical charter network that opened new schools as an alternative to district schools. Rather, the ASD was a state takeover apparatus with the authority to remove schools from local control and hand them over to private organizations, which would then hire their own teachers and leaders, select curricula, and imprint their own educational philosophy. Many of these organizations were from out of state, and as local residents would later point out, most were White-led organizations. Advocates saw the ASD as a bold attempt to transform long-failing schools, but few in the community would share that perspective.

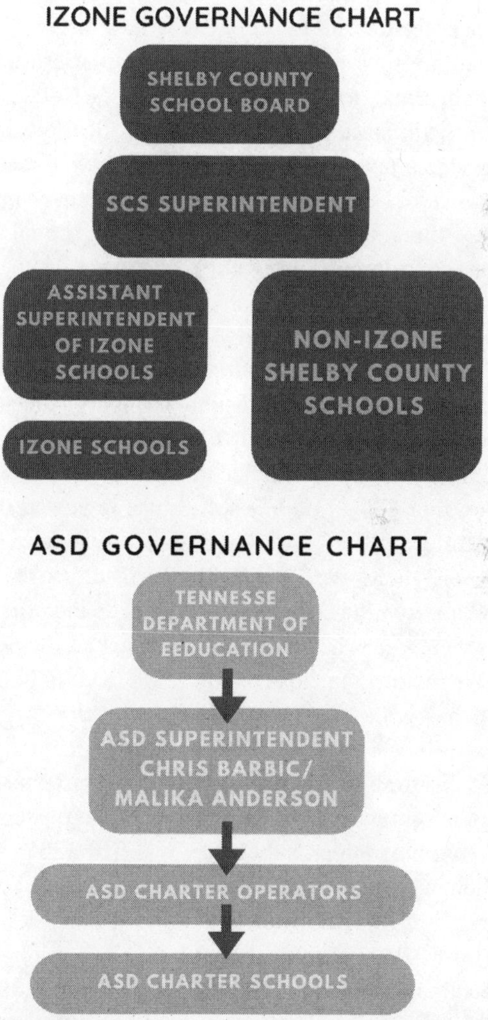

FIGURE 1. A chart showing the iZone and ASD's governance.

As the union rep spoke, she explained that schools incorporated into the iZone were unlikely to be absorbed into the ASD and would thus remain district schools. Accommodating the iZone was a small price to pay, she said, if it meant protecting neighborhood schools from state takeover: "We do not have the luxury to fight the iZone. The more important battle is against the ASD."[1] The message hit home. In the ensuing years, residents fiercely protested an educational reform they perceived as unjustly imposed on them by outsiders. These future protests, however, would no longer take aim at the district-led iZone. The new target was the ASD.

Across town, another meeting was taking place, although with no reporters, no police, and no residents holding signs. Katie Kling, a veteran teacher and instructional coach for Aspire Public Schools charter network, was discussing with a few colleagues the results from a recent assessment they had administered to a handful of their students. Appointed by the ASD to operate three schools, Aspire was among the more high-profile and well-regarded national charter networks to set up shop in Memphis under the auspices of the ASD. Kling, like many of Aspire's top staff, had cut her teeth on the network's nearly two decades of experience in East Los Angeles. They were no strangers to the work of running schools in neighborhoods where decades of decline and marginalization posed formidable educational challenges. They had arrived in Memphis a year earlier, confident in their ability to realize meaningful improvements.

But the data that Kling and her colleagues reviewed that September evening told a different story. After more than a year since launching their first ASD schools, there was little evidence of improvement, and even worse, internal observations revealed inconsistent and often weak instruction. Teachers were overwhelmed, and many lacked the needed skill and experience. "We're nowhere close to where we need to be," she lamented. As Kling and her colleagues looked at the evidence, one conclusion seemed inescapable: What had worked in LA was not working in Memphis. Teachers were unsure how to devise suitable lessons, had little idea how to teach struggling students without watering down the content, and were unsure how to use the materials that Aspire had provided them. A second conclusion, then, was that their teachers needed a more robust system of support that required less invention and on-the-fly decision-making. In the following months, Aspire would overhaul its entire system, including curriculum, instructional coaching, and professional development.

For the most part, researchers have acted as if the topics of these two meetings—system design and education politics—have little to do with each other. Indeed, the political processes that swirl around schools can seem disconnected from the work that goes on inside them, which often seems untouched by events beyond school walls. This book argues precisely the opposite: The political processes that transpire outside schools and the day-to-day work of improving schools are, in fact, deeply connected. Another way to put this is that while public education is inherently political, it is also a professional enterprise requiring expertise, experience, and knowledge. The puzzle we wrestle with in this book is how the political and professional sides of school reform can work in tandem.

This is not to say that researchers have ignored education politics or systemic improvement; rather, they have not sufficiently grappled with the connection between the two. For example, the account of the Memphis community meeting resonates with a particular brand of contemporary scholarship that sees reliance on charter schools, parental choice, and circumvention of the school board as part of a larger set of market-oriented reforms imposed on communities, such as New Orleans, Louisiana; Newark, New Jersey; Detroit, Michigan; Philadelphia, Pennsylvania; and Camden, New Jersey. Reformers and policymakers have depicted these policies as an effort to shake up underperforming systems, but some scholars have cast doubt on the supposed benefits and underlying intentions while noting what they see as their racialized underpinnings.

For example, a handful of contemporary researchers have argued that the labels and measurement systems used to legitimize aggressive reforms impose a narrow set of educational goals that fail to reflect community values or create space for alternative traditions of knowledge.[2] Terms like *chronically underperforming* and *failing* are said to ignore the social, cultural, and historical importance of neighborhood schools that cannot be reduced to outcomes on standardized assessments.[3] In this same vein, scholars have argued that the narrow conception of knowledge embedded in state assessments mistakenly casts non-White students as inferior or less knowledgeable.[4] As one author recently wrote, "Systemic change is needed to place families in a position to generate meaningful goals and outcomes for their children that then become metrics for measuring success in schools."[5] In other words, communities, not state departments of education or assessment experts, should determine what counts as a good school.

This critique is not limited to issues of measurement. Among the most pointed criticisms of contemporary reforms is that they strip Black- and Brown-led cities of political power and the right to self-determination.

While some reformers claim that the need to improve outcomes in urban schools justifies far-reaching changes to governance, critics have lambasted the curtailing of local control and the introduction of market-based reforms, which they see as driven by private (and often White) interests that are inattentive to community values. As one commentator wrote: "At times these transformations have more closely resembled hostile corporate takeovers than acts of racial emancipation."[6] The perspective is clear: Reforms that fail to empower local voices, leverage community resources, and explicitly address racial injustice are, at best, ill-conceived and, at worst, thinly veiled efforts to further disenfranchise marginalized communities.[7]

Yet the issues of system design and classroom practice that Kling and her colleagues debated that evening often go unmentioned in this scholarship. Concern about political processes, community control, and larger sources of inequity, important as they are, do little to answer questions about designing education systems in ways that enhance teaching and learning. As decades of school improvement research have shown, the complexity of classroom practice, school organization, and institutional change demands a robust combination of expert knowledge and experience. This point is central to school improvement researchers, yet it is seldom accounted for in contemporary political analyses of school reform.

Nowhere is the nearly total lack of attention to system design, school organization, and practice more evident than in the competing interpretations of the New Orleans Recovery School District (RSD). After the devastating destruction of Hurricane Katrina in August 2005, the city of New Orleans underwent a transformative change to its public education system. A new state law disbanded the long-standing Orleans Parish System with its locally elected school board and traditional neighborhood schools. In its place arose a new system—the RSD—characterized by parental choice, competition, and a massive influx of charter school organizations that assumed control of more than 90 percent of city schools. The transformation of governance, the pace of change, and the impact on students' day-to-day experience were unprecedented in US education history.

About these facts there is little disagreement. More controversial are the consequences of these changes. Motivated by the research findings from Douglas Harris and his colleagues at the Educational Research Alliance for New Orleans, economists and other researchers have drawn attention to what they see as promising educational outcomes, including gains in student learning, graduation rates, and college attendance.[8] In their review of the literature on charter school effects, Gamoran and Fernandez conclude,

"With cumulative effects estimated at between two-tenths and four-tenths of a standard deviation . . . the [findings] are substantially meaningful as well as statistically significant."[9]

More critical scholarship, however, has adopted a wider and less flattering lens on the impact of the New Orleans reform. Rather than focusing on educational outcomes, these researchers have noted the lower levels of satisfaction among the city's Black residents, the loss of Black political power brought about by the shifts in governance, the firing of 7,500 predominantly Black district employees, the outsized influence of private investment, and the loss of neighborhood schools.[10]As Dixson and her colleagues put it, "Despite reports in the mainstream media that public education in post-Katrina New Orleans is a success, we have attempted to speak back to that success narrative."[11]

Largely missing from these competing narratives have been the topics of teaching, learning, and the design of instructional systems. Harris, for example, argued that the main driver behind the RSD's improved outcomes was the closure of underperforming schools, which he compared with the previous system, in which ineffective schools stayed open indefinitely. That may be true, but it does little to enhance our understanding of what makes some schools effective, what is involved in improving weak schools, or what it takes to design a high-performing system. Professional learning, leadership, collegial structures, curriculum design, classroom practice, and the other components of what some scholars refer to as *educational infrastructure* remain unexamined.

RSD critics have also been largely inattentive to matters of practice, school organization, and system design. The focus on empowering local communities and grounding improvement processes in local history sheds little light on the professional knowledge and expertise needed to redesign public systems. Indeed, the dilemmas confounding Katy Kling and her Aspire colleagues stemmed less from the political dynamics surrounding the ASD and more from the internal architecture of their instructional system. These were questions about curriculum, pedagogy, professional learning, and leadership that are part and parcel of any successful reform effort and that cannot be solved entirely by local participation and democratic processes. Education is indeed a public and thus political institution, but it is also a professional one.

One group for whom this point was exceedingly clear was the leadership of the Shelby County iZone. Unlike the Aspire leaders who had arrived from California, the managers of the iZone were primarily local

Memphians, many of whom had attended the very schools they now sought to transform. They were also predominantly African Americans with intimate knowledge of Memphis neighborhoods and culture. Yet by their own admission, the district was suffering from deeply rooted pathologies that contributed to uneven and weak instruction, inadequate levels of professional knowledge, a bureaucratic and hierarchical culture, and an overall lack of capacity. Moreover, in the eyes of these same district leaders, community involvement was a mixed bag, as much a barrier to change as a catalyst for improvement. As local leaders, their concern was not making the system more democratic but making it more professional.

This book tells the story of the ASD and iZone. Politically, these two reforms were worlds apart. The iZone was a special enclave within a traditional district searching for ways to improve long-standing neighborhood schools. The ASD was a state-run district that removed schools from local control, relied heavily on charter school organizations and private investment, and circumvented local political institutions (see fig. 1). Educationally, however, the iZone and ASD were as much alike as they were different. Leaders of both initiatives confronted vexing problems of constructing coherent, rigorous, high-performing instructional systems while also closing enormous gaps in student learning. Their educational goals and the challenges they confronted in achieving them were often one and the same.

The ensuing account of the ASD and iZone lends support to the importance of reform processes that empower local communities while debunking arguments that see local resistance as simply the cost of doing business. Political scientists and education researchers who have made similar arguments about reforms in Newark, New Orleans, Detroit, and other cities will find this part of our argument familiar. Yet our analysis differs from this past research in two important ways. First, we show that politically divisive reforms falter not only because they are unjust but also because it is exceedingly difficult to build high-performing systems in contentious political environments. As we show in the ensuing chapters, one reason that reforms fail is that the time and energy spent battling critics is time and energy not spent improving teaching and learning. A second reason is that in a politically fraught environment, leaders have little choice but to pursue short-term gains that deliver instant credibility yet undermine slower and more meaningful improvement. Our point is that political shortcuts that circumvent local democratic processes can lead to educational shortcuts that shortchange the substantive work of reform.

The book's second argument, then, is that just as there are no good political shortcuts, nor are there good educational ones. In the current era, a high-performing system is not just one that increases test scores but one where teachers develop students' conceptual understanding of subject matter, content is on grade level even for students who are behind, classroom discourse is vibrant and dynamic, students grapple with complex tasks, and teachers work collaboratively to solve problems of practice. Constructing systems that consistently provide teachers with the guidance, materials, and incentives to embrace this work is an incremental and grinding process.[12] When the task is this tall, quick fixes are inherently self-defeating, both educationally and politically. As we discuss in later chapters, once the competition between the iZone and ASD reached a fever pitch, iZone leaders searched for ways to show that the district did not require outsiders to save their schools, whereas ASD leaders desperately sought the legitimacy that only improved test scores could bring. Leveraging their most experienced educators and savviest leaders, iZone leaders found ways to quickly increase outcomes, easily outpacing the rival ASD. Accolades and national headlines soon followed.

But iZone leaders would come to see those early years as a lost opportunity that did little to redesign a system in desperate need of fundamental change. Scores went up, but the work of adopting a new curriculum, retooling teachers and principals, and training a cadre of instructional coaches was left untouched. When asked about the iZone's initial and much-celebrated success, the district official in charge simply said, "I made so many mistakes." Several years would pass until new iZone leaders would embrace the slow, grinding work of system redesign that challenged entrenched norms and practices and that promised more meaningful learning opportunities for students. One takeaway from the ensuing account is that reform, whether rooted in the logic of markets, community, or social justice, is painstaking, incremental, and knowledge-demanding work.

Throughout the book, we avoid excessive use of jargon or technical terms that can detract from clarity and shared understanding. Nonetheless, a few key terms warrant explanation. First and foremost is the notion of "system," which, even in these first few pages, has made several appearances. When most people refer to "the education system," they are speaking of the entire enterprise of public education encompassed by a district, state, network, or some other jurisdiction. Used in this way, the term *system* includes everything from funding mechanisms to hiring processes, extracurricular activities, transportation, family engagement, curriculum, governance, testing, and more. When *we* talk about education systems, however, what we are typically referring to is the *instructional system*, which has a more circumscribed meaning. To speak of the instructional system is to call attention to the specific functions and processes—curriculum, pedagogy, professional development, assessment, and problem-solving procedures—that shape what is taught in schools and how it is taught. To talk about *system design*, another phrase readers will encounter, is to talk about how these elements are coordinated.

Some authors, ourselves included, use related terms, such as *educational infrastructure* or *instructional design*, to similarly highlight the way that a particular district, network, or state ties together materials, roles, routines, and processes to bring a particular educational vision to fruition.[13] This notion of "tying together," or what analysts often refer to as *coherence*, is critical for understanding instructional systems. A coherent instructional system is one in which key functions, such as curriculum, pedagogy, leadership, evaluation, data systems, and feedback loops, are all geared toward a common set of goals and a shared vision of teaching and learning. Similarly, a high-capacity system is one where learning goals are ambitious and where there are processes in place that cultivate the knowledge, skill, and support that teachers need to meet those goals. As intuitive as this may sound, realizing coherence in US education has long proven a formidable challenge that has derailed countless reform efforts.

We employ terms like *instructional system*, *infrastructure*, and *design* to shed light on the iZone and ASD's core ideas about teaching and learning, the materials made available to teachers and students, the strategies for developing teachers' knowledge and skills, and the mechanisms for integrating these various pieces into a coherent whole. To illustrate our argument, we occasionally refer to the design of other systems, such as Advanced Placement (AP), Montessori schools, and the International Baccalaureate (IB) program. Across all these examples, our intent is to situate the work of improvement in local history, values, and politics while simultaneously delving into the professional and knowledge-demanding nature of large-scale reform. At the core of our argument is the idea that building a more equitable system sits at the intersection of inclusive policies and coherent instructional systems. It is a tricky balance to strike, but a necessary one.

The remainder of this book proceeds as follows. Chapter 1 sets the context for the ASD and iZone by examining the political and social history of Memphis and the role of public education within it. The discussion touches on the century-and-a-half battle of African Americans to improve educational opportunity for their children and to obtain representation in the elected bodies where educational decisions are made and resources are allocated. The chapter serves as a reminder that the contemporary reform efforts that are the focus of the book were shaped by the region's long history of racial oppression and the fight for equal educational opportunity. Chapter 2 unpacks the political and educational assumptions that undergirded the designs of the ASD and iZone, along with the key vulnerabilities of each system. The chapter demonstrates that analysis of educational policy must attend to politics, system design, and the interaction between them.

Chapter 3 shows how the educational strategies adopted by ASD charter operators and iZone leaders unfolded across dozens of schools and hundreds of classrooms. The chapter highlights what designers of both systems came to understand as significant miscalculations in their educational strategies and the flawed reasoning behind them. Politics retakes center stage in chapter 4, which illuminates the multiple perspectives on the ASD and iZone, including those of ASD leaders and advocates, policymakers, and the local community. The chapter argues that communities view reforms through their own historical lens as much as for their educational content.

Chapter 5 examines the efforts of iZone and ASD leaders to redesign their systems in ways that embraced a long-term, incremental process for changing school organization, leadership, and instructional practice. The evolution of both the ASD and iZone highlights the gradual emergence of new ideas in which the work of teaching and learning is slowly transformed from an individual to a collective endeavor. The chapter argues that in many ways, this slow, grinding process and the grit that it requires are part and parcel of meaningful reform. We tie together the themes of politics, pedagogy, and system design in chapter 6, which brings the story and analysis to a close. Cutting across the entire book is the larger point that building new types of educational systems is at once technical work, requiring a wide breadth of professional knowledge, and political work that demands attention to the way in which those systems embody and empower the people they purport to serve.

CHAPTER ONE

From Reconstruction to Resistance

Black Education and Power in Memphis

In May 2011, the charismatic education reformer Chris Barbic was named the first superintendent of an unusual type of district that had recently been instituted in Tennessee. The Achievement School District (ASD) had been created to tackle the state's most underperforming schools that were seemingly immune to improvement and beset by what a local leader called "suffocating levels of poverty." For reasons that will soon become clear, the majority of ASD schools were located in Memphis and ranked in the bottom 5 percent of schools in Tennessee, a state that, itself, was among the lowest performing in the country. Barbic, whose television appearance on *The Oprah Winfrey Show* had made him something of a household name, was no stranger to the work of school improvement. His track record as the founder of one of the most heralded charter networks, YES Prep, suggested that he had the right combination of experience and determination that the job demanded. In his first press conference, he made it clear that he was unintimidated by the challenge: "I have spent my 19-year career in public education proving a simple hypothesis that all students, regardless of race or socioeconomics, can achieve at high academic levels when given access to the same opportunities and resources that students receive in great private and suburban public schools. I could not be more excited to return to Tennessee to invest the lessons I have learned in the well-being of the children in this great state."[1]

The creation of the ASD, coupled with the hiring of Barbic, created a buzz in education circles. High-profile commentators were impressed by the seemingly innovative idea of a state-run district composed of schools that had been removed from the authority of local school boards, which many saw as lacking the wherewithal and determination to make serious change. Observers were also intrigued by the central role that charter management organizations (CMOs) would play in operating and improving the ASD schools.[2] US Secretary of Education Arne Duncan signaled his support, noting that he was "deeply inspired by Barbic's work with YES Prep Public Schools in Houston" and that he would be "a valuable asset to Tennessee as they continue the courageous work of turning around their lowest performing schools." Duncan was not the only one to express optimism. National pundits applauded the arrival of the ASD, and prominent organizations gave their approval. A report from the Thomas B. Fordham Institute declared that "the ASD's most important contribution will be to demonstrate that a combination of autonomy, resources, leadership, and clarity of purpose can work miracles for thousands—maybe millions—of kids." The head of the Tennessee Charter School Incubator declared that Memphis was "becoming the epicenter of education reform."[3]

Three hours from Nashville, where Barbic's press conference took place, the leaders of Shelby County School District, the century-old district that had recently come to include Memphis, looked on incredulously.[4] The district had cycled through various reforms, and while not all were failures, they had fallen short of the lofty goals that Barbic would soon announce. The notion that a new set of educational actors, many of them new to Memphis, could obtain the type of results that had eluded generations of district leaders seemed implausible. But the arrival of the ASD and its confident new leader was also unsettling because were the ASD to succeed, what would that say about the district and city that had overseen these schools for decades?

Among the district officials asking these questions was Dorsey Hopson, the district's chief counsel at the time. Hopson was immersed in helping the district navigate a highly contentious merger of Memphis City Schools (MCS) with the surrounding suburbs, but within two years, he would be named the district's new superintendent, a position he would hold for five years. Among his central tasks as superintendent would be to prove that the district could improve its most underperforming schools no less effectively than the ASD and to debunk the notion that the district required an out-of-town savior. The district's response to the ASD would involve the formation of a semi-independent enclave within the district called the Innovation Zone, widely known as the iZone. Over the next several years, iZone and ASD leaders would engage in a public and high-stakes battle over which was the more effective school turnaround strategy. The

ASD and iZone were new entities, yet the relationship between them was embedded in 150 years of history.

Even before the ASD and iZone would dominate headlines across the city and state, leaders of both systems had reasons to be concerned. For one, they confronted enormous educational challenges. All their target schools served communities with staggering levels of poverty, born of decades of social and economic marginalization that had left students years behind their more affluent peers. Americans are used to hearing about the achievement gap, in which middle- and upper-middle-class students significantly outperform their less privileged counterparts. We know that better-resourced schools provide better programming, smaller classes, more experienced teachers, and more up-to-date facilities. We also know that affluent families pour resources into their children's education and development—tutors, music lessons, summer camps—that are out of reach for poor families.

But the nature of poverty in Memphis is both different and staggering. At the peak of our research into the ASD in 2014, child poverty rates in Memphis were at a high of 47 percent, compared with the Tennessee state average of 26 percent and the national average of 22 percent.[5] In comparison to its affluent suburbs, poverty in Memphis affects families, schools, and the city as a whole. Years of disparity and segregation have worn on Memphians, leading to high levels of crime, addiction, and a declining population. These sobering realities raised the question as to what educational strategies ASD and iZone leaders would deploy, what type of classrooms they envisioned, how they would organize schools, and how they would enhance the professional capacity of the teachers and leaders they would rely on to realize learning gains. Another question was where these principals and teachers would come from. A few years earlier, thousands of young people had flocked to New Orleans in an effort to rebuild the city's education system in the aftermath of Hurricane Katrina. Would, as some local leaders predicted, a similar wave of energetic youth lift the ASD and iZone to the level to which they aspired, or would the reforms need to depend on existing teachers and leaders?

For leaders operating in the first decade of the twenty-first century, there was no shortage of ideas to draw from. There were market-based frameworks holding that a combination of competition, student choice, and autonomy could drive improvement. The most common reform based on market principles involves charter schools, in which private organizations operate public schools free of district oversight and regulations. In comparison to traditional schools, charter school leaders have more latitude to choose their own curriculum, hire (and dismiss) their own teachers, and pursue their own educational philosophy. Charter advocates believe that when school leaders have the freedom (*autonomy* in current educational parlance) to respond to a competitive environment in which families have the liberty to choose schools, they will respond by designing better schools. Charters that fail to attract families will, at least in theory, go out of business. The press for improvement, in other words, comes less from state regulation and more from market forces.

There were other models to choose from as well. Emergent ideas about school improvement networks were highlighting innovative ways for schools to learn from each other while collaboratively designing and refining new practices. The idea of improvement networks would later attract the attention of Gates Foundation officials, who would make it the centerpiece of their philanthropic strategy. A nascent but rapidly expanding continuous improvement movement, driven in large part by the Carnegie Foundation for the Advancement of Teaching, was experimenting with ways for schools to iteratively test and refine a set of practical ideas that would incrementally drive improvement. The research–practice partnership movement was expanding beyond its origins in Chicago, where a consortium of universities had partnered with Chicago Public Schools to chart a research-driven path to improvement. iZone and ASD leaders did not need to invent an improvement strategy from scratch but rather to find and operationalize the right combination of ideas that would best meet the educational challenges that Memphis posed.

Alongside these educational conundrums sat an equally formidable set of political challenges. For all the excitement that the ASD had generated among reformers and national leaders, the reaction of the local community was another matter entirely. How would the predominantly African American local population react to the state takeover of their neighborhood schools and to the selection of out-of-state (and largely White-led) charter networks as operators of neighborhood schools? Moreover, as two educationally and politically distinct entities took shape, what would be the relationship between them? Would they find ways to work together and learn from shared experiences, or would the promise of collaboration be cast aside by competition and zero-sum political calculations?

However these issues would unfold, one thing was certain: They would be framed as much by the region's uneasy, highly racialized history as they would by the latest research or current educational trends. As we elaborate in the remainder of this chapter, the educational and political challenges confronting the ASD and iZone had been over a century in the making. In some instances, this history was readily evident, whereas in others, it was less visible but still highly potent. We begin our discussion, therefore, by providing a historical perspective that contextualizes the educational ideas that inspired these reforms and the political dynamics that either buttressed or undermined them. The intent is not to provide a new history of the South or Memphis (we leave that to the historians) but to show that policy, which is professionally sound and politically sustainable (or to reference a term we'll use later, *legitimate*), is rooted in and informed by a past in which education, politics, and community are intertwined. Put slightly differently, the question we tackle is how education can be a profession, rooted in expert knowledge and shared practices, while also being public, democratic, and tied to local values. Our starting point for this discussion dates back to an earlier period when the education of Black Memphians was also at the center of a fierce public debate and when the political and educational stakes were equally high—Reconstruction.

Part I: Freedom's Foundation: Black Education in the Reconstruction South

Education was a central pillar of Black Memphians' efforts to realize the promise of liberty after the Civil War. An effective, albeit short-lasting, alliance between newly freed Black people, Northern Christian missionary societies, and Southern state leaders contributed to remarkable progress in Black education, including the emergence of Northern-based missionary societies that educated freedmen, as well as the first publicly funded Black schools in the state.[6] Central to this effort was the federal enfranchisement of Black males and the formidable voting bloc they represented in Memphis, where they made up nearly 40 percent of the population.[7] For the next two decades, Memphis's Black community navigated the politics of Reconstruction by forging alliances with various White ethnic constituencies, turning out to vote, and tirelessly pressing their case for better schools within a segregated system.[8] During this period, new school buildings were constructed (although not enough), teachers were hired (although not nearly enough), and attendance of Black students in Memphis rose to a remarkable 72 percent by 1870.[9] Throughout the South, the effort to establish schools for the formerly enslaved was more than just about learning to read and write. As James Anderson put it in his seminal work on Black education in the South, "The struggle for education was an expression of freedom."[10]

These and subsequent efforts to establish educational opportunity were relentless and determined, but so was the resistance these efforts encountered. In what became known as the "1866 Memphis Massacre," White mobs burned down every Black school and church in the city. The attack left at least forty-six dead, and Black and White teachers fled the city in fear.[11] Other efforts to stonewall the opening of Black schools were less violent but equally damaging. School board minutes from 1863 to 1867 contain no references to Black schools or students as White officials were unwilling to even acknowledge the presence of Black students, let alone attend to their educational needs.[12] Further, through 1869, Memphis continued to enforce an antebellum law that state education funds for schools were for White schools only, thereby requiring the local Black community to foot the bill for their own schools while relying extensively on Northern charity.[13]

Despite these obstacles, Black Memphians' persistence, coupled with federal and state laws, eventually ended the debate about whether there would be Black schools (there would be). What was not resolved, however, was the question of who would control them. As one writer noted in her analysis of that period, "Within a decade, in Memphis and across the state, the discourse changed from *whether* Black students would be educated to *who* would teach them, *for what* purposes, and *how* this education could be managed and controlled."[14] This debate would continue for the next 150 years.

At first, Black students were taught primarily by White women who had traveled down from the North. But by 1870, both Black and White Memphians, each for their own reasons, sought to reduce the influence of these outsiders. Local Whites were eager to be rid of Northern interlopers, whose presence garnered considerable suspicion. Among African Americans, there was an increasing sentiment that the community should educate its own children. "Colored teachers for colored schools" became a rallying cry in newspapers and local meetings.[15] The movement was about more than wanting Black teachers in Black schools; it was a pointed response to the paternalism of White educators who considered African Americans incapable of managing their own educational affairs. This coalition, fleeting as it was, proved effective, and by 1884, all of the twenty teachers instructing Black students were themselves African American.[16]

But as will be seen in subsequent chapters, the question of who should teach the children of Memphis was far from settled.

Yet even as Black teachers grew in number and importance, their role was limited by a lack of power over educational decisions and a level of training that lagged behind that of their White counterparts. One estimate of the professional preparation of Tennessee teachers in 1900 found that 44 percent of Black teachers had not even completed high school, whereas for White teachers, the percentage was 28 percent. Moreover, because Whites controlled the electoral bodies and therefore the purse strings, they also controlled education policy and decision-making. Thus, while Black teachers were at the forefront of their people's quest for freedom, their power to effect change was limited. As one historian of that era describes it, "Black Tennessee educators were forced to maintain a delicate balance between the welfare of Black students, the dictates of those Whites who controlled the educational funds, and their own integrity."[17]

If who would teach Black students was one point of conflict, what content would be taught was another. Despite limited political power, Black citizens pressed and protested for a better curriculum and more resources. The controversy over the curriculum was part of a larger conversation about the purpose and goals of Black education, itself a reflection of divergent views of what freedom would mean for the Black citizens of the South. One vision of Black education focused on industrial and technical training. Across the South, a combination of Southern elites, a few Black allies (Booker T. Washington being the most famous), and a handful of Northern philanthropies (e.g., John F. Slater Fund, the Rosenwald Fund) sought to enshrine a system of Black education rooted in basic literacy, manual labor, and strict discipline. Their purpose was to prepare Black students for the lower rungs of an emergent industrial economy and, in doing so, preserve the economic and political hierarchy that had long defined the South. Indeed, it was the idea that education could maintain the social and economic order that ultimately persuaded a skeptical planter class to accept the idea of publicly funded schools.[18]

On the other side, a handful of Black activists and intellectuals fiercely contested this vision of Black education and its implications for their position in the economic and social hierarchy. W. E. B. Du Bois and other Black intellectuals saw equality and the eventual political and social empowerment of Black citizens as inherently tied to a classical curriculum focused on the arts and sciences that, in the words of Du Bois, would foster "intelligence, broad sympathy, knowledge of the world that was and is, and of the relation of men to it."[19] One scholar summed up the differing approaches to the curriculum as follows: "Would or should it include the full range of training, from elementary to graduate and professional education? Or would it consist of a smattering of basic elementary education and vocational/ technical/agricultural training for a people who were mostly farmers and unskilled workers and who, in the opinion of most southern Whites, were not capable of higher education?"[20]

These debates unfolded in Tennessee much as they did across the South. In 1879, the Tennessee state legislature, recognizing the need to prepare students for the technological changes wrought by the Industrial Revolution, supplemented the mainstream academic curriculum with courses in agriculture, home economics, and manual training. In Black schools, however, vocational classes such as shoemaking, tinsmithing, and basketry were the entirety of the formal curriculum, absent the courses in Latin, physics, and literature that were offered to White students.[21] This would not be the last time that the question of what should be taught in Memphis schools would surface as a point of controversy.[22]

This history is as important for methodological reasons as it is for historical ones. The scholars reporting on these events drew explicit connections between a political environment defined by issues of race, equity, and power and the educational processes that unfolded inside schools. Their point was not simply to document how White elites wielded their power over a determined yet vulnerable Black community but also to show the significance for students' and teachers' day-to-day experiences in schools. The ensuing discussion of the iZone and ASD follows this same path.

As fierce as the debates were about who should teach and what should be taught, the most contentious question was who would have the power to make those decisions. Indeed, if there is a single issue that is threaded throughout the decades of Reconstruction, Jim Crow, the civil rights era, and into the twenty-first century, it is the determined struggle of Black Memphians to achieve representation in the elected bodies that controlled public education and the fierce White resistance it engendered. It is for this reason, above all others, that in cities like Memphis, the politics of education are about far more than education.

In January 1880, Edward Shaw became the first Black man to be elected to the Memphis Board of Education.[23] Shaw joined with other Black activists to seek an increase in state-level spending on Black schools, curriculum reforms, and better pay for teachers. These efforts, fueled by Black electoral strength and political organizing, resulted in meaningful progress, including an 1888 board decision to establish a Black high school, Clay Street School, with an upgraded curriculum. Well into the twentieth century, scores of Black Memphians would go through Clay Street School and its successor, Kortrecht School.[24] These were monumental accomplishments that enhanced educational access and quality, but they were also short-lived. After a handful of electoral victories in the 1880s, the next Black person elected to public office in Memphis, educational or otherwise, was in 1960.[25] Indeed, by the beginning of the twentieth century, there was not a single Black representative in the Tennessee General Assembly.[26]

The meaningful accomplishments of Shaw and other Black leaders inform the events we chronicle in later chapters. One lesson is the extent to which African Americans were the driving force behind the effort to educate their own people. The traditional perspective depicting Whites (Northern and Southern) as the primary generators of Black education has diverted attention from the role of the local Black population in establishing and managing that system. As historian Kathleen Berkeley has noted: "[It was] Black Americans that took the lead in guiding the development of Black public education."[27] It will be important to keep this in mind as we consider the legitimacy, both social and historical, of reforms that transpired 130 years later.

The second lesson regards the highly politicized nature of the Black educational agenda. It is no exaggeration to say that every aspect of this emergent system—the construction of school buildings, the composition of the teaching force, the size of the classes, the number of days in the school year, and the nature of the curriculum—was fiercely contested. The growth in educational access and opportunity that emerged in the two decades after the Civil War was a product of Black Memphians' political maneuvering, skillful coalition building, and dogged persistence. When political scientist Clarence Stone wrote in 1998 that "all education reform is political," he captured not only the reality of the late twentieth century but also that of the previous one.

If Black agency and political activism are two important themes of this era, the third is that the press for educational equity took place in a political environment in which the levers of economic and political power were overwhelmingly controlled by Whites. This included White Northerners of the Reconstruction era who dismissed the notion that Black teachers or administrators could run their own system, local businessmen whose primary goal was to limit expenditures, civic elites who sought to maintain a White majority on the school board, and the total consensus of all Whites—Northern, Southern, Democrat, and Republican—that the schools should remain racially segregated. So absolute was the commitment to segregated schools that in the years after the Civil War, Southern Whites threatened to shut down the entire system of public schooling rather than tolerate a system where White and Black children studied together.[28] The fact that a hundred years later, they would abandon the schools and then the city for that very reason suggests they had every intention of following through on that threat.

In the Shadow of the Lost Cause: Schools and Black Power in Memphis

Black empowerment and activism continued into the first half of the twentieth century much as they did in the first two decades after the Civil War. In Memphis, Black political associations, newspapers, churches, and local leaders continued to leverage African Americans' formidable voting bloc to press for benefits and civil rights gains. Religious leaders, Black churches, workers, and community leaders fought against social injustices and enjoyed some occasional successes.[29] As one commentator of that era wrote, "Black Memphians were, to a very limited extent, able to use access to their votes as a tool for negotiating community improvements."[30]

Beyond political channels, more confrontational forms of activism included flouting segregation policies, physical resistance to police brutality, sit-ins, and other forms of civil protest. Renowned activist and Memphis resident Ida B. Wells-Barnett spearheaded efforts to raise international awareness about segregation and lynching through her writings and refusal to relinquish her seat in the White section of the train departing from Memphis in 1884.[31] African American intellectuals and leaders utilized education to counteract pervasive negative images of African Americans, particularly as "Lost Cause" mythologies depicting African Americans as uncivilized and without history proliferated in Southern education systems.[32] In her capacity as a founding member of the National Association for the Advancement of Colored People (NAACP), Wells-Barnett contributed to a national network of Black educators dedicated to resisting the White supremacist ideology proliferating in educational texts in the early twentieth century.[33] Perhaps the most prominent works to emerge from this period were the writings of Carter G. Woodson, who advocated for textbooks and curricula that portrayed the history and culture of African Americans in a dignified and accurate manner.[34]

In response to this Black activism, White elites marshaled the power of the state to thwart Black empowerment and self-actualization. Beginning around 1900, one of the country's most pervasive systems of segregation took root, leading to separate buses, schools, parks, theaters, and other public spaces, not to mention the host of facilities that were simply off limits to Black people, such as the county fair, the zoo, and the art museum.[35] Lynchings and mob violence peaked during the 1890s throughout the state and in Memphis and western Tennessee in particular.[36] Black political power was also curtailed by new municipal election laws that concentrated power in a smaller group of wealthy White males. The conservative Democrats who were now firmly in control of city politics (and typically sent their children to private school) reduced overall public expenditures, including funds for public education.[37]

Cultural and political conservatism were reinforced by an economy that relegated Black people to the lowest rungs of the economic order. Reliance on the cotton industry meant that Memphis did not develop an industrial base until far later than other US cities. Labor unions never established a foothold in the city, even during the height of union power in the 1940s and 1950s. When Black agricultural workers migrated from the plantations of nearby Mississippi, Arkansas, and Alabama, they found predominantly low-wage jobs in the service and commercial sectors. Even those manufacturers that did eventually come to Memphis after WWI did so to take advantage of low wages, low taxes, and weak unions. The education reformers who later came to Memphis to reverse these trends would encounter the educational implications of Blacks' economic marginalization and the intergenerational poverty it spawned.[38]

Memphis in the early twentieth century, then, presents a paradox. On the one hand, it is during this period that it emerged as a modern city in terms of size, development, and appearance. Migration from the surrounding areas greatly increased its population, and new buildings began to dominate a rapidly transforming city center. Moreover, the city's multicultural population laid the groundwork for the blues and soul music scene that would later become a defining facet of the city. Memphis Minnie, Frank Stokes, and Furry Lewis were among the early Black artists who brought blues music to Memphis's Beale Street from the Mississippi Delta. The turn of the century also saw the rise of vibrant Black neighborhoods and a notable Black professional class in areas ranging from law to medicine to real estate. The neighborhood of Orange Mound, widely recognized as the first subdivision built by and for Black homeowners in the country, was founded in 1890 as a symbol of freedom and pride for African Americans in Memphis. To the casual observer, Memphis would appear to be an apt example of what was increasingly being called "the New South."

But as historians of the South have noted, looks can be deceiving. Gerald M. Capers Jr. observed that by 1900, the modern physical appearance of Memphis belied a culture "rural in background, rural in prejudice, and rural in habit." Roger Biles similarly noted that while the migration from the surrounding countryside greatly expanded the city's size and stature, it also cemented Memphis's conservative culture. "These recent arrivals from the countryside who were responsible for giving the city a decidedly provincial air included in their cultural baggage such items as a nostalgic devotion to the southern Lost Cause, a propensity for violence, and belief in stringent codes of honor, fundamentalist religion, and White supremacy."[39] Historian David Goldfield captured the overall point, noting succinctly, "There was never any New South."[40]

Before Brown*: Schooling and the Segregated Social Order in Memphis*

The city's history is a window into its education system, both past and present. The activism, oppression, independence, segregation, and creativity that characterized Memphis throughout the WWII era characterized its schools as well. A few themes stand out. The first, of course, is the absolute and uncompromising commitment among Whites to segregated systems of schooling. Southern Whites often defended this in terms of tradition, but as Goldfield and other historians have pointed out, the motivation was largely practical. "The schools were the bulwark of biracialism, since illiteracy and the separate and unequal educational systems in southern cities were important in maintaining the subservient position of the Black community."[41] Indeed, lest there be any confusion about Whites' commitment to school segregation, Tennessee statutes made interracial education a criminal offense subject to fine and imprisonment.[42]

A second theme is that patronage and cronyism pervaded the system, long after other cities had removed schools from the center of political horse trading. Teaching and leadership jobs were handed out in exchange for electoral support and campaign contributions all the way into the 1950s. Only school staff with the right political connections enjoyed a semblance of job security.[43] Foreshadowing criticisms that would be leveled at the system decades later, a survey conducted by the US Bureau of Education in 1919 found that "without any doubt, to an unusual and disquieting degree, the schools of Memphis have been organized and administered on a personal and political basis rather than upon the impersonal one which seeks the answer to but one question, 'What is best for the children of the city?'"[44] Part of the problem was that public education was simply not a high priority for the city's most powerful groups. The economic and civic elite sent their children to private schools, the Irish relied predominantly on parochial schools, and other members of the White working class were more interested in low taxes than well-resourced schools.[45]

The third theme is thus of little surprise: Well into the 1950s, many Memphis public schools were underresourced, overcrowded, and academically poor-performing. This was true of both White and Black schools, but of course, it was truer of the latter. The same US Bureau of Education report that exposed systemic patronage also pointed to pervasive educational problems. Among the report's findings were that only 30 of 550 elementary teachers had graduated from a "recognized" college, and there was little to no oversight of teachers. Central High School was unaccredited, and the Black high school was "pitiable." The curriculum for both Black and White students was cast as "out of touch with life and too dependent on rote memory," a problem that future reformers would struggle to uproot.[46] Further, overcrowding forced schools to double the number of students per class and left over two hundred teachers without a classroom. In Black schools, students brought umbrellas to protect themselves from deteriorating buildings and leaky roofs. Per-pupil spending in 1926 in Memphis was $51.61 annually, whereas the average for US cities at the time was $76.30.[47] A study conducted by the Russell Sage Foundation in 1912 determined that the student enrollment rate in Memphis was lower and the dropout rate higher than in any comparable city. The report cast Memphis schools as the worst among US cities.[48]

Nearly a century later, when Memphis schools were managed primarily by Black leaders and teachers and attended predominantly by Black students, outsiders would level complaints about patronage and poor outcomes, in part to justify the state takeover of schools and in part to support the claim that local leaders were incapable of managing their own system. Forgotten by these critics is that those pathologies long predated the arrival of Black leadership.

Brown *and Its Aftermath: Massive Resistance and the Reshuffling of Political Power*

On May 17, 1954, US Supreme Court Justice Earl Warren delivered the unanimous decision declaring that state-sanctioned segregation of public schools violated the Fourteenth Amendment of the US Constitution. *Brown* sent shock waves through the South, and nowhere more so than in Memphis, where racial segregation was a form of civic religion. Local leaders immediately declared that they would not cede any ground in their ninety-year effort to maintain segregated schools. When Milton Bowers Sr., president of the Memphis Board of Education, was asked if he believed White schools would ever be opened up to Black students, Bowers replied that he "did not believe such would ever be the case here."[49] To the extent Bowers meant that *Brown* would have no impact on Memphis, he could not have been more wrong, but if he meant that there would never be meaningful integration of public schools in Memphis, he was largely correct. The ensuing decades would bring an enormous political realignment and huge demographic shifts; what they would not bring was the racial integration of schools.

Visitors to Memphis in the years following *Brown* would have found Bowers's remarks to be prescient. Memphis schools remained completely segregated until the end of 1950s, and only in 1961, under the threat of legal action, did MCS admit thirteen Black students into previously all-White schools in what was largely a symbolic gesture. In the ensuing years, modest and incremental numbers of Black students were permitted to enroll in White schools. By 1970, those same visitors might have detected some changes in the racial composition of Memphis schools, but only if they were paying careful attention. At that point, a full sixteen years after *Brown*, 55 percent of the Memphis student body was Black, but among the city's 155 schools, fifty-four were 100 percent segregated, and seventy-six were 90 percent segregated.[50] The message was clear: Memphis schools were not going to be integrated unless forced to.

In 1973, Judge Robert Malcom McRae Jr. of the US District Court for the Western District of Tennessee attempted to do just that. In response to a lawsuit filed by the NAACP, and following precedent set by the Supreme Court's decision in *Swann* (which upheld mandatory busing to accelerate racial integration), McRae established a plan to bus nearly forty thousand students daily "in the hope that [it would] be the terminal plan for this long-standing problem in Memphis."[51] A similar lawsuit, the *Northcross* case, unfolded in Shelby County. The effect of court-ordered busing changed the social, political, and educational dynamics of Memphis in ways that are felt to the present day. But one effect that it did not have was to create a system of integrated schools. By the 2012–2013 school year, 81.7 percent of students in Memphis City Schools were Black, while only 6.8 percent were White.[52] Political scientist Marcus manmann explained the failure of Judge McRae's plan in one short sentence: "Many Whites simply refused to be bussed."[53] Indeed, just as White elites in the 1870s were willing to dismantle public schooling rather than have an integrated system, a hundred years later, they were equally willing to abandon the public education system and, if need be, the city itself.

Which is precisely what they did. During the summer of 1972, close to ten thousand White students, nearly a third of the total number, left the city's public school system. By 1978, the total number of departing White students rose to forty thousand.[54] Overall enrollment of White students in MCS declined from 71,369 in 1970 to 27,173 in 1980.[55] In a 1981 interview, future superintendent and mayor Dr. Willie Herrington said, "The White community did not participate as planned in the desegregation program. The schools are even more segregated now than they were before."[56] Many of these students attended private schools that had sprouted up to meet skyrocketing demand while scores of families moved beyond city boundaries.[57] The buses continued to run, but for the most part, they transported Black students from one segregated school to another. Desegregation plans ran out of White students.

The consequences of Whites' exodus from the city have been both profound and complicated. One result has been a rise in Black political power within Memphis. Before the demographic upheaval of the 1970s and 1980s, Black activism had led to incremental gains in political representation, including the election of Maxine Smith in 1971 as the first Black member of the school board since 1880. But it wasn't until the massive demographic changes of the 1970s and 1980s that Black citizens gained control over the school board, city council, and mayor's office. The White exodus was helped by the availability of suburban houses, lower taxes, and an increase in jobs outside the city, but it was largely the threat of busing and racially integrated schools that motivated White migration to the suburbs. It is no coincidence that in 1991, when Black people made up the majority of the voting-age population, W. W. Herenton was elected as the city's first Black mayor. The election was decided by 142 votes, with 99 percent of Black voters casting a ballot for Herenton and 96 percent of the White electorate voting for his opponent. Herenton's victory, along with the addition of three Black council members, marked the end of over a century of White conservative dominance in Memphis.[58] One lesson from Herenton's election was that Black political power was less the result of changing social norms or White acceptance of Black leadership but, as was the case during Reconstruction, a product of their increased electoral strength.[59] Black power, in other words, was a direct result of Black political muscle.

A second lesson was that the rise in Black political power was offset by a lack of economic power. The economic and social character of the city was transformed in ways that would leave Memphis with a large number of poor citizens, a declining tax base, and a school system whose students presented an array of academic and social challenges. While Black Memphians could finally control a city in which they had been a major presence for 125 years, the city itself was, in the words of historian James Cobb, "more of a problem than a prize." As the city's financial situation became increasingly precarious, elected leaders made several attempts to establish revenue-sharing and joint-governance arrangements between Memphis and the surrounding municipalities. The proposals included city–county consolidation, the creation of a shared general-purpose government for Memphis and Shelby County, and school district consolidation.

It should be of little surprise that the referendums on these initiatives were roundly dismissed by suburban voters.[60] The message from county residents was that while they had been forced to relinquish control of the city, they had little intention of providing the resources needed to maintain it. The city's most recent effort to break out of its economic isolation took place in 2011 when a series of events led to a (very) temporary merger between MCS and Shelby County Schools (SCS). Unlike some of the other events that transpired decades ago, the story of the merger and subsequent demerger is widely known throughout Memphis and Tennessee. At the same time, it is best understood as the most recent iteration of the social and political themes that have played out time and again in Memphis.

Together, Apart: The Unification and Splintering of Shelby County Schools

The 2010 midterm elections ushered Republicans into office across the United States at both the national and state levels. In Tennessee, the "Red Wave" gave Republicans control of the governor's office and the legislature for the first time since Reconstruction. The implications would prove far-reaching on numerous levels, but for the twelve members of the Memphis School Board, the election results raised a particular concern. For years, Shelby County had expressed an interest in permanently separating its education system from that of Memphis. While the systems had long been educationally and administratively independent, each with its own board and superintendent, they were tied together in other ways. One was financial. City and suburban taxpayers contributed to a single, county-wide fund that was allocated to schools across the county according to an agreed-upon funding formula. In addition, residents of Memphis paid a separate tax that provided supplemental funds to MCS. The arrangement ensured that Memphis at least somewhat benefited from the disproportionate affluence of the suburbs, but in the eyes of many suburban residents, it meant that they subsidized city schools.[61]

But it was the second tie between city and suburban schools that was far more worrisome for many suburbanites. Tennessee state law classified SCS as a "county system" responsible for the education of all students within county borders. This meant that not only was the county legally obligated to provide financial support to Memphis schools, but also if the Memphis Board of Education were to surrender its charter, Shelby County would be required to absorb all Memphis schools. It was this law allowing for the potential consolidation of the two districts that was of foremost concern to those living outside the city.[62]

But laws can be changed. And so when Republicans assumed full control of the state government, it seemed only a matter of time before suburban residents would lobby for a new law reclassifying SCS as a "special district" solely responsible for students outside the city. As a special district, Shelby County would shed the threat of district consolidation while gaining the ability to keep suburban taxes out of city schools.[63] Suburban leaders denied that this was their intention, but a century and a half of history gave Memphians reason to worry.

The Memphis Board of Education was acutely aware of the political implications of the election, as well as the potentially devastating financial implications were SCS to achieve special-district status.[64] The gut-wrenching question for the board, and for the entire city, was whether to make a preemptive move by surrendering the board's charter before the legislature had time to act. Some Memphians were eager to act rather than let the suburbs dictate the course of events, whereas others saw the merging of the two school systems as a matter of historical equity. As one Memphis School Board member put it: "Memphis citizens are

70 percent of the county, and the county was built on city taxpayers' investment. Now that they have the ability to sustain themselves, they want to take the higher assessed property values that were built with city money and back out of the agreement to fund education for every child in Shelby County."[65]

But other Memphians were aghast at the idea of forfeiting the control they had fought so long to obtain. One school board member openly worried what would be lost if Memphis could no longer run its own school system: "If the charter is surrendered, what is going to happen to the teachers, their seniority rights, and even their rights to be employed if the city schools no longer exist? What is going to happen to the curriculum?" And yet others, reflecting on the lessons of previous decades, refused to believe that suburban Whites would ever tie their system to that of Memphis. In 1982, David Goldfield wrote, "Black political power is circumscribed by the absence of Black economic power."[66] Twenty-eight years later, his remark and the dilemma that it implies seemed no less relevant.

In the end, the board, the city council, and finally, the voters opted for financial security over political autonomy. Although a narrow majority of a divided board voted to surrender its charter, an overwhelming 67 percent of voters agreed to transfer control of MCS to the SCS board. The legal maneuvers, countermaneuvers, and court orders that transpired during this period are as extraordinary as they are well documented.[67] Yet the overarching themes and resolution of the situation fit comfortably alongside events of the past. Following the vote of the board and the citywide referendum, MCS ceased to exist as an independent political entity, and its schools were in fact integrated into a single, county-wide district: SCS. The expanded district encompassed all the county's K–12 schools, was governed by a single county-wide board of education, and was managed by a single superintendent. It represented the largest merger of districts in US history.

The arrangement lasted for all of one year. County politicians were not able to prevent the Memphis board from surrendering its charter, nor the eventual merger of the districts, but with ample allies in Nashville, they had other options. A new law was quickly passed that opened the door for suburban municipalities to secede from the newly formed district. As one commentator put it, "This essentially ensured that on the day that Memphis and Shelby County began operating a unified school district, the process of undoing it would begin."[68] By the start of the 2012 school year, six of the county's suburban municipalities had established their own small, independent districts. SCS, which now included Memphis, would continue to be funded by county-wide taxes, which at least assured a degree of financial stability.

Demographically, however, little had changed. Without the majority-White municipalities, the district was overwhelmingly Black and low income. Moreover, the region's educational landscape was now extraordinarily fractured, with fourteen ASD charter operators (that also opened their doors in 2012), six small municipal districts, and the Shelby County School District. The implications for the teacher labor force and regional coordination were stark. Many saw the demerger, as it was called, as laden with undercurrents of racism. An SCS board member explained, "The reason why the demerger happened was because of race. People felt like their kids shouldn't be mixed with our kids. People felt like their children were smarter and they don't want those problems. So we merged and then they demerged. And so now we have all these municipalities with their own districts, but we're stuck with all the low-performing schools that have social issues, mental issues, community issues."

Suburban residents had a different explanation that emphasized their desire for local control. One elected official stated, "I want Memphis children to have a good education, but I'm elected to make sure [my] 57,000 people have a high quality of life. So that's my primary responsibility." The comments of another suburbanite captured the sentiment of many: "People want to feel comfortable going to the principal. They want to feel comfortable going to see the teacher. They want to be able to reach out to their school board members. They go to church with them. They go out to the cafeteria and have Sunday dinner with them. They're in the community with them. There's that familiarity and that closeness that comes with it."[69] The comment refrains from overtly mentioning race, but as Siegel-Hawley and her colleagues note in their excellent analysis of this episode, race-blind language of this sort belies actions and policies that confer advantage and concentrate resources among those who have already benefited from over a century of past policies.[70]

History's Grip: How Memphis's Past Shapes Its Schools

In his discussion of Southern cities, David Goldfield wrote: "In no other region is the past so much a part of its present."[71] One can scarcely imagine a city where that is more true than in Memphis. The Memphis economy is different from the one that emerged in the early twentieth century—multinational corporations such as FedEx now shape the city's landscape—but what has not changed is the preponderance of low-paying jobs, scant benefits, and weak union protections. Decades of territorial expansion (a reliable tool for maintaining a White electoral majority), poor public transit, and a legacy of low taxes and minimal social services have led to a sprawling, low-density geographic configuration in which jobs are both poor-paying and scattered.[72]

The social and economic marginalization of Memphis's poorest citizens is not just the unfortunate by-product of individual choices within a free-market system. Rather, it is the consequence of a litany of policies—federal, state, and local—that have kept Memphis and its suburban neighbors worlds apart. White flight was abetted by federal programs, low mortgage rates, interstate highways, state policies, and local ordinances. Weak investment in public transit has kept city dwellers from seeking jobs in the suburbs, and housing policies have ensured that the majority of urban residents stay where they are. The vast majority of public housing initiatives have been located in the city, whereas a meager 16 percent of houses built in the suburbs are multifamily constructions that could accommodate low-income families.[73] It is little surprise that among the seven municipalities in Shelby County, Memphis has the lowest relative property values, the lowest median income, and the lowest tax revenue relative to the population.[74]

Across the nineteenth, twentieth, and twenty-first centuries, the region's civic elites have stated with unwavering clarity that they will not tolerate racially integrated schools or administrative arrangements that tie their children's education to that of Black children. This was evident during Reconstruction when White elites threatened to dismantle the nascent system of public schooling rather than accept racially integrated schools; it was reiterated in the post-*Brown* era when decades of legal and administrative delays gave way to a mass exodus to the suburbs, then again at the beginning of the twenty-first century when six suburban municipalities ceded from the larger Shelby County district. A great deal has changed since the 1860s, but opposition to racially integrated schooling has remained a durable feature of White civic leadership in Memphis. The task for Memphis's school administrators, principals, teachers, and the community itself, since at least 1990, has not been how to integrate schools but how to manage a system characterized by extreme segregation and poverty.

Part II: The Historical Roots Beneath Modern Reforms

Just as the ASD and iZone must be understood in terms of a century and a half of regional politics, the reforms' educational content is no less a product of history. Indeed, one can scarcely imagine the existence of an ASD in the 1980s or 1990s. A policy enabling the state takeover of local schools and the use of private organizations to manage them is a relatively recent addition to policymakers' toolbox. To understand the ASD and iZone means understanding *both* the political history of Memphis and the broader educational context from which these reforms materialized.

The last few pages of this chapter, therefore, highlight a few of the major reform initiatives that have unfolded in Memphis since 1990, including the efforts of its first Black superintendent, Dr. Herenton; the city's central role in the implementation of a national reform initiative known as *Comprehensive School Reform* (CSR); and a massive investment by the Gates Foundation in a program to enhance teacher quality. The chapter continues through Tennessee's successful bid to secure over half a billion dollars in federal funds as part of a program known as *Race to the Top*, which in turn led to the formation of the ASD and iZone. In juxtaposing Memphis's educational history with its social and political history, we aim to show that while a successful reform derives legitimacy and support from a community's past experiences and values, equally important are the lessons gained from decades of experience in educational improvement.

When Dr. Herenton became the first Black superintendent of MCS in 1978, he was well aware of the historical significance. In accepting the position, he stated that the task of improving the school system was "a collective challenge for [all] Black people."[75] A well-regarded and experienced administrator, Herenton relentlessly lobbied for a larger budget and proposed a litany of new programs that ranged from early childhood education to computer-based instruction to multicultural programs. The fact that Memphis schools, and Black schools in particular, had been underfunded for their entire history provided additional motivation for his campaign. He is rightfully remembered as a tireless advocate for public education in Memphis.

At the same time, it is unclear to what extent Herenton oversaw a school system that embodied his lofty ideals. Herenton advocated for a variety of reforms, such as implementing more rigorous promotion standards for students, enhancing home–school communication, improving discipline and safety, and providing extra opportunities for students to learn basic skills. Herenton's time in the superintendency was also defined by acrimonious battles with the local school board around funding. Time and time again, Herenton's ambitious (albeit expensive) plans to implement wraparound supports such as early childhood education, after-school and summer programming, and computer education programs were thwarted by the school board, city council, and state legislature. Like many people of that era, Herenton seemed to believe that an increase in resources would inextricably lead to better outcomes. When the resources failed to materialize, he eventually resigned from his position in 1990.[76]

The cornucopia of various programs and services proposed by Herenton and the difficulty he encountered in bringing them to fruition exposed some of the flaws of what researchers came to understand as a "Christmas tree" approach to school improvement, in which myriad, unrelated programs are added to schools, like ornaments to a tree, absent a coherent strategy for improving teaching and learning.[77] Further, the patronage that plagued Memphis for over a century did not disappear under Herenton's leadership. An external evaluation found that appointments were motivated as much by personal considerations as by professional ones. Neither Herenton nor Memphis invented the problem of patronage in public education, yet its pervasive presence in the city would complicate subsequent efforts by local leaders to establish an education system rooted in professional expertise.[78]

No superintendent could surpass Herenton's legendary status, but if anyone could come close, it was Superintendent Gerry House, who led the school system from 1992 to 2000. Widely respected in the city and state, House placed Memphis at the center of the national reform movement when she embraced a series of "break-the-mold designs" that formed the backbone of a large-scale CSR school improvement initiative. One of the most storied chapters in the history of US education reform, CSR sought to transform the performance of thousands of chronically underperforming schools across the country by moving away from the piecemeal, Christmas tree approaches of the past in favor of comprehensive and coherent designs that focused squarely on the improvement of practice. Backed by the George H. W. Bush administration, along with several prominent corporations (e.g., Xerox, ALCOA), CSR was an effort to inject new energy, innovation, and ideas into the school reform arena. Under House's leadership, half of all Memphis schools adopted one of the dozen newly minted CSR designs.

At their best, CSR programs provided schools with detailed plans to improve classroom practice while also explicitly tying leadership, administration, and school processes to teaching and learning. Changes in federal policy would eventually undercut the market for CSR, and many of the organizations that developed and helped implement the original designs were either forced out of business or compelled to change course. Yet CSR's core contention that meaningful improvement in schools requires an integrated, comprehensive set of changes—that is, a coherent instructional system—continued to endure. Some twenty years later, iZone leaders, pivoting away from quick fixes, would embrace the foundational idea of CSR in their effort to confront the overwhelming educational challenges posed by Memphis schools.[79]

The CSR movement, and other reforms of that era, did not arrive in Memphis (or elsewhere) by coincidence. Their origins go back to the 1960s and 1970s, when scholars began to produce compelling evidence that public education exacerbated inequality more than it ameliorated it. Researchers such as James Coleman, Dan Lortie, Milbrey McLaughlin, Elizabeth Cohen, John Meyer, and David Cohen were taking an unflinching look at the organization and culture of schools, the teaching profession's dominant norms, differences in achievement among demographic groups, and the effect of reform-oriented policies. The results were sobering. Instruction was portrayed as low level, teachers as intellectually isolated, and school management as disconnected from teaching and learning.[80] Moreover, the widely held assumption that variation in conventional resources—class size, libraries, teacher salaries, science labs, textbooks—explained variation in educational outcomes was shown (by Coleman) to be largely untrue.

Mounting evidence and simmering discontent led to new policies. President Bush declared in 1988 that he wanted "to be the education president" who would "lead a renaissance of quality in our schools"—a striking departure from President Reagan's threat, issued just a few years earlier, to dismantle the federal Department of Education.[81] It was during the 1990s, though, that the contemporary policy landscape came into view, setting the stage for the ASD, iZone, and many other improvement efforts. After the Bush administration, President Clinton introduced a set of federal policies intended to cajole states into developing coherent content standards, assessments, and accountability policies.[82] Backed by a broad coalition of stakeholders that ranged from business groups to the NAACP, a coalition of state governors, and military families (to name a few), these policies gained traction in successive Democratic and Republican administrations.

When George W. Bush announced his signature education policy, No Child Left Behind (NCLB), support was bipartisan and broad.

Standards-based reform's broad bulwark of support also stems from the fact that these policies have skirted controversial issues of race. As segregation has steadily ticked back up since its low point in 1988, most education policies have implicitly adopted a separate-but-equal philosophy, seeking to improve schools without altering their racial composition.[83] Indeed, when George W. Bush introduced NCLB, he famously stated that the policy would confront the "soft bigotry of low expectations"; implicit in his words was a distinct lack of interest in confronting the hard bigotry of racial segregation.

Yet without policies that required districts to measure outcomes, identify the performance of historically underperforming groups, and press schools to do better, there would have been no CSR, ASD, iZone, or any other effort to improve educational opportunity for students who have been left far behind by over a century of economic and social marginalization. Standards and accountability have been no panacea for Memphis, but as the previous pages have shown, the prior eras of public education were no golden age either.

The Half-Billion-Dollar Game Changer: Tennessee's Race to the Top Victory

Tennessee Governor Phil Bredesen, a popular second-term Democrat, had long promoted educational reform, going back to his days as Nashville mayor. Between 2003 and 2008, his administration pushed through a variety of reforms, including pre-K programs, increased teacher salaries, and more equitable funding formulas. But it was a devastating 2007 report from the Tennessee Chamber of Commerce, coupled with bottom-of-the-barrel National Assessment of Educational Progress scores, that spurred the governor to take aggressive action. The report gave the state a grade of D for overall academic achievement, an F for the achievement of low-income and minority students, a C for the rigor of its standards, an F for its degree of postsecondary and workforce readiness, and an F for what it called "truth in advertising."[84] Hardly a ringing endorsement for a governor who claimed to prioritize education. Determined to reverse course, Bredesen launched an all-out effort to win a potentially game-changing grant that had recently been announced by the Obama administration.

Race to the Top was not a mandate or a condition of Title I funding in the way NCLB was but an invitation for states to vie for an enormous injection of federal dollars into their education budgets. States that chose to enter the competition (and almost all did) were instructed to focus on four priorities: adopting college- and career-ready standards, building data systems that measured student growth, establishing hiring and retention policies that rewarded effective teachers, and turning around chronically underperforming schools. With grants as high as half a billion dollars and districts still reeling from the financial fallout of the Great Recession, the stakes were high.

On March 29, 2010, Tennessee was named as one of two states to win Race to the Top's first round of competition. Several factors led to Tennessee taking home the $501,000,000 prize. One was a major piece of legislation that Bredesen's team oversaw and that passed through the legislature with overwhelming bipartisan support.[85] The legislation, fittingly named First to the Top, required annual evaluations of teachers and principals, mandated that 50 percent of teacher and principal evaluations be based on student achievement data, and created the ASD, a special state-operated district dedicated to turning around chronically low-performing schools. Tennessee's proposal was also boosted by its 2008 adoption of the Common Core State Standards, which replaced the notoriously low-level Tennessee Comprehensive Assessment Program (TCAP) standards and assessment and had led to its F score for "truth in advertising."

Separate Strategies, Common Goals: The ASD and iZone Take Shape

The new teacher evaluation system was initially the most controversial part of the new law; the Tennessee Education Association (TEA) "expressed deep reservations" about student achievement measures accounting for 50 percent of teacher evaluations.[86] Indeed, so extensive was the attention given to teacher evaluation that the provision in the law establishing the ASD seemed to pass virtually unnoticed. Bradley Leon, who would later become Shelby County's deputy superintendent, was one of the few observers who foresaw the controversy that would later unfold: "I was struck that virtually all of the media coverage was focused on the governor's proposal for how teachers would be evaluated . . . This fight subsumed talk of the boldest reform: The Achievement School District . . . What if all teachers in Memphis became at-will employees and 60% of our district became charter schools? That these questions did not surface more prominently is simply puzzling."[87]

The ideas behind the ASD were bold and ambitious. First to the Top directed the Tennessee Department of Education to generate a list of "priority schools" comprising the schools in the bottom 5 percent of performance across the state.[88] The law granted the state's commissioner of education total authority over hiring, curriculum, and other educational matters in priority schools. Further, it enabled the commissioner to grant charters or other private organizations the responsibility of operating the schools. Explicit in the law was that ASD schools would no longer be under the jurisdiction of the local school board and that all staff members were subject to replacement. Schools taken over by the ASD would start from scratch. The ASD reached its peak during the 2016–17 school year, when it had thirty-three schools under its management, twenty-nine of which were located in Memphis neighborhoods.

Turning the ASD from a law into an operational agency fell to newly hired State Commissioner of Education Kevin Huffman. A former Teach for America executive, Huffman had earned a national reputation when *The Washington Post* named him "America's Next Great Pundit" because of his communication skills and wide-ranging knowledge of policy. From his hiring in March 2011 to his resignation in November 2014, Huffman made deep changes to the state's education policy landscape while also generating considerable controversy.

Among his earliest and most consequential moves was to hire Chris Barbic as superintendent of the ASD. As mentioned earlier, Barbic had been the founder and director of the Houston-based charter network YES Prep, which had gained national attention for its impressive graduation and college attendance rates among a predominantly disadvantaged student body. That Barbic's appointment garnered wide-scale praise from the likes of Secretary Duncan and other high-profile names in the education community is not hard to understand; who better to take on the task of leading the ASD than someone who had actually done the work. The claim that all children can learn is a familiar refrain in contemporary education circles, but Barbic was among the few who had demonstrated actual success in meeting this challenge. What he knew far less about, however, was the politics and history of Memphis and, still less, the consequences of curtailing local control in a city where the struggle for equal representation had left deep scars.

Between Huffman and Barbic, the ASD's educational philosophy quickly came into focus. Autonomy for school operators, minimal state interference, competition, and accountability emerged as guiding principles. Under Barbic's leadership, the ASD would authorize charters or (in a few cases) other nonprofit organizations to operate one or more ASD schools according to their own beliefs and strategy. That is, despite Barbic's and other ASD officials' considerable experience, the ASD central office would allow each of the fourteen organizations operating ASD schools to hire their own teachers, select their own curriculum, determine their own pedagogy, and in general, chart their own course.

What the ASD central office did do, however, was establish strict accountability measures that demanded rapid growth in student outcomes. ASD operators could adopt whatever strategy they wanted, but those who failed to demonstrate progress faced the threat of removal. There was one additional caveat. Unlike traditional charter schools, in which families apply and often have to enter a lottery to gain admission, *ASD schools would retain their status as neighborhood schools open to all within the traditional attendance zones*. While ASD schools would have new leaders, teachers, and curriculum, and operate under a new governance structure, one thing that would not change was the student body. This difference between conventional charter schools and ASD schools would prove to have enormous consequences.

The ASD, however, could only be a partial solution to the state's problem of underperforming schools. Limited capacity was one reason. There were over sixty priority schools in Memphis alone, which was far more than the fledgling ASD could handle. Money was a second factor. In addition to the Race to the Top funds, the state was flush with its share of the $3 billion School Improvement Grants (SIGs) that the Obama administration handed out to districts across the country as part of the 2009 American Recovery and Reinvestment Act. For Huffman, the SIG money offered an opportunity to bring his philosophy to districts over which he otherwise had limited influence. A third reason was political. The ASD represented a muscular state intervention in a region whose political culture valued local control. As Huffman later explained: "The idea of having district-controlled zones was always going to be more politically palatable than the state coming in and running schools itself." He was certainly right about that.

The state officially announced in 2012 that it would launch three iZones—one in Hamilton County, an economically diverse county that included the city of Chattanooga and a mix of urban, suburban, and rural areas; one in Davidson County, which encompassed Metro Nashville; and one in Shelby County, which included Memphis. With sixty-nine of the eighty-five priority schools located in Shelby County, its iZone was by far the largest and most consequential. In contrast to the ASD, iZones would be district-run initiatives that operated within a traditional governance structure under the aegis of a locally elected school board. With the SIG funds providing a million dollars per iZone school, districts found themselves with an unusual and well-funded opportunity. In August 2012, SCS launched its iZone as a special enclave within the larger district dedicated to turning around priority schools.

Conclusion

Few people could have predicted that the ASD and iZone would dominate headlines across the state for the next several years or that a state intervention into a handful of schools would generate extraordinary community resentment, heated neighborhood meetings, and sustained resistance. But to understand the iZone and the ASD means looking beyond the laws that created them or the intentions of their founders. It requires understanding the century-and-a-half battle for control of the bodies where educational decisions are made, policies set, and resources allocated. It means recognizing that the struggle for representation in educational institutions is inextricably tied to the larger quest for political power, self-determination, and equality. It also means seeing both systems as embodying a set of ideas about schools as organizations, about how students learn and what they should learn, and about how to orchestrate change in schools whose organizational blueprint dates back over a century. And most of all, it means understanding the connection between politics and history, and the work that goes on inside the schools, where teachers and students attempt to forge new patterns of teaching and learning.

CHAPTER TWO

Designing Systems and Building Coalitions

The Achievement School District (ASD) and Innovation Zone (iZone) were established to improve educational outcomes. To accomplish that goal, they would have to design instructional systems that would enable performance at a level that few US states, districts, or charter organizations have ever accomplished. As we elaborate in the second half of this chapter, designing a system of teaching and learning at this level represents a complex, multilayered challenge in virtually any set of circumstances, and even more so for ASD operators, all of whom were either new to Memphis or lacked experience running an educational organization. It was no less a conundrum for iZone leaders who were deeply familiar with the community but who were forced to lean on long-standing leaders and teachers in the hope that they could somehow realize better results than suggested by the district's past performance. Moreover, ASD and iZone leaders had to contend with over a century of history that had left many Memphians unimaginably poor and lacking many of the social and economic resources that contribute to academic success. From an educational perspective, they had their work cut out for them.

The challenge, however, was not just educational. Both the iZone and ASD also needed to engender support from multiple stakeholder groups in a city where cross-coalition collaboration has been rare and divisions run deep. A spirit of unity could hardly be taken for granted. Still, each system had political assets it could draw on. The ASD was bolstered by the support of powerful allies at the state and national level, and as a new entity, it was not weighed down by a history of poor performance. The iZone lacked those types of political connections, as well as the bells and whistles of a new innovation, but it could still rely on its insider status and deep connections to the city. At the same time, both the iZone and ASD had to grapple with the thorny conundrum of finding support in a divided region with little history of collectively working toward shared goals.

In this chapter, we examine the strategies that iZone and ASD leaders adopted to meet these formidable challenges and highlight the educational and political assumptions that undergirded them. The discussion sets the stage for chapters 3 and 4, in which we consider how these strategies unfolded across dozens of schools as teachers and leaders attempted to turn well-intentioned plans into classroom practice, as well as how system leaders attempted to rally public support in a highly politicized environment. It will come as little surprise that seemingly well-reasoned strategies devised by experienced educators encountered significant setbacks that forced a reconsideration of basic assumptions. Chapter 5 highlights the strategic adjustments that these leaders made as they learned from that experience.

Building Civic Capacity in a Divided City

Leaders of both the ASD and iZone had to ensure the support of key stakeholders, without which their educational goals would have little chance of success. Even the most well-constructed reform is of little value if it collapses in the face of opposition and instability. Key to that staying power is the coalescence of multiple interest groups around a shared educational agenda and strategy. The business community, parent groups, municipal leaders, organized labor, and educators are all critical players, but none can sustain a major reform initiative on its own.[1] In a field teeming with stakeholders, sustainability requires a coalition.

The ability of communities to build and sustain coalitions of this nature is what political scientist Clarence Stone refers to as *civic capacity*. Civic capacity entails a deliberate bridging of group differences in pursuit of a shared goal, along with the willingness to work together to realize that goal. As Stone's description makes clear, civic capacity is a political action: "Civic capacity is not a magical kind of consensus that simply emerges on occasion; it has to be created politically . . . Some education reformers may be uncomfortable with phrases like 'political action.' But politics also has an older meaning: The activity by which a diverse citizenry reconcile, put aside, or in some manner accommodate their differences in order to pursue their common well-being."[2]

Civic capacity can be thought of as existing in the interaction between a community—its history, politics, and interest groups—and a particular policy with its problem definition and plans for remedying it. The nature of civic capacity depends heavily on the particular community and policy at hand. For example, communities with little experience in building robust political coalitions to pursue shared agendas or that have a history of mistrust face a particularly steep challenge in generating civic capacity. At the same time, some reforms are more amenable to consensus while others exacerbate historic divisions. The 1950s National Science Foundation's curricular reforms failed to engender broad-based support because they exposed cultural divisions on issues such as evolution, religion, and human sexuality.[3] The swift political backlash led to the demise of a once highly touted but long-since-forgotten curriculum. Conversely, the No Child Left Behind Act was bolstered by an ideologically diverse coalition of supporters that included the business community, civil rights organizations, and many in the education reform community. The design of reforms matters not just for educational reasons but for political ones, too.

Some readers will note the connection between the concepts of civic capacity and legitimacy. Indeed, one way to understand civic capacity is as a political process that enhances the social legitimacy of a policy in the eyes of multiple stakeholder groups. Briefly, one can think of legitimacy as the degree of cultural support for an organization that flows from both its values and performance. The mark of a legitimate organization is the extent to which one is hard-pressed to envision the world without it, be it *The New York Times*, the Boston Celtics, or Google.[4]

Legitimacy has long occupied educational researchers, and it looms large in our analysis of the ASD and iZone. One way to think about this book's central question is how reform can be both effective and legitimate in pluralistic, diverse societies. In the 1970s, sociologists from Stanford published a series of papers arguing that schools operated without a well-defined knowledge base or set of proven techniques yet within a *cultural* context in which there were firm beliefs about the nature of "good schools."[5] In practice, this meant that while there was little codified knowledge by which school leaders could manage or evaluate teaching and learning, there were other culturally powerful ways that they could maintain social legitimacy and public support. New gymnasiums, libraries, science labs, graduation ceremonies, holiday festivals, and shiny textbooks may have little proven connection to student learning, but they are powerful "cultural myths" that engender confidence in public schools. So long as these myths held firm, there was little reason for educational leaders to worry about legitimacy or the need to build civic capacity. The system may not have served all students well, and enormous inequities hid just below the surface, but public confidence remained strong. As H. D. Meyer and Brian Rowan wrote, "Organizations such as schools and colleges . . . are held together more by shared beliefs—'myths'—than by technical exigencies or a logic of efficiency."[6]

But the 1970s have long since passed, and both theory and facts have evolved. The emergence and now full institutionalization of standards and accountability means that the public can (and does) evaluate schools based on measurable evidence of student learning. Legitimacy, in other words, is no longer just a matter of conforming to cultural myths but also a function of measured academic performance. Football games, proms, graduation ceremonies, school libraries, and science labs have maintained a degree of cultural cache, but their role in maintaining public education's social legitimacy has been offset by access to data on student achievement. For educational leaders, particularly for those in high-stakes environments like the ASD and iZone, the significance of this is clear: Outcomes matter.

A second change from previous eras is in the number and type of organizations that run schools. The growing dissatisfaction with traditional systems (in part fueled by the availability of outcome data) has led to a proliferation of new organizations that deliver educational services, including charter management organizations, private firms, state-run districts, school improvement networks, online schools, families organized into pods, and more. The traditional district and school board, once the only game in town, must now compete for students, teachers, financial resources, and legitimacy in an increasingly crowded institutional field.[7]

The implication of this for the leaders of the iZone and ASD was that maintaining public legitimacy was a two-pronged affair. They would need to muster the technical capability to improve outcomes while simultaneously attending to community norms and values that went beyond academic performance. This meant finding better ways to teach math, reading, and other content areas while also recognizing that in these neighborhoods, the social and historical significance of schools could not be reduced to a test score. This was not an either/or proposition; it was both. Moreover, the fact that these systems operated in a contentious and politically charged environment made juggling these demands all the more important and all the more challenging.

Top-Down Power, Grassroots Politics: The ASD Searches for Local Buy-In

As a state agency enshrined in the First to the Top Act (the law that created the ASD), the ASD's authority and legality were not in question.[8] The ASD is not alone in this regard. A combination of states' constitutional authority, resources, and enforcement capacity has enabled numerous state takeovers, and lawsuits intended to deter them have generally not been successful.[9] In short, the ASD had broad latitude to remove schools from local control, take over building facilities, and authorize charter operators to run them. From a legal perspective, there was little that opponents could do to stop them.

The ASD also drew strength from its ideological underpinnings. Market-oriented ideas about parental choice and competition, coupled with thinly veiled disdain for traditional districts, appealed to many across government, nonprofit, and philanthropic sectors. Even the Obama administration signaled its support, with Secretary of Education Arne Duncan calling the hiring of Chris Barbic a "deeply inspired choice" to lead the ASD's "courageous work."[10] Duncan's nod of approval was quickly followed by financial backing from a wide array of deep-pocketed allies. Beyond its $22 million share of the state's Race to the Top award, a separate federal grant funneled an additional $5.6 million into ASD schools.[11] National philanthropies, such as the Walton Family Foundation and the Laura and John Arnold Foundation, as well as Tennessee-based philanthropies, including the Hyde, Poplar, and Pyramid Peak Foundations, also chipped in significant sums of money.[12]

Organizations and advocacy groups sympathetic to the ASD philosophy—for example, the Black Alliance for Educational Options, the Tennessee Black Alliance, Memphis Lift, and the Tennessee Charter Association—heaped on support and praise. Adding to this was a network of like-minded training and support organizations, such as the Memphis Teacher Residency, Teach for America, Relay Graduate School of Education, and New Leaders, that supplemented their teacher and leader workforce while helping to build professional capacity. Writing for the Fordham Institute in 2013, Chester Finn and Amber Winkler offered an upbeat assessment: "The ASD is now leading the charge in developing talented building and classroom leaders, luring high-quality charter management organizations to the Volunteer State, and incubating new public school choices."[13]

The ASD was an attractive proposition to state education officials and even a handful of local representatives who thought that it would jolt the local system out of what they saw as a deep stupor. State Representative and Chair of the Education Committee Mark White stated, "It's my opinion that you've got to do anything you can to put competition in the system to where that which is not working will eventually go away. That's something you learn as a business. I believe that same thing works in the education system."

Commissioner of Education Candice McQueen saw the potential displacement of local teachers as a much-needed wake-up call. "I would say if a teacher has lost his or her job, they need to . . . retool to make sure they can meet the expectations of what we're now demanding." A long-serving local representative in Memphis who thought the district had grown complacent voiced his agreement: "The [Shelby County] school system stands there like the big guy on the block. It's this way or no way. That's the mindset." Most state-level Democrats, following Governor Phil Bredesen's lead, voted in favor of establishing the ASD, whereas Republicans, with little to lose from a policy that predominantly targeted the Democratic stronghold of Memphis, were virtually unanimous in their support.

Yet neither money, the support of the state legislature, nor national attention was a substitute for legitimacy at the local level. Even as state governments, federal authorities, and private groups have become increasingly active in the education sector, localism remains alive and well.[14] What Clarence Stone wrote twenty-five years ago is still true today: "It is at the local level that crucial support for reform is built, resistance mounted, and conflicts over education worked out."[15] Legitimacy, in other words, is still largely a local phenomenon.

None of this came as a surprise to Barbic and other ASD leaders, who clearly hoped that the district's undeniably poor performance would bolster local support. Although careful not to criticize local leaders, ASD officials stated time and again that the community deserved a higher-performing education system and that it was the ASD that would deliver the improvement. Barbic also pushed back on the perception that the ASD was taking schools away from the community, arguing that it was actually making them more local: "Essentially what we're doing is we're taking schools out of local control and actually giving them back to the community through nonprofit organizations that are running hyper-local networks of schools."

Moreover, Barbic made it abundantly clear that he had little interest in incremental or marginal improvement. Shortly after arriving in Memphis, he issued a statement that, in many ways, would define his tenure at the ASD. Speaking to a reporter in 2011, he declared that the ASD would lift schools into the top quartile of the state, as measured by the state's own accountability metrics. He continued, "And in three years if we haven't gotten that done, then I shouldn't be here. I think the ultimate accountability is that I shouldn't have a job." Barbic's claim was more than just bold; it was unprecedented. Research on school turnaround has noted instances of success and some promising trends, but rarely has it documented the extraordinary gains that Barbic predicted.

Critics mocked his audacity, but Barbic's intent was as much political as it was educational. His message to the local community was that it should settle for nothing less than transformative change and that reflexive support for the local district was misguided. As he explained in a 2015 interview, "To be clear, my expectation isn't that parents are going to jump up and down and say 'Yay, ASD!' at the very beginning of this process. I think a more realistic goal is for parents and communities to demand something better, to recognize that they deserve better than what's been happening in their schools." Still, Barbic seemed to intuit a key insight of policy analysis: What it takes to initiate a policy reform is not the same as what it takes to sustain it.[16] Recognizing the imperative, he stated, "We could just do what we want and cram this down people's throats. We could do that, and maybe we'd get greater results that way, but as soon as we left, none of the work would be sustainable. We're doing this as much as possible with communities, with the district, with the folks in the schools."

ASD leaders attempted to back these words with actions. They engaged local neighborhoods with community meetings, fairs, and picnics. Barbic, his Chief Deputy Malika Anderson, and other members of his staff sought connections with local religious leaders, community organizations, and even district officials. Ever the optimist, Barbic was hopeful that the community would see the ASD as an earnest effort to improve long-underperforming schools and, in doing so, to improve the life chances of children from marginalized communities. "We're building relationships with the local districts and superintendents, community leaders, teachers, and folks that are impacted by us," he said. "I think we've done a pretty good job."

Promises, Power, and Pushback: The ASD's Legitimacy Challenge

But neither Barbic's optimism nor his charisma could change the reality that bringing the community on board was a tenuous proposition. Notions of markets, competition, and parental choice that garnered the support of national organizations were unlikely to engender much enthusiasm from the local community. Nor was Barbic's status as a White outsider particularly helpful. Past research in cities like Washington, DC; Newark, New Jersey; and New Orleans, Louisiana, has documented the way in which upper-middle-class (and often White) residents look at a particular education reform and see one thing, whereas historically marginalized community members see something else.[17] For example, in his cogent analysis of the transition of Washington, DC, to a mayoral-controlled education system, Jeffrey Henig explained how attitudes toward mayoral control hinged on differing historical and cultural narratives. For upper-middle-class residents, many of whom were relative newcomers to the city, the promise of greater efficiency, accountability, and performance proved compelling. But local and predominantly Black Washingtonians listened "with a different set of ears" that were attuned to the city's fraught experiences with democracy and civil rights. Henig writes: "Against that backdrop, the message of school reform . . . was heard as one of racial disempowerment and the sacrifice of community-based jobs and institutions for the sake of corporate values (efficiency, lower taxes, managerial expertise)."[18]

In Memphis, the specifics differed, but the general point held. The features of the ASD that appealed to its (largely, although not exclusively, White) supporters would not necessarily carry over to the (predominantly Black) residents of the neighborhoods where ASD schools were located. Moreover, several factors tied the local community to the district whose schools the ASD was taking. Not only do the origins of the Shelby County School District date back over 150 years, but it is among the largest employers in the region; it has been an important institutional actor in the development of the Black professional class; and as discussed in chapter 1, it figured prominently in Black Memphians' decades-long civil rights battle. Further, the aftershocks of the departure of six suburban municipalities were still acutely felt around the city. Ramesh Akbari, a Memphis resident and Tennessee state senator, explained the negative perception that the ASD was likely to spark in the community: "When you have people losing their jobs and you have a school changing so dramatically and so quickly, then there's going to be a negative reaction." Or as another community member reflected, "The ASD is an outsider. SCS is home."

None of this negated Barbic's arguments about the district's weak academic performance or the need for improvement, but it did mean that residents' attitudes toward their local schools were deeper than ASD leaders fully appreciated. Yet there was one thing that the ASD could do to bring at least some people on board, and that was to deliver the promised results. The disruption to the local system and the usurping of locally elected representatives meant that for the ASD, fulfilling Barbic's promise of dramatic gains in student learning was not just an educational challenge but also a political imperative. Indeed, there was little else the ASD could do to convince local residents to see it as a credible effort to improve local schools.

The iZone's Fight to Improve and Protect Memphis Schools

If the legitimacy of the ASD to operate Memphis schools was up for debate, the rights of the local district were seemingly unassailable. In part, Americans generally accept the premise that it is the job of locally elected school boards to appoint superintendents who, in turn, oversee a local education system. There are a few other countries that delegate decision-making about basic educational functions—curriculum, pedagogy, budgets, hiring—to localities, but such has been the American way since the origins of the system in the mid-nineteenth century. In that sense, Shelby County Schools (SCS) is no different from the vast majority of US school districts.[19]

But the district's ties to local history and to its people run deeper than in other areas and in ways that differ from many suburban school systems. For Memphis's Black residents, the district is inextricably linked to decades of civil rights efforts, desegregation battles, and the rise of Black political power. Recall that no Black citizen had even *attempted* to seek political office from 1888 to 1951 until Dr. Joseph E. Walker sought a school board seat in 1951, followed by Reverend Roy Love in 1955. Alarmed by those near victories, White elites changed electoral regulations to prevent Black political progress. It was not until the election of Maxine Smith to the school board in 1971 and the appointment of W. W. Herenton to the superintendency in 1978 that cracks emerged in the armor of a century of White political supremacy.[20] The education system, in other words, was an inextricable part of Black Memphians' historic struggle for political power.

For all these reasons, countering the state's claim that the district was too inept to improve its own schools was an imperative with deep historical roots. That state officials made little effort to hide their contempt for the district and the need for an external intervention added further fuel to the fire. Note the words of one school board member: "When I talk to the legislature about a different legislative agenda [from the ASD], I have been told point-blank, 'You all had your chance. You're dragging the state down, so we are going to come in and fix you.' That is the attitude." The historic and political significance of the iZone was not lost on district leaders. As one official put it: "The iZone is trying to do something that wasn't formally said. People from outside of our state were coming to take the schools that were in African American neighborhoods with rich histories . . . So, part of our primary role is to help those schools."

Politics was not the only thing that tied Memphians to their schools. As employment opportunities migrated to the suburbs throughout the 1970s and 1980s, the education system became an increasingly important source of jobs, benefits, and social status that helped sustain the city's middle class.[21] With nearly fourteen thousand employees,[22] only FedEx employs more residents of the county. Additionally, Memphis schools are widely regarded as historic neighborhood institutions and sources of civic pride. Football games still draw former alumni from across the country, and various websites, YouTube videos, and documentaries celebrate neighborhood history, school championships, and the handful of residents who have achieved fame.[23] Memphis high schools maintain active alumni associations. An iZone principal and longtime Memphis resident described one of Memphis's most storied neighborhoods—Orange Mound—where both the ASD and iZone operated schools: "Orange Mound has a really rich, long history. It's a city within a city. Orange Mound and Harlem are the oldest African American communities in which African Americans own their homes. In the 1960s and '70s, before desegregation and busing of students, this was a thriving African American community with its own bank, its own grocery store. It was self-sufficient."

This history does not appear in the legislation that established the iZone. Yet it is through this lens that one understands the iZone not only as a way to improve outcomes in some of the city's most poorly performing schools but also as an opportunity to reassert the city's right to run its own schools, control its own destiny, and protect hard-won political gains. The iZone was about education, but it was also about identity, history, and politics. It was of little surprise, then, that Superintendent Dorsey Hopson tapped longtime local educator Dr. Sharon Griffin to be the first leader of the iZone. Whereas Barbic was an outsider, Dr. Griffin was among the city's most celebrated educators with a track record of success.

A native Memphian, Griffin began her tenure with SCS in the fall of 1991 as a teacher, later becoming a principal in Orange Mound and then eventually moving into the central office. A charismatic leader with an outsized personality and a loyal following, Griffin nonetheless maintained a stance of modesty and humility. When asked to comment on the success of the iZone, she simply said, "I made so many mistakes." With Dr. Griffin at the helm, the contrast between the iZone and ASD could not have been clearer. One board of education member put it this way: "The people in the iZone have been here; they know this community. They don't have to learn the community. They didn't have to do a whole lot of professional development on cultures." Although the board member did not mention the ASD, the implication was clear.

From Legacy to Learning: The New Test of Legitimacy

Were this story transpiring in the 1980s, there would be little more to say about the iZone's bedrock of support. The provision of jobs and economic security, the historic ties to civil rights and Black political power, and its long-standing position in the community would have silenced critics. In the current era, however, system leaders can no longer assume that the social and political forces of old will provide legitimacy as in the past. Put simply, in this day and age, results matter. Whereas previous education battles in the city have often been about increasing access to schools, the school board, and teaching and leadership positions, the current struggle is also about educational quality and outcomes. As Daniel Kiel, who traced the long legal history of desegregation in Memphis, put it, "Jockeying for governing power will prove historically meaningless if the opportunity to deliver higher quality educational opportunities . . . is squandered."[24]

That learning outcomes in many Memphis schools were weak was not a matter of debate; less certain were the reasons behind the poor performance. As education researchers have long known, economic and social circumstances go hand in hand with educational outcomes, and Memphis was no different. In Memphis City Schools (now Memphis Shelby County Schools) in 2010, over 74 percent of schools had a student poverty rate of at least 90 percent, and nearly 68 percent of schools were over 90 percent African American. Overall at that time, 85 percent of students in Memphis were Black, a staggering 87 percent were classified as economically disadvantaged, and the city's child poverty rate hovered at just under 40 percent. Unemployment, crime, and drug addiction were rampant.[25] For all these reasons, the achievement data from 2014 are unsurprisingly bleak: Nearly 25 percent of students in Shelby County achieved proficiency in math, and 32 percent achieved proficiency in reading.[26] By comparison, in the surrounding suburbs, 63 percent of students achieved proficiency in math, and nearly 69 percent achieved proficiency in reading.[27] The overall social and economic deterioration placed enormous pressure on the school system, which had to cope with students who brought an array of academic and social needs into the classroom.

Yet for some local residents, the economic and social conditions that plagued many Memphis neighborhoods were not the entire story. Voices from inside the community and even within the district cast doubt on the district's commitment to overcoming these challenges and finding ways to improve. None other than Superintendent Hopson questioned the motives that often seemed to motivate decision-making: "People say all the time, 'It's about the kids.' But when you really unpack what they are saying, kids may be number three of four on the list. It's about jobs, it's about contracts, it's about protecting this and protecting that. I think that is the reason we are in this position." This sentiment was echoed by Tomeka Hart, a native Memphian who served on the Memphis School Board and as an adviser to the governor: "There were good people on the board, but there were people who were in the way, continuing to be more obstacles than trying to move a school system in a way that it educates all children." Similarly, Dr. Nakia Towns, a long-serving state-level official, noted that the district's performance was a reason for serious concern and hard questions: "I think that it would be hard to argue that in Shelby County, there weren't years of [poor] performance that should have alarmed the community such that they would have rallied to invest in these schools." History, politics, and economics tied the district to the community, but questions about its professional capacity simmered below the surface.

Moreover, whereas many districts have a few underperforming schools toward which they can direct extra resources, Shelby County had a whopping sixty-nine schools ranked in the bottom 5 percent of the state. As Superintendent Hopson admitted, the district needed help: "I think that just because of the sheer number of schools that are here, we need some help." There is no doubt that the number of underperforming schools in the district was daunting, but no amount of outside assistance would relieve the district from the task of dramatically improving the teaching and learning in its own schools. The question was whether it was up for the challenge.

The Politics of Starting Over

The iZone's strong community ties were among its key assets, yet in other ways, they proved a liability. Like the ASD, the iZone strategy rested on wholesale changes in schools. Once a school was pulled from the larger school district and entered into the iZone, the existing principal and the majority of teachers would be replaced with other (and presumably better) leaders and teachers from within the district. The sweeping changes to school staff were integral to the iZone strategy for generating quick gains in a fraught and impatient environment, but they still risked a backlash among residents loyal to their neighborhood schools. Bradley Leon, the district's deputy superintendent, explained: "You're talking about basically fresh starting a school. You've got a bunch of teachers who are worried about losing their jobs, and you've got community members who care a lot about a school in their community; so, they leverage their board members to weigh in on their behalf."

Underlying the ties between the schools and community was an expectation that locals would have direct input into how schools would be run and, more importantly, who would run them. Further, there was an expectation that school doors would be perpetually open, allowing what one SCS official described as "free access to the building." Bradley Leon described the dynamics of selecting a new principal at one iZone high school: "The principal at Douglas High School, her father had been the principal, and she had been the principal for a very long time. When the iZone took over that school, the alumni association just wanted us to re-hire her as the principal. They did everything they could to select the principal."

The experience of Antonio Burt, a former iZone principal, is equally informative. Burt would later replace Dr. Griffin as the head of the iZone and, in many ways, prove to be its most influential leader, but when the iZone first took shape in 2011, he was still a middle school principal and not yet the household name he would later become. After several years as a teacher and coach in Memphis City Schools, Burt, like many iZone principals, was accepted to a year-long leadership training program at an organization called New Leaders.[28] When the iZone began operations in 2012, he was a natural choice to be among the first cohort of principals.

Burt wasted little time in instituting changes. Leveraging the hiring authority granted to iZone principals, he brought back only two of the school's existing teachers, deeming the wholesale change in faculty as the best way to upgrade professional expertise. "When I was first a principal at Ford Road, I only brought back two of the existing staff. The community didn't like that because those people have been there, taught some of their kids, and so forth. I caught a lot of backlash." Community concerns, he noted, were not always motivated by the need to improve teaching and learning: "The community demands tend to be around relationships. People that may have taught them or taught their kids, or someone that they went to school with. The school might have a 0.7 percent success rate and been on the state priority list for five consecutive years, but the demands are for the people in the building, which may not be in the best interests of kids."

The idea of community control is not unique to Memphis. Chicago experimented with community control in the 1990s and early 2000s by granting parents and neighborhood residents decision-making authority over an array of educational decisions, including the hiring and dismissal of building principals. Similar experiments were tried in New York City in the 1960s, in which neighborhood residents exercised considerable power over local schools. Some analysts see the elevation of local residents into positions of formal authority as a potential force for change, claiming that it represents a form of deliberative democracy that has proven successful in other areas. Commenting on the Chicago reform, education researcher Anthony Bryk stated that the reform was predicated on the idea that by "expanding local participation in school affairs, a collective responsibility for the schools' work would emerge," and this would "advance significant changes in classroom instruction and ultimately in student learning."[29]

In this sense, there was nothing unprecedented in neighborhood demands for involvement in school-level decisions. The problem was that district leaders wanted the iZone to be a system in which decisions were motivated by professional qualifications and expert knowledge. In sociological terms, the iZone was seeking to dislodge a system of community control with a system of professional control. An iZone administrator described the type of principals they were looking for: "The major emphasis is making sure the school leaders are instructional leaders . . . That's making sure leaders are able to drive results, influence the classroom, and problem solve."

It's no small irony that iZone leaders defended these changes the same way that ASD proponents defended the state takeover: by pointing to the schools' weak academic performance and the need for change. And like ASD leaders, district officials gambled that the promise of improvement would justify what some local residents took to be (and in a sense was) a loss of power. The question was whether they could deliver the results, and if the district's history of past performance was any indication, the answer was far from certain.

The ASD and iZone Fight to Own the Narrative

Despite similar academic ambitions and shared challenges, iZone and ASD leaders were well aware of the emerging competition between the two systems. Each side knew the other's vulnerabilities. In an effort to generate community support for the ASD, Barbic was quick to highlight the dismal state of the schools the ASD was taking over. Discussing his strategy to win over a skeptical community, he said, "Parents need to have the whole story before they start to make their signs and get upset. And when you get them away from all that and you just sit down and talk about how the schools are doing, nobody's happy about the performance in the school. So when you see 'save our school' signs, the question I always ask is 'save it from what?' Only 2 percent of the kids can read."

Similarly, when asked to comment on the iZone's early successes (which we discuss in chap. 3), Barbic was quick to point out that the assessment gains did little to build system-wide capacity: "If you look at where those [iZone principals] came from, all they did was create the next set of priority schools. So that strategy only works if you've got a talent pipeline to backfill where you're pulling those people from, and right now, that talent pipeline doesn't exist." Dr. Griffin and other iZone leaders would eventually conclude that Barbic's analysis was right.

At the same time, iZone leaders were equally aware of the ASD's vulnerabilities. When asked to comment on the ASD, one district leader reinforced the popular narrative that the ASD was a group of outsiders uninformed and uninterested in the local community: "You have individuals from places who have nothing to do with Memphis. You can't do that. You have to have people who are vested in the community and in those kids, and who understand the mindset of the children that you serve." ASD and district leaders would eventually arrive at a degree of cordiality and even mutual respect, "coopertition," as Superintendent Hopson would call it. But in the early years, when the stakes were high and the atmosphere fraught, each side sought ways to delegitimize the other.

Designing a High-Performing System in a High-Stakes, High-Needs Environment

Aware of threats to their legitimacy, managers of both the ASD and iZone confronted a stark reality. They would need to design instructional systems that accomplished what countless past reforms had failed to do: Improve learning outcomes in schools with a long history of poor academic performance and that served students who had been deprived of the social and economic supports that bolster academic success.

Designing high-performing instructional systems confronts education managers, be they in Memphis or anywhere else, with myriad dilemmas and challenges. These include basic questions about what curriculum to adopt, what assessments to use, and what pedagogical techniques to embrace. These questions lead to more complex ones, such as what knowledge and skills teachers need in order to use the curriculum effectively, which in turn raises questions about the type of learning opportunities that will help teachers develop those capabilities, as well as how those opportunities will be stitched into the daily life of the system. For example, instructional coaching has become popular in recent years, but while deploying a cadre of coaches can be an effective way to build capacity, it also creates another layer of the system to be set up and managed. Just as good teachers do not appear out of thin air, neither do good coaches. Similarly, hands-on instructional leadership is widely considered a key ingredient of an effective school, but instituting this requires large-scale retraining of leaders, the development of classroom observation protocols, and new systems of oversight and data management.

Additional dilemmas include striking the optimal balance between fidelity to the curriculum and adaptation to the needs of each classroom and student. Teachers often favor increased discretion, but absent the requisite professional knowledge, adaptation becomes a recipe for inconsistency. Highly specified lesson plans increase consistency but still require teachers who can use them adaptively in classroom settings. Our point is not that there is one best way to design an instructional system but that even in the best of circumstances, doing so is a complex, multifaceted, knowledge-demanding endeavor.

And these were not the best of circumstances. As noted previously, both the ASD and iZone confronted a student body in which poverty was high, outcomes low, and the educational challenge formidable (see table 1). Moreover, these results predated the state's adoption of Common Core–aligned standards, which greatly increased the intellectual demands of teaching and learning and pushed proficiency rates even lower.

Adding to the difficulty, both ASD and iZone educators would need to realize improvement in a stringent accountability environment that rewarded measured outcomes but offered no credit for intermediate indicators of progress and critical design features, such as changes to instruction and leadership, professional learning, and shifting beliefs. These factors are understood as conditions that establish the foundation for better outcomes, but they were unaccounted for by the results-only state accountability regime. Finally, and as we elaborate later on, both ASD and iZone managers would need to clear these hurdles in what would turn out to be a turbulent and highly politicized environment in which there was little room for missteps and every decision took on a life of its own.

TABLE 1. **First ASD and iZone Cohorts' Proficiency and Demographics in 2012–13**

	ASD	iZone
Proficient or advanced in English language arts	16.7%	16.2%
Proficient or advanced in math	19.6%	25.7%
Eligibility for free or reduced lunch	93.6%	97.1%

Note: Tennessee Department of Education, "Assessment Files: School-Level 2013," https://www.tn.gov/education/districts/federal-programs-and-oversight/data/data-downloads.html.

Decentralization as Strategy: The ASD Bets on Providers to Go It Alone

ASD leaders were under extraordinary pressure to quickly deliver meaningful results. Funders and supporters expected success, and a skeptical community would accept nothing less. Yet the ASD strategy was not to leverage the considerable expertise of Barbic's highly accomplished team, to consult outside experts, to partner with local universities, or to help bolster the capacity of the local district (an approach later taken by the Massachusetts Department of Education). Rather, it chose to rely on a handful of charter operators to design and implement their own plans for curriculum, instruction, and leadership. Informing this approach was a theory of management and accountability that was at once outcomes-oriented and, as one ASD staffer put it, "devoutly agnostic" about the details of any particular educational strategy. ASD leaders believed that a combination of autonomy and accountability would spur innovation, creativity, and performance—and would do so quickly. In other words, school operators could design any type of school they wanted to, so long as they got the job done.

The belief in autonomy and the aversion to bureaucracy were deeply felt by ASD managers, many of whom were products of the charter movement, where these ideas are sacrosanct. Far from an abstract set of beliefs, this philosophy guided day-to-day decisions in the ASD. As Barbic put it: "My job as ASD sup' is to make sure that at the end of the day we're looking at the results. If it's all direct instruction and the school's getting great results, fine. If it's all project-based learning, and they're getting results, that's fine too. If it's textbooks and they get results, we're not going to judge. The philosophy is that if you put decision-making power in the hands of educators that actually know what to do with that, they can create high-performing schools."

The idea is neither new nor without intuitive appeal. Empowering talented and committed professionals to make decisions based on their experience and the needs of their students will yield better results than a system where decisions are made in a central office disconnected from schools' day-to-day work. At least that's the theory. The concept has its roots in the quality management movement of the 1980s, which held that workers on the front line are better positioned to make improvements to the manufacturing process than managers who are less attuned to the dynamics of the shop floor. In educational settings, the notion is that teaching is so context specific, communities so variable, and student needs so diverse that efforts to manage educational processes from above are futile. As Barbic's deputy and eventual successor, Malika Anderson, put it, "The magic happens when it's driven by the folks who are closest to kids."

But what if the magic didn't happen? What if ASD officials misjudged charter operators' ability to meet the formidable challenge that priority schools posed? In fact, ASD leaders expected some operators to come up short, and Barbic and his team made it clear that they would not hesitate to cancel the contracts of underperforming operators. Indeed, they saw their willingness to shut down operators as distinguishing them from traditional districts (and one district in particular) in which schools are seldom closed because of poor performance and ineffective leaders and teachers are rarely held to account. Anderson explained, "The fundamental difference between the ASD and other districts serving low-performing schools is that we believe all students can succeed with the right support. When a school fails its students, we hold the operator accountable to make changes. If failure continues after three years, a governance change will happen."

While the ASD's commitment to this principle was not in doubt, less clear was whether Barbic and Anderson fully grasped the political and educational implications of replacing a charter operator (and thereby the school's leaders and teachers) or, even more difficult, multiple operators. At that time, however, there was little concern about such matters. The ASD philosophy was applauded by charter operators (it was a main reason they came to the ASD in the first place) and was appealing to those who believe in market-based approaches to reform. Walking around the ASD offices at the time, one sensed a palpable undercurrent of confidence.

ASD managers also encouraged diversity among charter operators. Unlike some reforms—the Comprehensive School Reforms (CSRs) mentioned in chapter 1 being a prime example—that seek to establish coherent systems through the adoption of a common curriculum, shared pedagogical approaches, and uniform systems of professional development, the ASD valued variation. Indeed, a key idea behind the ASD strategy is that diverse educational approaches are needed to meet diverse student needs. As one ASD staffer put it: "If we are going to serve all the students that are zoned to us, we need to have a lot more options . . . We should be actively seeking out a variety of settings so that all kids can feel successful and be interested in school."

Yet one consequence of delegating most educational decisions to over a dozen independent operators was that it rendered irrelevant Barbic's own experience as the founder and manager of a well-regarded charter management organization (CMO). The same was true for Anderson, who had cut her teeth as a top district official in Washington, DC, as well as other ASD staffers, several of whom had worked in New Orleans in the aftermath of Hurricane Katrina. All of them had years of hard-earned experience, but the system they designed made that experience virtually useless. Indeed, as Anderson would put it, they viewed guidance from above not as a resource to improve performance but as a bureaucratic obstacle to be avoided at all costs: "This [approach] is going to enable the schools to perform much better and much faster than they would within a bureaucracy where all of the decisions are centrally made."

Uncharted Territory: The ASD Gambles on Charters in the "Big Leagues"

Despite ASD leaders' confidence, the strategy was not without vulnerabilities. The primary risk was the charter operators themselves. Some, such as Aspire and Green Dot, were experienced but unacquainted with the local environment, whereas others had local roots but were inexperienced in running an entire charter system. Not one was experienced *and* local. Common to all was that the ASD presented a challenge that few charter organizations are designed to tackle: turning around neighborhood schools.

The difference between a neighborhood school and a typical charter school may seem inconsequential. In some ways, charter and traditional schools have much in common; the length of the school day is typically about the same, they both teach about 180 days of the year, the design of buildings is often the same, they often use similar curricula, and both are accountable to state accountability regimes. Research has found that in many charter schools, teaching and learning are utterly conventional.[30]

Yet it is also true that charters typically deploy mechanisms that shelter them from elements of public school environments that can pose significant educational challenges. For example, although charters have a legal obligation to admit all classifications of students, they are usually authorized to recruit students without the constraint of attendance zones, giving them access to a broad pool of families actively seeking out educational opportunities for their children. Moreover, the ability to impose early registration requirements, limit specific types of services, and demand parental involvement allows charters to engage, on average, with a more stable and academically motivated population while reducing the number of students whose language or disabilities require additional resources and expertise.[31]

These advantages did not apply to ASD operators. Tennessee legislation required ASD schools to recruit the majority of their students from within the school's existing attendance zone while forbidding the early registration requirements that allow charter operators to establish a stable student body.[32] With the student mobility rate hovering around 37 percent, ASD operators would need to cope with the arrival of new and unfamiliar students throughout the school year, as well as a wide spectrum of student needs.[33] No local student could be turned away or counseled out, and schools would have to adapt their approach to meet the needs and sensibilities of families, not the other way around. Malika Anderson explained the difference: "Operators know that these are public neighborhood schools, and so if something doesn't work, if the student doesn't fit into your program, it doesn't mean the student changes, it means the program changes. For a lot of operators, that's different." It was, in hindsight, a considerable understatement. Barbic echoed this point: "This is uncharted territory. There are very few charter operators in the country that are experienced and successful at school turnaround. We are asking successful operators to work in completely different environments, to modify their models and their entire academic approach."

For teachers and leaders in traditional public schools that serve high-poverty communities, these challenges are entirely familiar and central to their daily experience. But for charter operators accustomed to long waiting lists of eager families, these circumstances are contrary to the very approach that made them successful to begin with. Even Barbic came to realize that he and his team had underestimated just how big a challenge the ASD posed for even the most stalwart organizations. "This is the big leagues," he would later say. "If you think you're ready for the big leagues, come to Memphis."

The question on which the success of the ASD hinged was whether this particular group of charter operators was ready for the big leagues. If they could demonstrate success, the ASD could silence its critics and justify its presence in the local community. Moreover, the results would have national implications because policymakers, funders, and charter advocates were all paying close attention. Just two years earlier, Secretary of Education

Arne Duncan, speaking at the National Charter Schools Conference, challenged the charter sector to enter into the school turnaround arena: "I am challenging you to adapt your educational model to turning around our lowest-performing schools. I need you to go outside your comfort zones and go to underserved rural communities and small cities."[34] ASD charters were among the first to take up the challenge.

For the ASD, however, it was not enough that charters would venture outside their comfort zones (that was a given) or that they would begin to adapt their educational model. The political environment and the ASD's tenuous legitimacy in the city meant it needed strong results, and it needed them quickly. Another way to put this is that while one would expect operators new to Memphis or new to turnaround work to need a few years to build the requisite capacity and accumulate experience, the political clock ticked at a faster pace. The ASD was betting on charters not only to figure things out but to hit the ground running. Barbic and Anderson touted the ASD philosophy as giving autonomy to those who know what to do with it; whether that applied to the charter operators the ASD had entrusted to deliver results remained to be seen.

Rewiring the System from Within: The iZone Reinvents the Usual Suspects

Like the ASD, the iZone needed a strategy to significantly improve schools that posed educators with an array of formidable problems, for which past interventions had proven inadequate. The same levels of poverty, isolation, and community deterioration that ASD charter operators had to contend with confronted iZone leaders as well. On one level, their educational predicament was the same.

Yet in other ways, the nature of the iZone's educational conundrum differed. While many ASD principals and teachers had to learn the culture and needs of the local community, iZone leaders had the opposite problem. For the iZone to achieve its goals, the same people operating in the same system, under whose watch failure had occurred, would need to radically reinvent their professional identities and skills. Further complicating matters was that many of these educators had studied, worked, and been socialized into the culture and practices of the old system in which direct instruction, test prep, and basic skills were commonplace. The iZone's leader, Dr. Griffin, explained: "Many of the people that are in my schools are native Memphians. What is hard for these teachers and leaders to say is 'I don't know.' Yes, we know the cultural narratives of communities, but you can't ever stop growing as an educator." Could the people who were, in some sense, the problem transform themselves into the solution?[35]

Responding to this challenge, Dr. Griffin crafted a plan that would turn out to be remarkably effective, at least in the short term. She started small, designating only seven elementary schools to enter the iZone in the first year, thereby avoiding the complexity of large-scale change and the seemingly insurmountable challenge of improving a large, urban high school. The work of designing a broad effort encompassing all levels of schooling would be tackled at a later date. Second, Griffin utilized her intimate knowledge of the district to recruit seasoned and effective school leaders with a track record of success. For those hesitant to leave their existing schools or to risk their reputation in more difficult circumstances, signing and retention bonuses offered a compelling incentive.[36]

Griffin then established conditions that most principals can only dream of: She allowed these handpicked principals to select their own teachers from across the district while reassigning those they didn't consider up for the challenge. A salary bonus of up to $3,000 rewarded teachers for taking the plunge.[37] Moreover, principals were permitted to introduce whatever materials, practices, and strategies they thought would improve student outcomes. The school day was extended by an hour in order to provide additional learning time. With its own identity, resources, and rules, the iZone quickly evolved into a unique subsystem within the larger district. Bradley Leon, Dr. Griffin's supervisor at the time, explained the underlying theory: "We believe really strongly that if you've got a principal coming into the iZone, they're going to choose their own team because they're coming into a harder situation." Barbic couldn't have said it any better.

While recruitment and autonomy were the main thrust of the strategy, the iZone did establish some central support systems. A small Instructional Leadership Team (ILT) was constructed to support school leaders, and an Instructional Support Team (IST), composed of about ten content experts and classroom coaches, worked directly with iZone teachers. In the early years of the iZone, the ILT and IST played a marginal role, but in later years, when the entire system was overhauled, they would prove to be of great importance.

Conclusion

In terms of governance, the ASD and iZone could not have been more different. The iZone was a local, district-run initiative that leaned on long-standing district employees, whereas the ASD was a state-run enterprise that removed neighborhood schools from local control and depended on private organizations to run them. Viewed from this lens, the iZone was utterly conventional and the ASD highly unusual. Educationally, however, the strategies bore striking similarities. Both were motivated by a "talent-and-autonomy" philosophy that believed in finding the right people and getting out of their way. Just as the ASD promised autonomy to charter operators, so did the iZone promise its school leaders freedom from traditional district rules, policies, and most forms of central guidance.

The strategies had a similar combination of strengths and risks. On the one hand, neither the ASD nor the iZone needed to develop a centralized organizational capacity. For the ASD, this meant there was no need to develop a comprehensive instructional design, or what some analysts call *infrastructure*, that touched on central office capacity, curriculum, instruction, leadership, professional development, and so forth. Monitoring and oversight were restricted to compliance with legal requirements. This is not to say that ASD leaders thought those issues to be unimportant, simply that they delegated them to school operators. The same was true for the iZone. A strategy that hinged on recruiting highly qualified leaders and teachers did not require any consequential changes to the larger district—no new curriculum to be adopted, no wholesale change to professional development, no massive retraining of teachers.

Second, for both the ASD and iZone, the strategy avoided conflict. As Barbic made clear, there was no need for ASD charter school operators to agree on strategy or philosophy so long as they produced results. One charter operator could rely on traditional instruction, whereas another could utilize project-based learning. Similarly, the iZone avoided the unavoidably contentious and inevitably public process of achieving consensus on pedagogy, curriculum, and other controversial decisions that inevitably involve the school board and draw in the public. This is a significant advantage for public agencies that are averse to controversy and accountable to diverse constituents. Third, because the strategies (particularly that of the iZone) rested in large part on the abilities of tried-and-true teachers with little need for retraining or supervision, there was potential to realize quick results. Retooling scores of new teachers and leaders would have been a more systemic approach, but it was not a way to deliver measurable improvements in the short run.

On the other hand, the strategies were not without risk. For the iZone, a reduced role for community members accustomed to exerting considerable influence on educational decisions would undoubtedly ruffle some local feathers. Second, despite leveraging the city's most effective teachers, there were still questions about the district's overall professional capacity. Even community leaders opposed to the ASD wondered whether the same district that had failed to stem decades of decline could suddenly reverse course. The district's own leaders admitted to needing help, but the iZone would succeed or fail based on the decisions and capabilities of its own people.

The iZone strategy was also ill-suited for growth. Were the iZone to add additional schools, district administrators could find themselves hard-pressed to recruit suitable principals, and even if they could, those principals would quickly run out of highly qualified teachers with which to staff their schools. Furthermore, were the new principals' and teachers' previous schools to decline (as Barbic had predicted), a promising strategy might turn out to be no more than robbing Peter to pay Paul. The problem was both educational and political; if the success of iZone schools came at the expense of other district schools, then it would cast doubt on the legitimacy of the iZone as a viable improvement strategy while lending credibility to the notion that the district needed outsiders to save its schools.

For the ASD, the risks were similar but more pronounced. The ASD strategy assumed that attitudes toward the district were so negative, and the desire to try something new so great, that local residents would accept the idea of outsiders taking over neighborhood schools. The problem, of course, was that the history of Memphis and the perspective that it wrought made the ASD a tough sell, to say the least. The second risk lay in the assumption that a collection of independent charter operators could, on their own, muster the expertise, organizational capacity, and wherewithal to realize substantial improvements in learning outcomes. Barbic may have been the face of the ASD, but at the end of the day, its success was largely out of his hands.

CHAPTER THREE

New Systems Encounter Old Problems

When analysts and commentators discuss educational programs and interventions, they often ask, "Did it work?" It is a reasonable question motivated by a desire to ensure that the investment of time, effort, and money actually had the desired effect. Tracking outcomes also creates the opportunity for program designers and educational leaders to learn from experience and to make needed adjustments to their strategies and underlying ideas. US education is several decades into the results-oriented part of its history and is, for the most part, better off for it. In prior eras, inattention to results and limited ability to measure them allowed systemic inequalities to escape notice and for suspect assumptions about school improvement to go unchallenged.[1] The current focus on educational equity is, in good part, a result of our ability to measure and compare student learning outcomes.

Yet one theme of this chapter is that asking "what works" is too simple a question to produce educationally meaningful answers in a field where implementation and outcomes vary by context and where what counts as "working" is considerably more complex than it may seem. For example, one of the most perplexing aspects of the Achievement School District (ASD) narrative is that reputable charter organizations with decades of hard-earned experience struggled to achieve the success in Memphis they had accomplished elsewhere. The strategies that operators like Aspire and Green Dot had developed over years of work in cities like Oakland, Stockton, and Los Angeles failed to gain traction in the neighborhoods of Memphis, and the experience that a celebrated local educator brought to his ASD organization similarly failed to translate into results.[2] One interpretation of these outcomes is to say that the ASD "didn't work" and to leave it at that. The problem with this type of "did it work" question, however, is that it sheds no light on the "why" and "how" of instructional improvement, without which we can't learn how to design more effective systems,

Like the ASD, the Innovation Zone (iZone) also presents an educational puzzle that cannot be solved by asking, "Did it work?" After three years of stunning results that captured headlines across the state, iZone leaders overhauled their educational approach, abandoning the core idea of school-based autonomy. If the iZone was in fact working, and rigorous evaluations claimed it was, why would district leaders abruptly reverse course? Some might argue that this is a case of district incompetence or misguided decision-making, but this and subsequent chapters argue that there was sound educational reasoning behind the decision. The topic of this chapter, then, is not just whether the ASD or iZone worked, but how their respective improvement strategies, and the implicit theories that informed them, played out in a highly politicized environment and in schools that posed an extraordinary set of educational challenges. Working, we argue, lies at the intersection of instructional systems and social and political environments.

In addressing these questions, this chapter touches on another: What is the relationship between teacher effectiveness and the design of instructional systems? ASD charter operators and iZone leaders fought tooth and nail to find effective and experienced teachers who could produce desperately needed results. Indeed, central to the competition between the ASD and iZone was the race to recruit the most effective teachers or, in contemporary parlance, to find "talent." Yet as this chapter illustrates, if educational systems are not designed to enhance teacher expertise and to organize teaching as a collective endeavor, their success is entirely dependent on recruitment efforts, which, among other things, severely limits their ability to expand operations. It is true that to be effective, instructional systems require good teachers, but as the ensuing discussion shows, a core characteristic of a high-performing system is that it cultivates the very expertise on which it depends.

In the remainder of this chapter, we illustrate the way in which these issues unfolded within ASD and iZone schools over their first three years of operation. Our analysis examines the clash between the ASD and iZone's underlying ideas and the social and political environments in which they worked. We report findings relating to the statistical impact of the ASD and iZone on student learning in large part because those findings drove public opinion and the resulting political dynamics. Yet this chapter is not ultimately about a narrow conception of "what works" or parsing program impact on student outcomes; it is about exploring different approaches to constructing instructional systems and the educational and political implications of those approaches.

One overarching point of this chapter, then, is that instructional systems that depend on the extraordinary feats of individuals working in relative isolation are no match for a trio of challenges that include extreme student need, a high level of intellectual rigor, and stringent accountability. ASD charter operators varied in their experience and philosophy, but each would learn that the degree of guidance and collaborative work embedded in their instructional systems was insufficient relative to the challenges confronting their teachers and principals. A second conclusion is that the first is particularly true as systems increase their scale of operations. The iZone was widely perceived as the more effective system, with eye-popping outcomes that amazed even veteran observers, yet questions about its underlying strategy emerged as it struggled to manage a larger and more variable set of schools.

The What over the Who: Instructional System Design in the ASD

At its peak during the 2016–17 school year, the ASD comprised fourteen charter operator organizations running a total of thirty-three schools, twenty-nine of which were in Memphis. These schools were spread across the city, from the historic neighborhood of Orange Mound in central Memphis to the Frayser community in the north, and down to South Memphis, home to the Riverview neighborhood (see fig. 2). While all operators were tasked with realizing dramatic gains in student outcomes, their strategies for achieving that goal varied. Some charter operators adopted a project-based learning approach in which students and teachers designed and then engaged in open-ended, complex projects over a period of weeks. Another operator employed an approach aligned with the "no excuses model" that features conventional instruction, regular testing, and a heavy focus on student behavior. Yet another charter operator placed a strong emphasis on fostering students' civic responsibility, with the hope that students would develop into local change agents. Some charter operators relied on traditional textbooks, whereas others employed more specialized

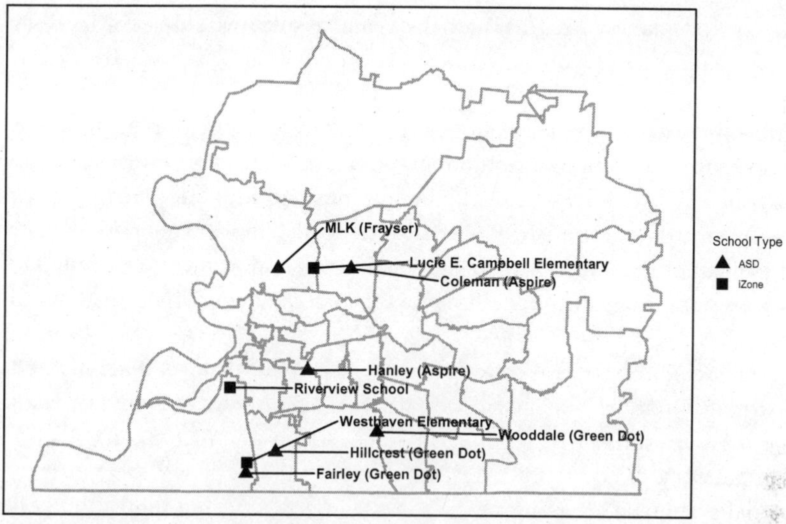

FIGURE 2. A map of Memphis showing the location of the iZone schools and ASD schools (and their CMOs) discussed in this chapter.

Note: From Memphis Data Hub, *Shelby County Zip Codes* (EGIS, 2018), https://data.memphistn.gov/dataset/Shelby-County-Zip-Codes/98jk-gvpk/about_data; Memphis Data Hub, *Shelby County Schools Shapefile* (EGIS, 2023), https://data.memphistn.gov/dataset/Shelby-County-Schools-Shapefile/xhgg-d4u5/about_data.

programs. When it came to teaching and learning, variation was the name of the game in the ASD.

In the research that informs this book, we tracked the experiences of six ASD charter operators (each of which is named in fig. 2) from 2013 to 2016. We examined their initial strategies and assumptions, their perceptions of how those strategies were working, and the adaptations they later made to their plans and ideas. Here, we focus primarily on the experience of three operators that collectively shed light on the challenges faced by ASD operators and their efforts to overcome them. The three include two charter networks that operated high schools, Martin Luther King Jr. College Preparatory High School (MLK) and Green Dot Public Schools, and a third, Aspire Public Schools, that operated three elementary schools. Aspire and Green Dot are national organizations that came to the ASD with track records of success and strong reputations but little knowledge of the local context. MLK was founded and managed by a well-respected local educator with deep roots in the community but who had never run an educational organization.

At first glance, MLK, Green Dot, and Aspire would seem to offer something for everyone. For those who believe in tried-and-true charter networks unencumbered by district bureaucracy, unconstrained by collective-bargaining agreements, free to hire and fire, Green Dot and Aspire would seem like optimal choices. For those who think that success lies in strong ties to local communities and intimate knowledge of neighborhood culture, MLK, with its local leadership and network of civic organizations, fits the bill. In an age when much importance is attributed to *who* is operating educational systems, the ASD presented a smorgasbord of dishes.

This chapter takes a different approach. What shapes teaching and learning, we argue, depends less on whether schools are operated by charter organizations or traditional districts, less on union contracts, district bureaucracy, or community ties, and more on the design of their instructional systems. That is, more than the *who*, it's the *what* that ultimately matters. The story of these three ASD operators, and in many ways the ASD overall, is in large part one of instructional systems that, each in their own way, leaned too heavily on individual expertise and, in doing so, delegated an excessive burden to individual teachers. This is not to minimize the impact of the divisive political dynamics of the state takeover (chap. 4 is devoted to that topic), the importance of schools as neighborhood institutions, or the significance of historical context, and it certainly is not meant to detract from the extraordinary effort and commitment of the individuals who worked in these organizations. Our point, rather, is to say that the quality, rigor, and equity of teaching and learning are, in good part, a question of how instructional systems are designed, how the work of teaching is organized, and how capacity is cultivated. As the remainder of this chapter shows, that is a professional problem, and as chapter 4 shows, it is also a problem of politics.

The Insider–Outsider: Bobby White and the Promise of Local Leadership

For Dr. Bobby White, taking control of MLK was both unexpected and personal. Whereas most ASD charter operators were led by outsiders, White was a native Memphian with deep roots in the Frayser neighborhood where the school was located. He had attended MLK (formerly known as Frayser High School) as a student and worked as a teacher, coach, and principal in Shelby County Schools (SCS). The opportunity to run a charter high school in the Frayser neighborhood was a chance not just to operate or improve one school but also to make a difference in a community to which he had a deep connection. He explained:

> For us to be local, Black, serving 98.9 percent Black children in a reform movement that is led by large or established CMOs, makes us stick out like a sore thumb. We're not Green Dot. We're not Aspire. We're not Scholars or KIPP or YES Prep; just Bobby White and his folks—people who are from Memphis, who care about the children in Memphis, who feel like we understand how to do this work.

White recognized that as a lifelong district employee, he was an unusual candidate to operate an ASD school. Many in the community were skeptical about the ASD, and White's decision to operate an ASD school raised more than a few eyebrows. He knew what people were saying: "As someone who is so connected to the community, to all of a sudden do the same work that the outsiders were doing, people were saying, 'What happened to Bobby White?' You're a district guy, you're not reformer, you're not TFA [Teach for America], you're not a New Leader.' I had the district's DNA running through my blood, so people thought I could not play the part of the reformer."

But while White's past was with the district, he saw his future with the ASD. He worried that remaining a district employee would not provide an opportunity to make meaningful change. He had seen other principals settle into their role while losing the drive to make a difference: "I was comfortable. I could've stayed in the same spot and become one of those old-school principals that sits in the cafeteria all day eating lunches and shaking children's hands, and nothing ever happens." White was also aware of the historical significance of a local, Black leader playing a central role in a movement that was dominated by White-led organizations. He saw the ASD as an opportunity not just to turn around his former high school or even positively affect the Frayser neighborhood but also as a way to assert himself within a context where Black students were often the target of change but Black leaders were rarely the change agents. He notes, "I'd come to grips that this movement was here and that if some folks that didn't look like me were not a part of this movement, it would pass us by. Years from now we would be upset with ourselves because we were not on the front line of this battle, trying to serve the lowest performing students in our city."

White's commitment to the community not only motivated him to become an ASD charter operator but also informed his ideas about school turnaround. Whereas some other operators relied on a well-honed vision of classroom instruction, materials, and established routines, White's primary resource was his intimate knowledge of the neighborhood and his broad network of community partners. He stood apart from other ASD operators, and from the ASD itself, in that he enjoyed significant legitimacy within the neighborhood he served. Even the most strident ASD critics acknowledged that White's bona fides were beyond reproach. It made sense, then, that White would focus on school culture and community-based partnerships that he believed were integral to academic success: "You have to create a spiritual-like buzz around higher expectations and the possibilities that are within the people who come through those doors every day. They have to begin to believe that they are special and that they can do something that nobody has ever challenged them to do, or that no one thought that they would ever be able to do."

White firmly believed that community involvement and commitment to student success were as important as what went on inside the classroom. The more technical elements of instruction took a back seat to the social and cultural aspects of schooling. He noted, "Look, this is going to take a concerted effort. The entire community needs to be pulled in. You need all the partners in order to serve the needs of the students, so they won't have these barriers that keep them from learning . . . Without [the community], I just don't believe you're going to get academic success."

The emphasis on culture and community did not mean that there was no focus on teaching and learning. Led by a small team of veteran educators, MLK adopted a college- and career-ready curriculum that was aligned with the Common Core State Standards (CCSS) and the ACT college entrance exam. A pacing and content guide provided general guidance but contained little pedagogical detail about how to organize and run a classroom in an environment where expectations were high and students were far behind. Professional development seminars covered fundamentals of teaching and learning, and teachers were encouraged to employ the "I do, we do, you do" instructional strategy, in which the teacher models a particular skill before gradually handing it over to students.

When pressed to explain how the school would achieve a high level of professional capacity, MLK leaders explained that expertise would emerge from a collaborative school culture. Said one leader: "Think about a pyramid. You have one person train a teacher and then when we have new teachers, that teacher will train the next teacher . . . They will not need us anymore. We will have teachers helping lead each other, a community of learners." It's an appealing image, perhaps possible in certain circumstances, but at MLK, it meant that the core task of constructing lessons and meeting learning objectives was largely delegated to individual teachers. Yet White and his top staff saw a commitment to teacher autonomy as the key to attracting the city's most capable educators. One of MLK's instructional leaders explained: "We're not asking teachers to read from a script. We are asking teachers to look directly at our standards to see how the standards align with what it is that you're teaching. The autonomy lies in being able to relay the information to students in the way they feel students would best learn."

The lack of local knowledge and cultural context that hindered other ASD charter operators was MLK's primary strength. Indeed, White seemingly had much in his favor—deep community roots, a network of local organizations to partner with, decades of educational experience, and an abundant amount of goodwill. Still, one important question remained unanswered: whether White and his team could turn these resources into the student learning outcomes that both he and the ASD desperately needed. What was not in question was that for Dr. Bobby White, the stakes were high: "The stage is so big. We took over one of the worst schools in our state, if not the country. We just have to do things better for these babies, but then you put all of that other stuff on top of it and the weight of it for me is immense. Man, we can't fail."

Green Dot: Experts in Turnaround, Novices in Memphis

Unlike other ASD charter operators, Green Dot Public Schools had already tried its hand at turning around existing neighborhood schools (although not in Memphis) and was familiar with the complexity of turnaround work. At the same time, the network's regional director, Megan Quaile, faced formidable obstacles that differed from those confronting Dr. White and MLK.

Fairley High School was eighteen miles south of the Frayser neighborhood where MLK was located, practically walking distance from the Mississippi border. Located in the Whitehaven neighborhood, home to Graceland, civil rights leader Benjamin Hooks, and many famous rappers and music producers, Fairley had experienced a precipitous decline that placed it on the state's priority list. In the year before joining the ASD, Fairley's performance was near the bottom of the state in several categories, with proficiency rates in Algebra I of below 30 percent and rates of under 20 percent in English.[3] The challenges confronting Quaile and the pressure to succeed were enormous.

Green Dot brought a different constellation of resources and challenges to the work from MLK. Unlike White, Quaile and her colleagues lacked knowledge of the local context, which, as one leader conceded, placed them at a disadvantage: "I think understanding the context is our weakness. We haven't been here enough to really understand the context . . . I just think that there is a mentality or a mindset in Memphis that is different from what we are used to. Some people thought that this was going to be an easier gig than it was. Turnaround is not easy work."

But if Green Dot's top staff lacked White's familiarity with the local context, its leaders had far more experience in running a charter network. A lesser emphasis on community partnerships was offset by an instructional model that focused on enhancing students' cognitive engagement, building a supportive learning environment, fostering active classroom discourse, and providing students with complex academic tasks. To help teachers realize this vision, Green Dot provided a smattering of curricular materials, instructional strategies, and assessments. The curricular materials included a course overview document, curriculum maps, a sample unit plan, and a lesson planning template. Moreover, network leaders promoted, although didn't require, a suite of instructional practices that they considered effective. A combination of workshops, coaching, joint planning, and co-teaching was meant to build capacity.

At the same time, there were limits to the extent of this guidance. Green Dot did not provide a detailed curriculum with daily lesson plans or units. Instead, the strategy was to support teachers' instructional decision-making around the design of units and lessons while monitoring pacing, content coverage, and adherence to Green Dot's general philosophy. As one network leader put it: "We don't pigeonhole our teachers and say, 'These are the strategies you can choose from.'" Teachers were provided with general resources and ideas but were then expected to assemble them into a coherent and effective instructional program.

While Green Dot's instructional system was more developed than that of MLK, both organizations relied on recruiting extraordinarily capable teachers who could construct and deliver lessons that would meet the formidable needs of students, maintain intellectual rigor, and realize dramatic gains in tested learning outcomes. The nitty-gritty work of instruction—constructing academic tasks, diagnosing student-specific needs, selecting texts, representing content, grouping students—was delegated to individual teachers. Green Dot may have provided a more robust vision and elaborate set of tools than MLK, but instruction was still, in large part, a do-it-yourself project. As one leader put it: "We can put systems in place, but if we don't have the right people at the table, it won't matter. My biggest concern is whether we are going to get the right people."[4] It was not the people, however, who would prove to be the problem.

Aspire: Big Ideas on Thin Ground

When Aspire arrived in Memphis in 2012, it was already a well-established, fifteen-year-old organization with thirty-seven schools and over thirteen thousand students in California. Like other out-of-state operators, the organization was drawn to Memphis because of its large number of low-performing schools and because of what they saw as a "citywide approach" to solving educational problems. Aspire's vision for teaching and learning was nothing if not ambitious. Leaders envisioned classrooms in which students actively engaged in problem-solving, argumentation, and inquiry. Rote learning and direct instruction were not part of the plan. Regional Director Allison Leslie explained: "We believe in the importance of students talking to students during the lesson and using evidence to defend their ideas. That's what we define as rigor. Rigorous teaching is when students are able to do that, whether it's student-led solutions in math, working in a reading group together, shared inquiry, or a whole-class discussion where they refer to the text."

Other Aspire leaders reiterated Leslie's student-centered vision of instruction and aversion to didactic pedagogy. The director of special education noted that Aspire sought to "create opportunities for scholars to learn not only from the teacher but from one another," whereas Chief Academic Officer Katie Kling emphasized the importance of small-group instruction, teacher–student conferences, and shifting the cognitive load from teachers to students. She elaborated on the changes to classroom instruction she envisioned: "We historically have loved this 'I do, we do, you do' model. First, the teacher models it, then we do it together, and then the student does it independently. But we can't continue to do that if we want our kids to be able to think and reason. We can't say to kids, 'Okay, this is how you do a division problem. Copy the steps that I did exactly. And now from now on, every time you do division, that's the way you're going to solve your problem.'"

To turn these ideas into practice, Aspire provided teachers with an array of classroom tools and curricular resources. These were, in turn, complemented with professional learning opportunities that included a two-week summer institute; weekly professional development; and a system of instructional coaching that, much like Green Dot's, involved observation, feedback, and co-teaching. But as was the case with every ASD operator, the Aspire system was not without its vulnerabilities. Two, in particular, stood out.

First, the network's eighteen years of experience could not mask its lack of familiarity with the local context or the community's apprehension. Dr. White's years of work in the community had earned MLK the benefit of the doubt, but the same could not be said for Green Dot or Aspire. Aspire's director of strategic partnerships, a local himself, knew that after decades of educational experiments that never seemed to live up to expectations, Memphians were wary of outsiders making promises: "Citizens in Memphis have been overpromised and under-delivered. So people are slow to trust. They want to understand who people are, what they believe, and to see the work that you put behind it. The best way that we can earn that trust is through competence." In sociological terms, outsiders began with a legitimacy deficit that could only be remedied by action and results.

A second challenge emanated from Aspire's lofty vision of classroom practice. A truism of instructional design is that the more ambitious the vision of teaching and learning, the greater the challenge of building the requisite professional capacity. This was doubly true in this case because Aspire teachers had to bring ambitious ideas to fruition with students they didn't know, who were academically behind, and who had rarely experienced classrooms demanding this level of critical thinking and independent work. Moreover, while Aspire boasted a variety of instructional resources and support, it, like Green Dot and MLK, relied heavily on teachers to integrate its wide array of materials into coherent lessons and units. Aspire's leaders frequently stated that they eschewed instructional mandates (just as MLK and Green Dot rejected "scripts" and "pigeonholing"), but the fact that few of these teachers were acquainted with the Aspire model meant that they confronted a steep learning curve in an environment where there was little patience for incremental progress.

In terms of background, experience, and philosophy, these three ASD charter operators differed from one another in notable ways. MLK focused heavily on culture, community, and its intimate knowledge of the neighborhood, whereas Aspire leaned on its experience, wide array of materials, and established processes. Green Dot also featured a multifaceted, albeit somewhat less specified approach that had been honed over years. Two were high schools, and one was an elementary school. Yet considered through the lens of their instructional systems, similarities were apparent. All three were counting on their teachers to shoulder the day-to-day work of identifying students' learning needs, remediating large gaps, and maintaining a high degree of intellectual rigor. In this way, their approach mirrored the overall ASD philosophy: Recruit talented individuals and provide them enough leeway to figure things out.

The strategy, however, was not without risk. Be it MLK's community-centered approach, Aspire's inspiring vision of classroom life, or Green Dot's tried-and-true experience, in each of these systems, success hinged on teachers establishing the basic instructional blueprint for their classrooms and compiling and using the necessary instructional resources to deliver daily lessons. In more forgiving environments, this is a less tenuous proposition; indeed, teachers all over the world do this type of work day in, day out. But in an environment beset by intergenerational poverty, large learning gaps, and extreme pressure, teachers' ability to cope with these challenges remained an open question, one on which the future of the ASD rested.

The iZone: Heroes of the Moment, a Precarious Road Ahead

Dr. Sharon Griffin knew that the iZone had no choice but to outperform the ASD, and as a Memphis native with years of experience in SCS, she knew how to do it. Griffin and her colleagues quickly selected principals whose experience, track record, and extensive knowledge of the local context positioned them to hit the ground running.[5] Those principals then handpicked teachers whom they could rely on to make rapid gains, and teachers who were seen as lacking the necessary skill and commitment were reassigned to non-iZone schools. Whereas most ASD charter operators were either new to Memphis or new to managing a charter management organization (CMO), iZone principals and teachers were in familiar territory. The iZone strategy, not unlike that of the ASD, was to identify the best people and get out of their way. The difference was that iZone leaders knew exactly where to find them.

In the pages that follow, we present three elementary school principals—Rodney Rowan, Jaron Carson, and Latasha Harris—who were at the forefront of the iZone's effort to best the ASD and silence critics. Readers will note their extraordinary commitment and relentless effort in the face of equally extraordinary challenges stemming from forces beyond their control. No less remarkable is these leaders' attention to classroom instruction and their willingness to work hand in hand with teachers and students with an intensity that belies the laissez-faire style of leadership often associated with US schools. Our discussion of these three principals brings us back to our earlier question about what it means for an educational intervention to "work" or for a leader or teacher to be "effective." In a political environment where assessment outcomes mattered above all else, there is little doubt that these three principals were nothing short of spectacular. Rowan and Carson, in particular, succeeded in lifting their schools out of the bottom 5 percent and registering remarkable gains in mathematics and reading while never taking their foot off the gas. In the Memphis of 2017, they were heroes.

At the same time, this story of unmitigated success is more complicated than it seems at first. In two of the cases, the educational vision driving leadership decisions was geared heavily toward test performance, with little appetite for ideas or practices that would threaten outcomes. As we will see in chapter 5, while that approach was a remarkable asset in the early years, it would later become a vulnerability when new iZone leaders sought to institute a set of pedagogical principles motivated by more than just test performance. In this sense, these principals, each in their own way, reveal an environment where the political capital afforded by quick assessment gains worked at cross-purposes with the task of building instructional systems that supported deep changes to teaching and learning.

Rodney Rowan: Hands-On Instructional Leadership, Test-Driven Focus

A lifelong Memphian, Rodney Rowan describes himself as a proud product of Memphis City Schools. Following a nine-year stint as a classroom teacher, Rowan steadily progressed through the leadership ranks, serving first as an instructional facilitator, assistant principal, and then resident principal with the organization New Leaders. It was as the principal of a struggling elementary school, however, that he earned recognition as a successful turnaround leader with the ability and determination to improve outcomes in challenging circumstances.[6]

Rowan quickly developed into a hands-on instructional leader who maintained a laser-like focus on teaching and learning. Indeed, in many ways, Rowan represents the type of principal that education reformers have long sought to cultivate and that many believe is critical to improving performance. Rather than allow teachers broad discretion to teach according to personal style, Rowan assiduously monitored instruction in his classrooms and was quick to step in when he saw a teacher deviate from what he considered to be best practice. He noted, "I don't take my hands off of anything related to instruction . . . I am going to spend the first month of school or the first two months of school really just modeling for teachers what I want to see them doing. Only once that is internalized will I give them a little latitude."

It was not surprising, then, that in 2012, Dr. Griffin tapped Rowan to lead one of the iZone's original schools. Griffin's selection of Rowan quickly paid dividends as he transformed a once poor-performing school into a "trophy school" for the district, quadrupling its proficiency rate in math and more than doubling it in reading.[7] Griffin would again turn to Rowan in 2016 to take on a new challenge. Westhaven Elementary had recently merged with two other elementary schools to form one of the largest elementary schools in the district. The merger had been contentious because it involved closing two historic neighborhood schools that brought with them years of poor performance and a student body that bore the consequences of long-standing social and economic marginalization. As Rowan explained, the cultural challenges were immense: "I can't stress enough the challenges around culture. Just the culture of learning . . . the attitudes, the beliefs, and the values of everyone who is affiliated with the school." The learning gains that Westhaven would realize under Rowan's leadership spoke to his skill, commitment, and relentless determination.

The dramatic rise in outcomes also reflected Rowan's belief that effective teaching and learning were one and the same with good test results, and he left little doubt that his primary goal was to drive up test scores on the state assessment. He insisted that students worked on tasks that mirrored the assessment, pored over test results to identify lapses in performance, and designed his own assessments to mimic the state test. Practices and pedagogies that did not raise scores were unwelcome. "You have to practice how you play," he said. A few years later, iZone instructional coaches would try to persuade principals that test scores are not synonymous with learning and that a core set of pedagogical principles should drive instruction. But Rowan would have little use for such distinctions: "If they're passing the test, they're learning," he said. "Everything that you do in life is centered around some standardized norm."

Jaron Carson: Improving Practice in the Trenches and on the Fly

The New York Yankees paraphernalia on the walls of Jaron Carson's office make it clear that he is not a native Memphian. Born in Westchester, New York, Carson's early career goals were focused on athletics more than they were on education. But when a career in professional sports failed to materialize, Carson decided to put to use an education degree that he had earned at a Memphis-based college. After a couple of years of subbing and teaching in SCS, an unexpected invitation came from New Leaders to apply for a year-long leadership training program. Carson's wife urged him to apply: "I told her, 'Well, it's not going to matter, because I won't make it past the first round anyway.' But all of a sudden, I make it past the second round, and they tell me I'm in the cohort and that we start that year. I spent a year learning from the best in New Leaders, underneath one of the best mentor principals. The next year, I got a school."

Like Rowan, Carson adopted a hands-on style that proved remarkably effective. He noted, "I was in classrooms all the time. If I saw something go wrong, I could affect it in real time. I do a lot of teaching with my teachers. If something's going wrong in the classroom, I'll say to the teacher, 'Excuse me, Miss. Can I jump in with you?' and she would say, 'Oh, come in, Mr. Carson, come in.' And now we're team-teaching, we're closing the gaps."

By the end of Carson's first year, his new school had catapulted from the lowest ranking in the state (level 1) to the highest (level 5) and was recognized by the state as a Reward School. Carson would maintain the school's level 5 status for a remarkable four consecutive years, during which time his reputation in the district would soar. When, in 2015, Carson told Dr. Griffin that he wanted to become an iZone principal, she allowed him to choose between one of two schools. "I said, 'Where is it the most challenging?' And she said, 'Frayser.' I said, 'Well then I want to go there.'"

The Frayser neighborhood was home to both iZone and ASD schools, and it presented formidable challenges for teachers and leaders alike. Carson's new school, Lucie E. Campbell, had experienced the same pattern of decline and poor results as other iZone and ASD schools. The year before Carson took over, proficiency rates in third through fifth grade ranged from 14 to 24 percent in math and from 22 to 35 percent in reading. Still, Carson was confident he could repeat the same success he had engineered at his former school. That is, until he received word that Lucie would be absorbing all the students of Brookmeade Elementary, the second-lowest-performing elementary school in the state that the district had decided to close. The fact that Lucie would nearly double the size of its student body certainly added to the challenge, but it was the impact on school culture that proved most devastating:

> When Brookmeade got here, it was something I had never seen before. Students who were just totally out of control. They'd never had structure before, they really didn't understand rules, regulations, and boundaries; it was a culture shock. That year we had 518 suspensions and 18 expulsions. I had kids bringing weed to school, bullets, fighting teachers, running out of the building, tearing up classrooms. We called the police in the first two months maybe thirty times. The kids were used to doing what they wanted, whenever they wanted, and I was trying to teach them that there are boundaries.

While somewhat less test-focused than Rowan, Carson was also reluctant to take risks that could compromise assessment outcomes. Like Rowan, he saw aligning instruction and assessment with the state test as the best way to maximize performance, and he instructed his teachers to use the months before the test to reteach material that he feared students had forgotten. Moreover, Carson had little patience for materials or practices that did not immediately prove effective in the classroom. If students struggled with a part of the curriculum or a particular lesson, he wasted no time in searching for alternatives. Carson spoke about how he and a teacher, struggling to convey the concept of place value to students, spent hours on the internet looking for alternative approaches: "We got on YouTube and started looking, and we went over about four or five different strategies. All of a sudden, we found that last strategy on Khan Academy. I said, 'I think this is going to work.' . . . So I walked up to the front of the class with her, and sure enough, when she put it on the board, light bulbs went off."

Carson's determination that no student fall behind and that seemingly ineffective lessons be replaced on the spot made sense in the early years of the iZone when there was little room for error and time was of the essence. As was the case with Rowan, Carson's ability to drive up test scores protected his school from ASD takeover while giving the iZone and the district much-needed political capital. In subsequent years, however, iZone instructional leaders would express misgivings about pulling lessons off YouTube and the Khan Academy website, urging principals to allow teachers the time to learn the district's new curriculum, which would pay off in the long run. But for principals like Carson, there was little reason to alter an approach that, from their perspective, had served them so well.

Latasha Harris: Leading Slow and Steady Change

Before taking over one of the most challenging schools in Memphis, Latasha Harris was a rising star in the SCS system. A graduate of the University of Memphis, Harris began her teaching career at the storied Frayser High School—later absorbed into the ASD and rebranded as MLK—where a young and ambitious principal, Sharon Griffin, was orchestrating remarkable improvement. A few years later, Harris followed Griffin to a new school, where she gained further experience in school turnaround work. Having gained the confidence of district managers, Harris advanced to the position of regional literacy coach, and from there, she advanced to the larger role of professional learning coach. After a year of training at New Leaders, Harris expressed her desire to lead one of the city's most challenging schools. Few schools fit that description more than Riverview K–8 in South Memphis.

As was the case for all iZone schools, the challenges went beyond low test scores and poor academic performance. Harris described what she found on her first day as principal of Riverview: "Before the school entered the iZone, it ranked last in the state of Tennessee. There is a lot of crime here, and it's gang infested. The environments that the children are coming from are very difficult. Attracting staff is hard because a lot of people are turned away by the community and by things that they have heard about the culture of the school. Attendance is a huge issue." There was no hyperbole in Harris's description of the neighborhood. A combination of street gangs, regular gunfire, and prostitution had led the local district attorney to designate the neighborhood as a nuisance zone, and with a median income of under $10,000, it was among the most impoverished census tracts in the country.[8]

The challenges that the neighborhood presented were rivaled by difficulties inside the school. In addition to poor academic performance and chronic absenteeism, a culture of mistrust permeated relations among staff and students: "When I arrived, the teachers didn't trust the administration, the students didn't trust the teachers. The entire culture was just damaged." Whereas Rowan and Carson dominated their schools with larger-than-life personalities, Harris adopted a distributed leadership style built on collegiality, consensus, and shared decision-making. "I am not one to make a decision and then just pass it on to everyone else," she said. "I get the input of people who are going to be most affected by the decision." Moreover, despite an environment that rewarded immediate results, Harris demonstrated remarkable patience that underscored her long-term approach to improvement. She purposefully refrained from practices that she thought artificially bumped up scores, resisting pressure to pursue immediate gains at the expense of slower but more meaningful changes. She noted, "We are not going to see immediate results because there are a lot of things that have to be unlearned by our students and teachers. I do believe that if we stay committed to the curriculum, some great instruction can take place. We just have to be consistent with it. It is going to take some time."

Whereas Rowan, Carson, and many other iZone principals tailored instruction and assessment to the state test, Harris held firm to a conception of learning that was motivated by more than just test performance. When asked about what she wanted to see during math lessons in her school, she articulated a vision of learning that most math educators would applaud: "I wouldn't want to hear a student say, 'If I multiply both the numerator and denominator by four, then I get four-eighths, then I know they're equivalent.' No. I want to hear the student say that one-half and four-eighths are equivalent because when I put them on this number line, they were on the same spot. Or if I drew a model for one-half and a model for four-eighths, I'd see that the one-half and the four-eighths occupy the same space."

Harris's approach was not designed to realize the extraordinary gains that Rowan and Carson engineered with stunning speed, and her slow and steady approach may not have generated the same degree of political capital. But as much as any school leader we encountered in Memphis, Harris embraced the grit and the grind of enhancing instructional expertise and bolstering professional capacity. In later years, when the iZone struggled to generate expertise across a considerably larger number of schools, Harris's commitment to ambitious instruction and fostering teacher expertise would serve as a reminder of what can be accomplished by a leader unwilling to game the assessment or sacrifice core pedagogical beliefs.

The iZone Registers Remarkable Growth and Praise

Evaluations of the ASD and iZone made it abundantly clear that Dr. Griffin's strategy was paying immediate dividends for the district. The experience and expertise of leaders like Carson, Rowan, and Harris led to growth in student outcomes that was remarkable for its magnitude, reach across subject areas, and speed. A Vanderbilt University–based research team reported that between the 2012–13 and 2014–15 school years, relative to priority schools not incorporated into the iZone or ASD, Memphis iZone schools generated statistically significant gains in math, science, and reading. The authors summarized their findings as follows: "iZone schools are having positive, statistically significant, and substantively meaningful effects on student achievement across all subjects."[9] Subsequent research found that the iZone's core strategy of hiring the most effective principals and teachers accounted for about 40 percent of its positive impact.[10]

The consequences of the iZone's dramatic gains were political as much as they were educational. Newspapers across the state ran stories of the iZone's remarkable success, and Sharon Griffin cemented her status as a local celebrity. State-level authorities took notice, as did national organizations and district leaders from across the country. Delegations from Indianapolis, Indiana; Washington, DC; Detroit, Michigan; Knoxville, Tennessee; and Oakland, California, as well as the Aspen Institute, traveled to Memphis to discover the secret behind the iZone success story.[11] Articles and opinion pieces in *The Tennessean*, *The Commercial Appeal*, and *Chalkbeat* marveled at the iZone's remarkable performance. As one local reporter wrote, "To the surprise of many, students at what were the lowest-performing schools in Tennessee are showing they can learn."[12] The icing on the cake came in October 2015 when Dr. Griffin was named Tennessee Supervisor of the Year by the State Department of Education. "If I had ten Sharon Griffins, we could change the world," said Shelby County Superintendent Dorsey Hopson. In a not-so-subtle reference to the ASD, Dr. Griffin noted that "I look like the people I serve."

The ASD Struggles amid Educational and Political Turbulence

Meanwhile, ASD charter operators were struggling. Shortcomings in the design of their instructional systems, high levels of teacher and leader turnover, and constantly changing state standards combined to undermine organizational stability, instructional practice, and ultimately, learning outcomes. Many core assumptions that informed operators' designs failed to come to fruition in an environment that proved more difficult than they had anticipated. Yet one particularly devastating issue, which we begin with in the following section, was outside operators' control—multiple years of flip-flopping around state standards and assessment.

Changing State Standards

In 2007, the Fordham Institute and the US Chamber of Commerce each released reports that ranked Tennessee's performance standards as among the worst in the country. Seven years and a great deal of hand-wringing later, Tennessee was poised to adopt the far more rigorous CCSS and Partnership for Assessment of Readiness for College and Careers (PARCC) assessment. The plan, which was integral to the state's successful Race to the Top application, was for the new standards and assessment to be piloted in 2012–13, expanded the following year, and fully rolled out by 2014–15.[13]

The gradual release made sense as a state strategy, but for the ASD (and iZone), the transition fell between the first and second year of operations. Publicly, ASD leaders expressed enthusiasm, but privately, there was concern about the timing and its impact on results. Aspire, for example, elected to immediately align its system to the CCSS, accepting the fact that first-year assessment results would suffer (which they most definitely did). Other charter operators were reluctant to take this risk and elected to make the transition the following year. Of course, the transition from low-level standards to the far more rigorous CCSS was a significant leap for all schools in Tennessee, the iZone included, but the disruption to fledgling organizations still finding their footing in a new environment was enormous.

Perhaps had the new standards unfolded according to plan, the ASD operators could have managed the transition with minimal disruption to their organizations. Instead, years of chaos ensued (see fig. 3). Opposition to the CCSS was gaining momentum, both nationally and in Tennessee, and a growing number of state politicians and right-wing activists were calling for the state to abandon a policy they saw as a federal intrusion into local affairs.[14] As political pressure grew, Governor Bill Haslam, in the spring of 2014, reluctantly ordered the Tennessee Department of Education to halt the implementation of the CCSS and to review proposals for a new set of standards and accompanying state test. The state legislature followed suit by repealing the law that had established Tennessee as a Common Core state. Finally, in advance of the 2017–18 school year, Tennessee adopted the Tennessee Academic Standards and the TNReady assessment. Most critics consider the standards, which have since remained in effect, to be at an adequate level of intellectual rigor and, ironically, not that different from the CCSS.[15]

Five years of flip-flopping had created much uncertainty for schools across Tennessee, but for the ASD and its charter operators, the damage

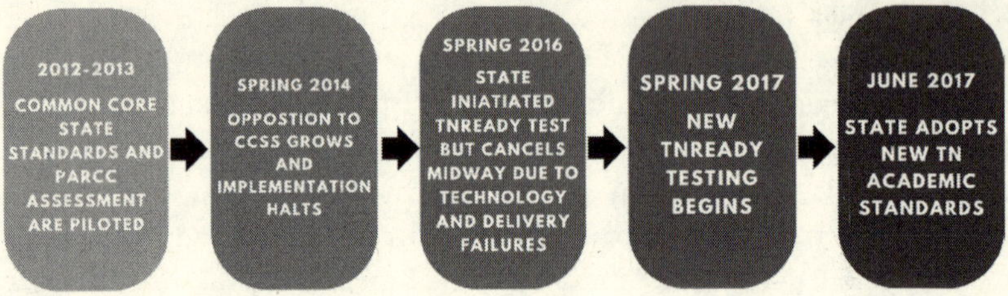

FIGURE 3. A visual chart demonstrating the changes in Tennessee's state standards from 2012 to 2017.

was irreparable. Operators were forced to hastily alter materials and teacher training programs in ways that seemed chaotic and haphazard. The leader of one ASD operator organization noted the effect on operators' ability to design instructional systems: "This is the worst time to build a curriculum. Entering year three and you still don't know what the finish line looks like. It's awful." Perhaps in a less politicized environment, district leaders could explain to the public about the educational consequences of moving the goalposts year after year, but for the ASD, struggling for legitimacy and desperate for results, such explanations rang hollow.

Teacher and Student Mobility

While the uncertainty regarding the state assessment was a destabilizing factor, it was far from the only problem afflicting ASD operators. An environment where they could not control enrollment and were forced to contend with large numbers of special-needs students overwhelmed teachers and undermined organizational strategies. In particular, coping with nonstop student mobility proved to be an enormous challenge for charter operators whose past experience had not prepared them for this level of instability. The director of one ASD operator expressed his frustration: "Last year was our third year, which we would have said going in was going to be the dream year because students would have adjusted to our culture and be close to grade level academically. Instead, it was very similar to our first year because of all the new students who arrived on our campus."

These are familiar problems for leaders and teachers who work in traditional schools that serve marginalized communities, but for most ASD operators, this was uncharted territory. As one district leader put it when hearing about operators' struggles: "Welcome to my world." Even for Green Dot, the only charter operator whose network had experience with turnaround work, the degree of student mobility was unanticipated. One Green Dot leader put it this way: "Part of the problem is that we're getting a ton of kids all the time who either haven't been in school or who were selectively disenrolled from other schools. What happens to school culture when 10 percent of kids didn't get the proper onboarding orientation, and they come in the middle of the year already behind?"

In addition, a steady churn of teachers further destabilized ASD operators. This was partially by design because the ASD strategy, like that of the iZone, involved the replacement of a large number of teachers in their first year of operation. However, while teacher turnover fell sharply in the second and third years of the iZone (also by design), among ASD schools, high levels of teacher turnover *continued* into the second and third years. Vanderbilt researchers suggested that were it not for the high rates of teacher turnover, the ASD might have been able to actually demonstrate student learning gains.[16] Making matters worse, a high level of principal turnover further derailed operations. One study found that over a six-year period across the ASD, only once did the principal turnover rate fall below 50 percent, and in the fifth and sixth years of the ASD, the rate climbed to a shocking 70 percent. By comparison, iZone principal turnover was below 40 percent in four of the six years of the same study.[17] One can scarcely overstate the significance of these numbers.

Another contributing factor was the subtle shift in power dynamics that forced ASD operators to accommodate the preferences of families, even if that meant compromising on fundamental principles. In typical charter settings, where parents can revert to the traditional neighborhood school, charters can stand by their philosophy, knowing that they need not be all things to all people. Indeed, this is integral to the underlying theory of charters and other reforms that seek to leverage the power of markets and choice.[18] While charter operators understood that the ASD would not afford these luxuries, knowing in theory and coping with the reality proved to be two different things. An executive director of one ASD operator explained the challenge:

> In a traditional charter, parents buy into what you're doing. If it doesn't go well, a traditional charter can say, "You're not doing what you promised to do, so you're no longer a student here." As an ASD school, we don't have that option. We're the neighborhood school—if you live in our neighborhood, we're your school. That means parents' engagement level is lower, and we're teaching in a way that's very different from what was taught in this building prior to our arrival. That makes it really hard.

Overwhelmed by the pressure to increase outcomes, the depth of student need, the ever-changing state assessment, and the seemingly revolving door of teachers and leaders, charter operators' lofty visions of teaching and learning failed to materialize. Plans that anticipated experienced teachers strategically selecting from an array of resources, empowered by their autonomy and free of bureaucratic constraints, proved more compelling in theory than in practice. One by one, charter operators arrived at the conclusion that their overwhelmed teachers simply were unable to meet what proved to be unrealistic expectations.

MLK's Shallow Pool: Staffing Shortfalls Undermine Turnaround Efforts

At MLK, Bobby White and his leadership team were experiencing unanticipated difficulties. One problem was the inability to recruit the experienced cadre of teachers White had confidently predicted would jump at the opportunity to join his team. But White's confidence turned out to be misplaced as few experienced local teachers expressed interest in teaching at MLK (or other ASD schools). He reflected on his miscalculation: "The teacher talent pool is not nearly as deep as most folks would think . . . We don't have people beating at our door to be a part of our team."

Without the experienced and highly effective teachers that White had envisioned, he had little choice but to hire an inexperienced staff that brought scant professional knowledge into a context that required expertise and resilience. Not surprisingly, a combination of poor classroom management, weak instruction, and disappointing outcomes followed. White would eventually realize that an effective school turnaround strategy cannot be based exclusively on teacher recruitment, but at the time, he continued to bemoan what he saw as an inadequate teacher labor force. "For me it's about the age and the maturity of our teachers. In a perfect world, I wouldn't have a school full of first- and second-year teachers. There's no way I'd have that."

While White and other charter operators may have overestimated the appeal of working at an ASD school, the fragmentation of Memphis's education landscape made teacher recruitment a highly competitive endeavor. In addition to the salary bonus enjoyed by iZone teachers, SCS offered tenure, job security, and a full array of benefits that the union had achieved through collective bargaining. ASD operators not only were nonunionized but also competed with each other for the most qualified teachers. What White and others saw as Memphis's "shallow" teaching pool was, in many ways, a product of the competition between fourteen ASD operators, SCS, and six surrounding municipalities.

For MLK, the consequences of relying on first- and second-year teachers were both predictable and devastating. Absent a detailed curriculum, a specified set of classroom practices, or a robust system of professional learning, White had few means to support inexperienced and struggling teachers. The autonomy that he touted as key to his strategy quickly turned into a liability. As a member of his leadership team put it, "We allowed the teachers autonomy . . . [but] then when it was time to analyze the [results], it was all so skewed. Each teacher did their own thing." Perhaps in some contexts, highly accomplished teachers doing their own thing is a viable strategy, but at MLK, it was a recipe for disaster.

Aspire's Dilemma: High Ambitions, Weak Capacity

Compared with MLK, Aspire had more organizational experience, a deeper toolbox of curricular supports, and a cadre of instructional coaches. It wasn't enough. Expectations for vibrant classrooms, the extraordinary needs of students, and the ever-looming threat of accountability (tied to constantly changing tests) quickly overwhelmed Aspire's teachers. For Katie Kling, who led the organization's education team, the bottom line was that classroom instruction was far from where it needed to be: "We've really underestimated how hard this was going to be. What I saw in a third-grade lesson today, there was literally no reading happening, no text in front of kids. We're upping the ante in terms of [the] sophistication of what we were doing, and we underestimated exactly how hard this is."

As struggles and weak results accumulated, Aspire's leaders increasingly realized that many of their assumptions about instructional design were not applicable to the ASD context. For example, a staple of the Aspire system was a collective approach to devising lesson plans in which a team of teachers would divvy up the work by different content areas. One teacher might write the English language arts (ELA) lessons for the week, another the math lessons, a third social studies, and so forth. The process was meant to be at once collaborative and efficient. But midway through Aspire's second year, Kling saw the strategy as fundamentally flawed. Teachers were delivering lessons they had scarcely glanced at and that they didn't understand: "As a teacher, I'm getting these lessons that I made no sense of and I don't really understand; yet these are my lessons that I'm supposed to be teaching for the week. Not only have I not done any prep work, but I don't really understand the content."

Moreover, Kling feared that the usual remedies of increasing professional development or providing extra coaching were unlikely to generate the needed improvements in teaching and learning. The underlying problem was that a combination of student need, Aspire's pedagogically ambitious goals, and the limited degree of instructional support placed extraordinary and, ultimately, unrealistic demands on teachers. "I don't think it's a PD issue," said Kling. "There's more to it than that. It's a human capacity issue. I don't care how long you've done it, especially with the new, rigorous assessment and new standards. It won't matter how much PD we do. We heard from people over and over, 'I have too many things I'm trying to do.' It's too much."

Green Dot's Struggle: Aligning Instruction with Teacher Capacity

Green Dot leaders were observing similar struggles in their classrooms. Despite the network's experience and array of curricular and professional resources, leaders were confronting evidence that their underlying assumptions about instructional design did not apply to the ASD. Chrystie Edwards, director of academics and teacher effectiveness, recognized the gap between the complexity and demands of the work, on the one hand, and teachers' experience and professional knowledge on the other: "We made a lot of incorrect assumptions about teachers' level of preparation and previous experience. That has led to inconsistent results and a lack of teacher effectiveness. I think we need to define what lesson preparation looks like in Green Dot; this is what good teaching looks like; this is what professional collaboration looks like. We have to establish the minimum expectation and really define that for teachers."

The problems were particularly acute in the area of special education (SPED). Teachers struggled to marshal the content knowledge, pedagogical skill, and management techniques for a student population that posed even greater challenges. Green Dot's director of special education was forced to ramp up support and guidance to help teachers cope with the day-to-day work: "I'm still working with the SPED teachers on basic education processes. The content part is missing . . . Providing direct instruction and lesson planning are areas of growth for them. A lot of training still needs to be put in place. We have a lot of work to do."

Compounding these difficulties were issues with teacher recruitment and retention, as well as the uncertainty around the state assessment. Consistent with the larger ASD trends, each year brought a substantial number of new and often inexperienced teachers who were unfamiliar with the Green Dot system and unprepared for the classroom challenges that awaited them. One Green Dot leader explained the difficulties confronting the network: "You've got a first-year teacher in physics, math, or in the specialized courses, and that can be challenging to support . . . And then with all the issues with testing, we can't even identify teachers' specific needs because we're not looking at consistent measures of student proficiency."

When Promises Fall Short: The ASD's Crisis of Legitimacy

The struggles of ASD charter operators and their teachers were evident in the ASD's disappointing learning outcomes. Across the board, operators failed to produce the transformative results that Barbic had promised, and in some cases, they seemed to take a step backward. The same 2015 Vanderbilt report that documented the iZone's impressive gains found that the ASD had no statistically significant impact on any of Tennessee's three tested subjects. The report's release just days before the ASD was to announce additional school takeovers was educationally disheartening and politically devastating. Headlines juxtaposed the ASD's failure next to the striking success of the iZone. *The Tennessean* described the ASD as under fire, and *The Commercial Appeal*, the state's other leading newspaper, ran similar stories.[19] ASD critics were quick to press their advantage. Stephanie Love, an SCS board member and vocal ASD critic, called for an immediate end to ASD takeovers, whereas State Representative Antonio Parkinson, a fierce ASD opponent, stated wryly, "Now the intervention needs an intervention."[20]

ASD leaders responded that it was too early to judge the effects of the ASD and that reform takes time. Congressman Mark White, chair of the State Education Committee and ASD advocate, wrote an op-ed piece emphasizing the overall improvement of priority schools while playing down the competition with the iZone. Perhaps had the community accepted the ASD vision from the outset, or had it been developed in close collaboration with the community, the public would have exhibited more patience. After all, the notion that an initiative based on a novel governance structure and the involvement of organizations new to the region would take time is not without merit. Researchers often state that successful turnaround efforts can take as long as five years to increase assessment outcomes.[21] But in the case of the ASD, the absence of what we referred to earlier as *civic capacity* meant that the educational clock and the political clock ticked at different speeds, and deep-seated doubts about the ASD's legitimacy left little margin for error and little tolerance for weak results.

The ASD's struggles and the iZone's perceived success weakened Barbic's hand in his negotiations with the district. Although the legal power of the ASD was undiminished, a growing crisis of legitimacy eroded his willingness to take additional schools from the district. He explained his predicament: "I told the operators that the iZone outperformed you. You've not given me the juice to go into [Superintendent] Dorsey Hopson's office and pound the table and say these are our schools. I can do that when we're kicking their ass in results, but we didn't . . . And based on the results they've been able to achieve, we're going to give them right of refusal because they've earned it."

The effect on ASD operators was devastating, both in terms of morale and in their ability to expand their networks. Several charter operators, particularly those with outside funding, had constructed a financial model that assumed continued growth, but now that growth was in doubt. Allison Leslie discussed the impact on the Aspire network: "There are very few schools left for us to be matched with, or if they're left, they're schools that are underenrolled. Chris [Barbic] has said over and over, 'How could I, with a straight face, say, "Give me those iZone schools," when the iZone has outperformed the ASD?' He's tied a lot of his decisions to how we performed in the first year, and now he can't make a case for anything bold and dramatic because we haven't performed to expectations." Leslie's point is well taken. Conditioning the future of the ASD on first-year results was, at best, wildly optimistic—if not outright unrealistic. Yet, with a skeptical public, impatient funders, and a national spotlight all focused on the ASD, what choice did Barbic have? As we discuss in the next chapter, the community backlash and the pressure on the ASD would only grow.

Growing Pains: The iZone Confronts the Challenge of Scale

While local headlines and community activists celebrated the victory of the iZone over the ASD, district leaders were quietly expressing concern. Success had brought pressure to expand, and what started as seven schools

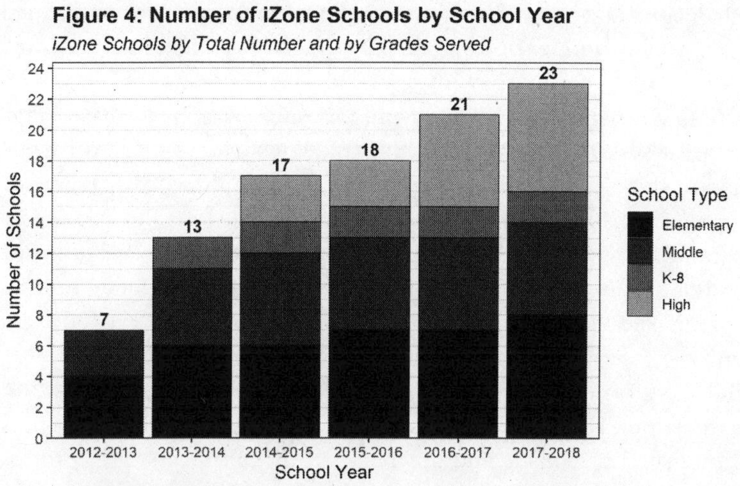

FIGURE 4. The number of elementary, middle, K–8, and high schools in the iZone from the school years 2012–13 to 2017–18.

in 2012 grew to thirteen the following year, seventeen in 2014, and eventually twenty-three schools by 2017.[22] In 2014, three high schools joined the iZone, bringing with them a host of new challenges (see fig. 4). The combination of growth and new state standards raised difficult questions. One was whether the pool of talented principals and teachers that was instrumental to the iZone's success would run dry now that the iZone was substantially larger. A more fundamental question was whether the iZone represented the beginning of meaningful, system-wide change or was nothing more than a boutique initiative ill-suited to the needs of a district with over sixty priority schools.

The answer to the first question came quickly. While the first three cohorts of iZone principals were seasoned veterans, subsequent cohorts included principals with far less experience.[23] The implications were stark; instead of handing the reins of iZone schools to accomplished leaders, such as Rowan, Carson, and Harris, the iZone was granting substantial autonomy to principals with far less expertise. One district leadership coach likened the strategy to "giving an inexperienced race car driver the fastest car. It's not going to end well," he said.

Dr. Griffin and other leaders also began taking a hard look at the quality of teaching and learning in iZone schools. A member of the iZone leadership team concluded that principals were avoiding the hard work of building instructional capacity and instead looking for ways to game the state assessment: "It was teaching to the test and just skill driven . . . It had nothing to do with real teaching and more to do with games." No longer satisfied with the first few years of test results, Dr. Griffin didn't pull any punches: "It's just been really eye-opening. We just don't see anything around planning, anything around understanding how the standards should manifest in classes. It's almost like everybody is at point zero."

Sobering observations about the quality of instruction led to difficult questions about the larger strategy. Recruiting the district's most accomplished principals and teachers had been successful in producing a dramatic increase in assessment outcomes and generating citywide support, but that success increasingly seemed contingent on a small scale of operations, a low-level state assessment, and a heavy emphasis on teaching to the test. But with a new and far more rigorous assessment on the horizon and the number of schools increasing rapidly, iZone leaders began to lament what they understood as a short-sighted strategy. Bradley Leon compared the iZone to a game of whack-a-mole:

> We had an amazing principal at A. Maceo Walker Middle School. We hired her for the iZone. She recruited all of her staff at A. Maceo Walker, and she went to Treadwell, where she had a twenty-point gain in the very first year. You know what happened to A. Maceo Walker? It dropped by fifteen points. From a district perspective, yeah, you can fix the school over here, but it's going to be a whack-a-mole situation.

As the iZone grew in size, so did iZone leaders' worry. Dr. Griffin reserved her most scathing critique for her own failure to foresee the current predicament: "The pool was shallow because I had not developed people. I was taking great principals from schools that they had turned around, putting them at these struggling schools, but I've run out of these great principals, and I am now in a dilemma where I don't have the human capital on the ground. I don't have a bench."

Conclusion

In many ways, both the iZone and ASD pursued strategies that eschewed the long-term work of system building, curriculum development, and enhancing system-wide capacity. The approach was both convenient and politically expedient, particularly for the iZone. Leveraging existing capacity (i.e., moving effective principals and teachers from one school to another) removed the burden of redesigning central office supports, building consensus on a common pedagogical approach, and most of all, uprooting unproductive and ineffective practices throughout the district. The short-term payoff of this tactic was enormous, but the long-term consequences were troubling.

For ASD operators, the imperative to hit the ground running meant that there was neither time nor organizational bandwidth to make substantial changes to their initial strategies. Charter operators, and the ASD itself, would later realize that they had started their work at the bottom of a steep learning curve that would force them to reconsider many assumptions underlying their basic strategies. In the early years, however, there was little choice but to lean on what they had done in the past and hope for the best. Barbic, who at the outset had envisioned ASD operators "humming along," increasingly recognized that the task was harder than any of them had initially appreciated: "We could tell people it was hard, we could talk about how this was different from typical charter schooling, but until you open up the school and get the students and start understanding what the work is like, you just can't appreciate how hard it actually is."

When it came to making an immediate impact and gaining credibility, the iZone strategy proved far more effective. The 50 to 65 percent teacher turnover rate that plagued ASD operators in the second and third years was less of an issue for the iZone, where turnover hovered around a high yet manageable 30 percent.[24] The iZone's ability to recruit and retain effective teachers, coupled with its smaller size and absence of high schools (in years one and two), strong public support, and local knowledge, led to immediate gains that the ASD was unable to match. For a district that was under the threat of state takeover and contending with public outcry over the loss of schools, rebuffing claims about its incompetence was paramount.

Yet the political victory came at the expense of a more meaningful, long-term educational strategy. The weakness in the original iZone approach was not that it started small but that it did not design an instructional system that could support teaching and learning at a greater scale of operations. Indeed, in some ways, the initial iZone strategy was rooted in some of the most deeply entrenched pathologies that have long-plagued American education and that stand in the way of more meaningful and wide-scale change. In relying on the individual abilities of leaders and teachers, both ASD operators and iZone leaders perpetuated the isolation and individualism that stymie collective action. As the education researcher Richard Elmore once wrote, for organizations that lack processes to systematically improve their core work, success "depends more on who gets in and who stays than on what happens to them while they are actually working in the organization."[25]

While this realization would eventually lead ASD and iZone leaders to make important changes to their strategies, it is hard not to look at these early years, and the fraught political environment that defined them, as an opportunity forgone.

CHAPTER FOUR

Contested Reform

The Political Terrain of School Change

Education is, of course, a profession, and like all professions, the role of expert knowledge looms large. This was among the central points of the previous chapter, in which we showed that instructional designs that relied on the individual efforts of teachers working in formidable environments failed to produce changes in teaching and learning. The demands of maintaining the intellectual rigor of the curriculum, meeting accountability goals, and attending to the social and academic needs of students overwhelmed teachers, who required more coordinated, integrated, and robust systems of support, or what some scholars call an *educational infrastructure*.

As a public institution, however, education is also political, and thus so is the work of school reform. One reason for this is that educational goals are inherently ideological. Equity, civic engagement, pluralism, and critical thinking are, at their core, value-laden pursuits, not to mention more controversial issues such as race, religion, and sexuality. A second reason for the political nature of education reform is that it touches on the concerns of multiple interest groups with differing priorities and interests, ranging from organized labor to the business community, civic leaders, and parent groups. Seemingly everyone has a stake in public education.

In chapter 2, we introduced civic capacity as a political process by which broad-based coalitions are created in support of tackling shared problems. Civic capacity, we argued, resides at the intersection of policy and community. Social problems, such as drug abuse, crime, pollution, and homelessness, can be seen in different ways that reflect what political scientists refer to as distinct *problem definitions*. Crime, for example, can be understood as a result of inadequate policing and tough sentencing or as a reflection of systemic racism, inadequate housing, and insufficient employment opportunities. Some policies embed a problem definition and solution that resonate among interest groups, whereas others arouse social divisions and past grievances. The state of Massachusetts's takeover of schools in Lawrence engendered support from the city's large immigrant population, in part because their experiences and worldview made them more receptive to state intervention.[1] Conversely, the historical experience of many Black Americans has made them, relative to other demographic groups, wary of aggressive state interventions that curtail local authority.[2] Similar policies engender different responses from different groups.

Writing in 2025, the idea of civic capacity can seem detached from the realities of the American political landscape. With partisan money pouring into school board elections, books struck from school libraries and curricula, and prayers at football games being adjudicated by the Supreme Court, the notion of collective action in pursuit of shared educational goals appears quaint if not out of touch. Yet the history of US education, and even that of Memphis, is not without promising examples. Consider the early efforts to build support for the Common Core State Standards (CCSS). Advocates framed the idea in a way that appealed to civil rights activists, business leaders, and organized labor. A dual emphasis on equity and the global economy engendered the support of the right-of-center Fordham Foundation, the left-leaning Center for American Progress, the National Association for the Advancement of Colored People (NAACP), the National Governors Association, and both national teachers' unions.[3] While cracks in this coalition would later emerge, the diversity of interest groups supporting the Common Core has been central to its survival. Similarly, the success of the charter school movement can be attributed to a coalition that once included free-market advocates, foundations, business interests, New Democrats, and a handful of civil rights organizations.[4]

This chapter employs the concept of civic capacity to examine the social and political dynamics that shaped public interpretations of the Innovation Zone (iZone) and Achievement School District (ASD), system leaders' efforts to manage those narratives, and the challenges they encountered. While our focus is weighted toward the ASD, we also discuss the political dynamics surrounding the iZone, the shadow that each system casts on the other, and ultimately, the implications of a contentious political environment for public education in the city. Although the discussion reveals considerable antagonism and seemingly irreconcilable differences, the previous examples remind us that even at a time when political divisions seem pervasive, communities can find ways to overcome differences in pursuit of common interests.

Reversing Failure or Repeating History? How the ASD Divided a City

State officials and ASD managers understood that as a state takeover apparatus, the ASD was unlikely to win popularity contests in Memphis. Kevin Huffman, the state education commissioner at the time, had few illusions that the state's aggressive insertion into local affairs would be warmly received. Ten years of experience as an executive at Teach for America (TFA) had prepared Huffman for what he saw as the cost of disrupting underperforming systems. "Bring your thickest skin," he warned future state commissioners. There was little doubt about Huffman's commitment to the ASD. As a member of Chiefs for Change—a group of seven state education chiefs that supported school choice, the closure of chronically low-performing schools, and tough accountability measures—Huffman was closely aligned with reformers who advocated an aggressive shake-up of the existing system. Looking back on his four tumultuous years as state superintendent, Huffman was unapologetic for ruffling some feathers: "We've had massive changes in our education system. Any time you have that volume of change and that speed of change, you are going to get pushback. I don't think that it's surprising."

As Huffman's choice to run the ASD, Barbic was not entirely naive about the political dynamics with which the ASD would need to contend. Stirring the pot and arousing some discontent among entrenched interests was, in his view, the cost of doing business: "This is incredible, bold transformational change," he said. "People are going to push back. If you're going to do anything of consequence in this work, it doesn't come without some level of controversy. We've just got to be comfortable with the fact that there's going to be a backdrop of noise." The noise would turn out to be more than a backdrop.

Beneath the bravado was a strategy premised on the belief that the community had lost patience with the district's long record of poor performance and was ready to embrace a radically different approach. Seen through the lens of civic capacity, ASD leaders framed district incompetence as a unifying problem everyone could agree on. Barbic pressed this narrative relentlessly, repeatedly telling local communities that they deserved better. He and other ASD officials cultivated relationships with the leaders of local organizations, churches (of which there were many), and community groups. They established Neighborhood Advisory Councils, which ASD leaders depicted as an attempt to allow community representatives a voice in making prudent matches between charter operators and neighborhood schools taken over by the ASD. In early 2014, Barbic was still optimistic: "We're doing this, as much as possible, with communities, building relationships with the local districts and superintendents, community leaders, teachers, and folks that are impacted by us. I think we're building community support for the structural change that we're making." The belief that the ASD would steadily win over skeptics was widely held among Barbic's staff. The ASD's head of public relations expressed confidence that Memphians would eventually come around in support of the ASD. He saw pushback as a sign of healthy public engagement. "If people are angry, that's okay," he noted. "We want people to participate, so if they come out and they have a ton of questions, they don't know what's happening, but they stand up for their schools, that's okay. Over time, we'll shift that raw energy into advocacy for great schools, a demand for great schools and involvement and engagement in great schools."

But neither unrelenting advocacy nor confidence could change the fact that the ASD had been dealt a politically tough hand. The main obstacle, of course, was Memphis itself, a city shaped by the legacy of discrimination, Jim Crow, massive White flight, and the recent secession of six predominantly White municipalities from the larger district. Generating civic capacity in Memphis is a tall order. For ASD officials, however, there was little choice but to embrace the challenge. Without community support, both educational success and political viability amounted to a tenuous proposition. The point was not lost on local residents. As one Shelby County School Board member said of the ASD, "You may have the money, you may have the clout, but without us, you don't have the missing piece of the puzzle. You need this community." Her words would prove prescient.

Breaking the Cycle: The ASD as a Catalyst for Disruption

For ASD supporters, not all of whom were White outsiders, the case for an educational overhaul could not have been clearer. They saw the ASD as intervening in a stagnant system, empowering parents, and inserting a much-needed element of competition into public schooling. This perspective resonated strongly among Republican backers and the business community, but also among those who saw the district as inattentive to student needs. Indeed, frustration with the district as an unresponsive bureaucracy was a common theme among supporters. State Representative Mark White captured a common sentiment among ASD advocates: "Here's the way I look at it. You look at the budget of the Shelby County School System—you're not performing—okay, you've got this massive school system. You're turning out a product that's not doing what it should be doing. They would say 'if we just had more money.' But then you look around, and money is not the answer. The same people were doing the same thing year after year."

Advocates maintained that not only was the ASD a needed intervention into a failing system, but it was also designed to empower parents. "Hyperlocal" was among Barbic's favorite terms with which to describe the ASD. Indeed, the notion that the ASD was empowering parents was a sacrosanct belief among ASD officials and charter operators. The community liaison for Aspire, himself African American and a native Memphian, offered an impassioned defense of his organization to those in his own community who saw the ASD as stripping away hard-earned political gains: "We see ourselves giving that school back to the community. You see it as taking away because it's a Shelby County school. You're feeling like your school is being stripped away by an outside entity. I argue that it has not. I argue that because we are here, because we're smaller, you have more control, more say over the work. We listen more closely to the needs of the community and neighborhood."

One would be hard-pressed to find a more cogent argument for the ASD, and there were people in Memphis of different backgrounds for whom this message resonated. But there were also a great many for whom these explanations rang empty and whose perspective led them to an entirely different conclusion.

The ASD as Paternalistic Imposition: "You Can't Fix Us"

The depiction of the ASD as a champion of otherwise powerless parents and a path to better education was one plausible interpretation of the ASD. But it was not the only one. Another narrative, more accessible and firmly rooted in locals' lived experience, portrayed the ASD as a paternalistic and disenfranchising enterprise insensitive to local history and culture. It was a narrative motivated by the historical significance of a locally elected school board, its ties to past civil rights battles, and the critical economic role the district played in the city. The details of the ASD may have been new, but many locals recognized a familiar storyline.

Numerous local representatives, educators, and civic leaders disputed a problem formulation that attributed poor academic outcomes primarily to district incompetence. The problems, in their view, were less tied to the failures of the district bureaucracy or a lack of parental choice but rather to generational poverty, systemic racism, and decades of neglect, or what Ladson-Billings refers to as "the historical, economic, sociopolitical, and moral decisions and policies that . . . have created an education debt."[5] One local school board member's comments illustrate what that debt looks like in Memphis: "If you have a community where 96 percent of your schools are failing, you need a guidance counselor at each school full-time. You have 90 percent of those kids who are from single-parent households. You have 90 percent of those kids who are at or below the poverty line. You may have 30 percent of the kids who have an IEP [individualized education program], but 55 percent may very well need an IEP. But you're telling me I can't get an assistant principal or a full-time guidance counselor?"

Even if there was simmering discontent over the district's complicity in decades of poor performance (as discussed later), the city's history and the lived experience of its Black residents made trust in the ASD difficult to cultivate. A district official explained, "I think it is understandable for our African American population not to trust the state, ever. Slavery existed in this state for hundreds of years, then Jim Crow for a hundred years, and Doctor King was killed in this city but 'oh, now you're here to help?'"

Indeed, numerous residents suspected that the true agenda behind the ASD was to take control of the district's more-than-one-billion-dollar budget.[6] Echoing Noliwe Rooks's notion of "segrenomics," a prominent school board member contended that the takeover of local schools was driven by money rather than a genuine concern for the life chances of the city's children: "I think that all of this new reform is about money. That is money that otherwise would have gone to Shelby County Schools that is now going to a separate entity as salaries, as operations, and a number of things."[7]

Differing problem definitions, varied lived experiences, and pervasive skepticism meant that ASD officials and locals often talked past one another. Whereas advocates saw the ASD as empowering communities, for many long-standing residents, the schools were about interpersonal relations, the generations of families who attended them, and the culture and history that lived inside them. The cultural scripts that sociologists in the 1970s said were integral to schools' social legitimacy were alive and well in Memphis. White-led charter schools (which most were) that belonged to out-of-state networks didn't exactly qualify as local, and a reform imposed by Nashville on Memphis most definitely did not. When asked about the ASD, a community leader noted that Memphis's cultural history was best understood as a neighborhood-specific phenomenon. She returned to the example of Orange Mound: "Orange Mound is the oldest African American homeownership neighborhood in America. The ASD came in and said that they were targeting schools there. Orange Mound is a community whose alumni are so strong; they have groups throughout the country. They were not happy about the ASD taking their schools, just like others throughout the city."

But above all, it was the overriding sense of paternalism that drove resentment toward the ASD. The notion that outsiders with little knowledge of or roots in the community needed to "save" locals from their own incompetence was, for many residents, intolerable and all too familiar. Said one community leader and lifelong Memphian: "They say these teachers you have known all your life are not good enough. We are getting rid of all of them. We are bringing in some twenty-two-year-olds who can do all these great things for your kids, and by the way, the majority of them are not going to look like you. I think that is destructive and offensive."

And finally, there was the matter of results. Had ASD operators been able to deliver the promised outcomes, it would have provided at least a modicum of credibility. In this sense, then, results were far more consequential for the ASD than for the district and its iZone. Whereas local systems are buttressed by their ties to neighborhoods, their central role in the local economy, and the sheer fact that they've been around longer than anyone can remember, the ASD could only point to the possibility of dramatically better results to justify its existence, solidify its organizational identity, and legitimize its methods.

So, when the promised outcomes failed to materialize, the damage to the ASD's local standing was enormous. One community activist and school board member put it this way: "If you're not doing any better with the schools, why should we continue to give you our schools? You can't fix us." An ASD staff member acknowledged how the discrepancy between early promises and actual results eroded support: "The perception in the community is that we've overpromised what we can do in terms of student outcomes." Even Barbic came to realize that bold predictions about radically improved outcomes had set the ASD up for failure, noting, "When some of the bigger operators were coming in to pitch themselves to the community, they could have shown a little bit more humility. They were kind of shitting all over the district in a way that the district very much heard and felt. Then to come in and not crush it right out of the gate, I think folks could have handled themselves a little bit differently." Barbic's point is well taken, but of course, it was he who promised that ASD schools would reach the top quartile within five years and, in doing so, set a bar that would prove far out of reach for the ASD and its partners.

The Limits of Advocacy

By 2015, as the ASD entered its third year, community anger reached a fever pitch. Heated meetings were held at schools slated for ASD takeover, with school board members and parents calling for resistance. Neighborhood Advisory Councils continued to meet, but frustration grew when the ASD would seemingly ignore their recommendations not to take over a school. In what would turn out to be his final year at the helm of the ASD, Barbic appeared overwhelmed and discouraged by the level of animosity. By May of that year, optimism had given way to resignation: "They're not buying what we're trying to sell. There's apathy. There's misinformation. There's who the messenger is. Fear of change. I think there's lots of reasons. People are generally skeptical of things to begin with because their neighborhood has gotten screwed over and over again. We're up against that."

As the backlash against the ASD gained momentum, some charter operators and ASD supporters wondered whether Barbic and his colleagues had done enough to win over the community. Yet swapping the message or the messenger would not have changed the fact that the ASD was an uneasy fit with the worldview of many Memphis residents or that anti-ASD sentiments easily slid into existing narratives rooted in a century and a half of history. State-level officials continued to insist that the controversy was an inevitable by-product of disrupting the status quo and that there was little reason to change course. Huffman compared the local pushback against the ASD to the dynamics in New Orleans, where even strong results had not silenced dissent:

> Look at New Orleans. If you would have told people ten years ago that New Orleans schools would get the growth that they have had on assessments and

> graduation rates, people would have said that's incredible. Yet the fact remains that there is massive political community pushback in New Orleans. It just demonstrates just how hard this work actually is. Reformers think, well, if we just get greater results, it'll go away. That's not true. People in the political world think if you just have enough community meetings, it will go away. That's not true either.

ASD leaders, charter operators, and advocates voiced various versions of this message. They argued that more time was needed; that it was just a small group of vocal critics causing the problems; and that if there really was any larger-scale push back, it was mainly the result of misinformation and ignorance. Aspire's Allison Leslie held firm to this view: "I think the resistors are mainly teachers, politicians, and the school board. But when I think about students and parents, once they understand what's happening, they're actually interested in learning more and figuring out how to make the school the best school it can be." Green Dot's leadership worked tirelessly to win community support, but one leader expressed frustration with what they saw as misguided opposition: "I had a parent actually stand up and say to me, 'Our school is not in the bottom 5 percent. Leave us alone, we're okay without you.' And to me that's really sad that your child is in a school that is one of the worst fifty schools of the 1,700 in the state, and yet you want us to not be here to make that school better."

These points are not without merit. It is true, for example, that some local politicians, school board members, and a few school leaders and teachers were particularly vocal in their criticism of the ASD. It is also likely that some parents did not fully grasp just how poor academic outcomes had been in their children's schools before the ASD's arrival. Several iZone principals said the same thing. Likewise, ASD operators' contention that many parents came to appreciate their schools and develop positive relationships with teachers is not difficult to believe. ASD staff worked relentlessly to build trust with families and community members, and the daily interactions among school personnel, students, and parents often seemed to make broader political tensions seem like what Barbic once described as "background noise."

But even if the community needed to reckon with the urgent need for school improvement, they were not the only ones who lacked understanding. ASD leaders, charter operators, and their advocates failed to grasp that for many Black residents of Memphis, the value of a locally run school system could not be reduced to test scores or even the quality of teaching and learning. In Black communities—particularly in the South—education is inseparable from the long struggle for civil rights. The locally elected school board, despite its inefficiencies and penchant for parochial concerns, represented a hard-won political victory in a region that had systematically disenfranchised African Americans for over a century. For Black Memphians, that history—and the collective identity shaped by it—offered potent reasons to resist the ASD.

Political scientists have long argued that new policies can generate new political incentives and identities that, in turn, spur new forms of collective action.[8] When those identities are reinforced by over a century of policies and politics, the incentives are stronger and the collective action more forceful.

Looking back, it is difficult not to see the ASD as a missed opportunity. Barbic, Anderson, and other ASD central office staff brought years of experience and a track record of success. They raised large sums of philanthropic resources and were relentless in their drive to make change. Many of the charter organizations brought innovative ideas and practices to a city clearly in need of them. Local educators such as Bobby White abandoned secure and comfortable positions to improve educational opportunities for local students. Yet rather than bringing the community together in support of a common goal, the ASD polarized a city already divided by its past. Worst of all, the political discord took a steep educational toll on charter operators already struggling to meet students' overwhelming needs.

Who Decides: The iZone's Push for Professional Control

The political dynamics of the iZone did not generate headlines or packed community meetings. Nobody compared the iZone to slavery or called its leaders colonizers (as they did the ASD). But as noted in chapter 2, the fact that the iZone strategy involved replacing local principals and teachers meant that it was all but certain to engender opposition. District officials had little interest in allowing neighborhood activists and school alumni to select school leaders, teachers, or other personnel for iZone schools. Their vision was of a "professional system" where expertise, credentials, and outcomes—not personal relationships or community ties—guided decision-making. It is of little surprise, then, that the early years of the iZone generated backlash. Deputy Superintendent Leon reflected on the struggle to appoint new principals to iZone schools over community objections: "We had an Alumni Association Committee that comes from the Melrose High School Alumni Association. We would take candidates through our interview process, and then they would interview the people. It was in those conversations that they made it clear that we shouldn't hire a woman. I was like 'that's not right, and this is not your role.'"

In another instance, Leon confronted community anger when Rodney Rowan was named as the principal of Westhaven Elementary. Local activists wanted a principal with deep connections to the neighborhood, despite the fact that Leon saw Rowan as the best candidate for the job. "These folks didn't know what they were talking about," said Leon. "They had very parochial concerns about certain things that they wanted to control directly." Nor did community tensions dissipate after Rowan took over as principal. His decision to replace most existing teachers with ones he saw as more qualified—a step that virtually all iZone principals took—was met with anger and dismay. He described the dynamic: "There was a lot of resistance. People remembered Westhaven from a long time ago. The dynamics were different. High-stakes tests didn't exist then. I interviewed a lot of the people that the community recommended. I actually went to schools to watch them teach, and I knew that they just were not a good fit for the work that I was trying to do. iZone work is a different kind of work. You have to have a unique skill set to be successful."

More than just an effort to improve schools or avoid ASD takeover, the iZone was also an effort by district leaders to rein in a system of patronage and community control while strengthening the importance of expert knowledge and professional credentials. One can hear echoes of the ASD argument in the words of iZone leaders. Leon's assertion that the district should determine staffing because "you need somebody with expertise and thoughtfulness to make the decisions" is not altogether different from Barbic's contention that the community should trust the ASD to deliver the results it needed. Both iZone and ASD leaders would at times lament that "people don't understand." The unspoken continuation of that sentence being "but *we* do."

From Opposition to Opportunity: "Without the ASD There Wouldn't Be an iZone"

In theory, one could argue that the ASD and iZone represented similar efforts to improve schools by curtailing community control. But only in theory. Because while it is true that both the ASD and iZone limited local decision-making about educational issues, the iZone—unlike the ASD—would not only quell community concerns about loss of control but would quickly emerge as a source of enormous community pride. How did the iZone turn a potentially negative political dynamic into a groundswell of local support?

One reason is straightforward: results. The Vanderbilt studies showcasing the iZone's strong impact on student learning captured statewide attention, standing in stark contrast to decades of reports chronicling the district's poor performance and decline. In a city long associated with crime and poverty, the iZone gave the community a reason to take pride. Few understood the importance of restoring that pride better than Antonio Burt, who made it a central focus of his tenure as an iZone principal. "I had to try to bring pride back to the neighborhood . . . I had to offer programs that didn't exist. We had majorettes, drummers, chess clubs, xylophone club, so people started bringing their kids back there that didn't even live in the neighborhood . . . That's the approach of iZone schools across the city, changing the landscape of the city and giving people something to be proud of."

Beyond strong outcomes and chess clubs, the iZone's legitimacy received a boost from an unlikely source—the ASD. Educators, parents, and community members rallied around the iZone not just because of its academic success but also because it was the homegrown antidote to the state's unpopular and ineffective takeover apparatus. As Bradley Leon put it: "The politics have shifted. Initially it was 'where can we thwart the ASD,' but now everyone wants to be in the iZone." Articles, blog posts, and stories about the iZone besting the ASD proliferated. *The Tennessean* ran a story under the headline "Memphis iZone schools outpaced state-run turnaround efforts."[9] Another news outlet's lead story stated, "Vanderbilt study: iZone more effective than ASD in turning around struggling schools thus far."[10] Burt explained how the perception of success shifted the political dynamics around the iZone: "The recognition throughout the city and state, and on a national level, has only magnified how people want their school to be a part of the iZone, and now a lot of teachers want to be a part of it, too." Remarkably, the iZone turned school turnaround into a high-status enterprise.

The iZone was more than a successful district turnaround initiative, or even a source of community pride in the way that a championship high school football team might be. Rather, it was an explicit rejection of the state's underlying narrative that the city lacked the commitment and wherewithal to manage its own education system and that the task should be left to others. In a Southern, Republican state with a long history of oppressing its Black citizens, the iZone was an expression of Black power.

ASD as Catalyst: Pressure That Sparked Reform

The political dynamic surrounding the iZone–ASD competition had practical implications. District managers reported that without the ASD, it would have been difficult for the district to make important changes, such as closing failing schools and replacing ineffective principals and teachers. Bradley Leon explained: "Our school board routinely wouldn't do the things that it would take to really turn schools around for political reasons. But once you have the leverage of an ASD that is otherwise going to take over your schools, the school board's willing to do a lot more. Without the ASD, would the board have said 'sure, you can go ahead and fresh start the schools, sure, you can provide performance, resigning and retention bonuses, and an additional hour to the day'? No way."

In fact, while the anti-ASD rhetoric in the community was rising, some district leaders were quietly expressing their gratitude for creating the conditions that allowed the iZone to flourish. Others noted the beginning of a long-overdue community conversation about the quality of the city's public schools (as some ASD officials had predicted). Dr. Griffin was explicit in stating that the ASD provided the district with much-needed motivation to improve: "The ASD has forced us to really look at proactive ways to support schools. We're typically so reactive when the schools fail, but how about on the front end we say, 'Red Middle School is not at the bottom yet, but I notice their third and fourth-grade results dropping with those new standards. We better put a coach or an experienced teacher in there, add an hour, or do some kind of intervention.' So, thank you for the pressure, ASD, because it is actually going to save some lives."

In one remarkable incident, district leaders were able to use the ASD threat not only to win over skeptical parents but also to engender the support of the local union that, in other circumstances, would have fiercely opposed the displacement of teachers and leaders from iZone schools. A district official recounted the dynamics at a community meeting: "We were bringing a school into the iZone, and there was a (community) meeting with lots of opposition. It was a huge community issue, and people were coming up to the mic. And, no joke, the head of the union came to the mic and begged the parents to accept the iZone because it was our last refuge before the state would take the school. The head of the union!"

None other than Superintendent Hopson acknowledged that the ASD had created a sense of heightened importance that had previously been lacking: "The concern of your school being taken over is a big motivator. I think it has really made people more aware and accountable, and forced them to step their game up. Without the ASD there wouldn't be an iZone . . . There is a real sense of urgency right now." Even members of the most fiercely anti-ASD institution—the Shelby County School Board—conceded that the ASD had ratcheted up parent engagement and community involvement. One board member spoke candidly: "The ASD pushed SCS [Shelby County Schools] to really look at what was going on with our schools. It's actually opening the eyes of the people to say, 'Hey, we didn't know this community was as messed up as it is.' Parents are getting more involved in the education of their children. They're reading, they're researching, listening to the news. They're asking questions."

It would have been easy to dismiss these comments had they come from ASD advocates in search of a silver lining, but the fact that they came from lifelong employees of the district makes them hard to ignore. Indeed, to the extent that Griffin, Hopson, Burt, and Leon were right that the district needed what one official referred to as "a kick in the pants," then it offers some support for the contention that competition can catalyze improvement.

But if adversarial politics had its benefits, it also came at a cost. Those costs were borne by ASD leaders, who increasingly had to divert their energy to fending off attacks; by charter operators, who were forced to invest resources in defending their credibility; and by the city itself, which spent considerable time and effort engaging in conflict rather than collaborating around a shared mission.

Community Politics as the Hidden Curriculum

Over a generation of sociological research has shown that organizational structure, leadership, and practice are shaped by what organizational theorists refer to as the *institutional environment* in which organizations reside. The core idea is that for organizations to be seen as "legitimate" and "appropriate," their practices need to conform to societal norms and values. In other words, while we may typically think that organizations survive or fail based on whether they "get the job done," in reality, what it means to be effective or capable depends no less on the larger cultural context.

But what happens when organizations operate in environments in which values are openly contested and competing conceptions of what counts as appropriate vie for dominance? Complex and contested environments of this nature exert considerable pressure on organizational governance, practices, and identity, often forcing difficult compromises and complex administrative arrangements that cater to widely differing demands.[11] It would be difficult to imagine an environment more complex, contested, and politicized than the one that ASD operators were forced to navigate. A community that was explicitly questioning its right to run local schools, students who presented an overwhelming array of needs, and a state that was demanding dramatic gains in student learning outcomes put charter operators under extraordinary pressure from multiple directions. In a less turbulent environment, operators could have focused their attention on increasing professional capacity, improving instruction and leadership, and enhancing curricular materials. But in the ASD, they had no such luxury. Instead, they poured resources into strengthening their position in the community, shoring up support, and assuaging fears about their intentions.

At Aspire, for example, leaders understood that their association with the ASD turned people against them and, in doing so, undermined the image they hoped to cultivate. "Everybody associates all of us with the ASD," said Leslie. To counter this impression, they invested heavily in efforts to enhance their credibility in the community and demonstrate their commitment to the neighborhood. A member of Aspire's leadership team reiterated the importance of garnering community support: "It's all been about community partnership. From people in the community who have been here a long time, to the churches, community organizations and partnerships, and parents. We want to include them in the partnership that is this school." In the historic Orange Mound neighborhood—home to Aspire's first two elementary schools—Leslie and her team left no stone unturned in their effort to build relationships. Leslie recounted the all-encompassing nature of the effort:

> I have to call Representative Hardaway and Representative Parkinson. I have to share results and updates with local pastors in each of the communities that we're in. I have to go to community meetings to make sure that they feel like we're open and transparent, engaging the community and participating in things that are going on. I'm still in a phase of proving myself to members of the

> community who may not have children at the school, but who influence the narrative of the neighborhood. I need to do this. It's not optional.

At Green Dot, school leaders were taking similar steps to distance themselves from the ASD's negative image. They were especially concerned that community hostility might hinder recruitment efforts critical to their financial viability. As with Aspire, the investment of time, energy, and resources was substantial. One leader explained, "I just hired a director of strategic partnerships whose primary purpose is to develop our strategy for community engagement and community partnerships, and to create meaningful relationships with community organizations that are coordinated to support our work. So that's a major shift and deepening of focus that we're going forward with. It's a huge amount of time and money that we didn't anticipate." Green Dot's effort to increase its presence in the community and to establish its credibility was multifaceted. The director of strategic partnerships explained the breadth of activity: "We literally and figuratively beat our drum as much as possible in the community. We have actually taken the band and gone and played in front of Geeter K–8. We've followed buses from the feeder schools, so we know where the kids live, so we'd know where to send a mailer. We have gotten signs and stood on the corners where our elementary schools are. We're passing out literature to parents, we're shaking hands with kids and inviting them to come to an event at the school. We're very present in the community."

It is not unusual for districts or charter management organizations (CMOs) to organize community events of this nature. Charter schools, in particular, depend on a positive reputation in order to attract families that might otherwise attend their traditional neighborhood school. But these were lean organizations already struggling to meet lofty academic goals, manage the myriad tasks associated with launching a new organization, and cope with a fraught environment that presented an endless array of challenges. The leader of one charter network that eventually withdrew from an agreement to operate ASD schools explained the shock of encountering community antagonism. "This has been humbling for me. We've been quite shielded from a lot of the politics and press in our home state. We have waiting lists of over 300 people to get into our schools."

For the leaders of organizations like Aspire and Green Dot who elected to remain, the organizational and individual costs were considerable. Green Dot's director of strategic partnerships explained the impact it had on her and her family: "I work six days a week now and sometimes seven days a week. I've had 16-hour days in this process. I've had my mother and my son up here stuffing envelopes. My husband is canvassing the neighborhood, going to the small businesses to talk to them about what we're trying to do. It has turned into my family's job."

At Martin Luther King Jr. College Preparatory High School (MLK), Bobby White faced a somewhat different calculus. While Green Dot and Aspire had to build community relationships from the ground up, White could draw on the goodwill and credibility earned through a lifetime of work in the neighborhood. Yet even he acknowledged that MLK's association with the ASD meant he couldn't take community support for granted: "When you align yourself with people that the community doesn't trust, you become somewhat untrustworthy yourself. They wanted to know if we can trust Bobby White now that he's with the White folks. Is he still that guy that is so pro-community and so pro-Black and Brown students, empowering them and raising them up to be great one day? Or is he now a businessman and all he's thinking about is how much money he can make? I had to make sure that the community knew that I was still that guy."

For White, extending the school's work into the community was also part of an educational philosophy that viewed community involvement as a cornerstone of academic achievement. At the same time, White understood that community outreach was essential to securing MLK's legitimacy in the neighborhood—a legitimacy that, despite his strong reputation, was not guaranteed. "We have to reach out to the community on multiple media platforms," he noted. "I have a commercial that's out right now. We have Facebook pages, a website, letters going out to parents. I'm speaking at community venues weekly. We have an event called Frayser Day. I'm speaking there, and we'll have a booth there. Just making sure the parents know who we are and the work that we're doing."

ASD operators engaged in an extraordinary array of activities. They forged ties with local religious and community leaders; took part in neighborhood sports leagues, picnics, and other social events; created jobs for residents; offered a variety of adult services; and undertook additional initiatives that both expanded and redefined their mission. These adaptations were not conventional extracurricular efforts but rather a broadening of organizational goals rooted in the cultural legacy of individual neighborhoods and situating school reform within a broader economic and social context.

None of the operators complained about the outlay of time, money, and effort that they had not anticipated. Yet for organizations whose internal processes and core instructional practices were still evolving, these investments came at a steep cost. Community engagement did not replace the ASD's expectation that charter operators should produce dramatic gains in student achievement, and disappointing academic outcomes underscored the need to make substantial changes to their instructional systems. As Barbic eventually acknowledged, deep community involvement carried a significant educational trade-off: "I think there could be a lot of time and energy spent on reacting to folks in the community who are upset with what we're trying to do. The protests outside the school or the battle with unions and that sort of thing. I understand that sometimes those things have to happen, but every minute you're spending worrying about that, you're not worrying about quality of instruction and quality of leadership and quality of talent in the school."

Barbic's point is well taken and speaks to our argument that politics and pedagogy go hand in hand. Community anger and resentment penetrated the organizations charged with improving teaching and learning and, in doing so, diverted scarce resources from what was already a formidable challenge. Yet the ASD's polarizing effect extended beyond school operators, affecting the broader community as well.

What Memphis Might Have Built: The Coalition Forgone

A scan of headlines and media coverage around 2015 would have led the casual observer to believe that two irreconcilable camps were battling over starkly different visions for public education in Memphis. On one side was a pro-ASD camp that championed competition, minimal bureaucracy, and charter operator autonomy. On the other was a pro-district camp that supported traditional public schools, which were doing the best they could under difficult circumstances. From this perspective, the two sides appeared locked in a winner-take-all battle, with little common ground on which to compromise.

But a more nuanced reality hid below the surface.[12] Numerous community members noted that despite their objection to the ASD, the community needed to confront the district's inadequacies and the community's own role in allowing performance to deteriorate over decades. Opposition to the ASD, it turns out, did not imply complacency. Particularly striking was the extent to which this perspective stretched across the social and racial lines that seemed so entrenched in the city's history and politics. A few examples illustrate the point. Tomeka Hart served two terms on the Memphis City Schools Board of Education, including as board president, and had been a member of Governor Phil Bredesen's Race to the Top team that had crafted Tennessee's successful application. Hart, despite previous experiences in TFA and a close association with the reform movement, saw polarization as detrimental to the city's educational agenda: "I think one of the worst things that's happening is it's ASD versus iZone. It doesn't have to be that way. We have yet to figure out how to do this with kids in mind . . . Everyone really needs to see themselves as true partners in the work of turnaround."

Similar perspectives could be found inside the Tennessee Department of Education. One official who quietly expressed reservations about the divisive nature of the ASD strategy noted that the local community was also complicit for not demanding improvement. A leader from a nonprofit organization critical of the ASD also conceded that the community needed to confront the inadequacy of the local system: "It would be awesome if we could have a bigger conversation around student achievement and the lack of high-quality educational options that are available here in our city. We have to focus on what's taking place in our traditional public schools." Even Superintendent Dorsey Hopson spoke about the need to shift the civic conversation from one in which students were "third or fourth" on the list of priorities to one in which they were first.

Most striking of all, however, were the voices coming from inside the ASD. The early ASD years were marked by a zealous commitment among staffers, but by 2016, doubts about the legitimacy and effectiveness of the model had crept in, particularly among those who were African American, local, or both. Chantavia Burton, compliance manager for the ASD, expressed a different vision of reform that engaged the community on equal terms: "In my ideal world the intervention would have come from the community. I feel like it should have been generated from them, kind of pulling back the veil and saying this is the realities that your students are experiencing. Let's problem-solve together about what the needs are and where we want to go."

Yet it was the comments of Barbic's top deputy and eventual successor, Malika Anderson, that most clearly revealed the depth of doubt within the agency's leadership. A strong advocate for decentralization and school-level autonomy, as well as a disciple of prominent reformer Michelle Rhee, Anderson was no stranger to the politics of school reform. But after years of witnessing the local opposition the ASD provoked, she began to question whether the agency was ultimately harming the very community it aimed to serve. The ASD had many critics in Memphis, but few voices carried more weight than that of Anderson:

> It is not enough to say that what happens in the classroom is important but then to ignore all of the other contributing factors that make our jobs in the classroom harder. I want to figure out the ways that we can positively impact the systems of inequity that are contributing to these failing schools. I really do think that unintentionally we made things worse by not paying attention to equitable hiring practices among teachers . . . We are going too far restarting every school. Replacing 80 percent of the teachers, most of whom were Black and Brown, is crazy.

Anderson also became increasingly aware that the politics surrounding the ASD were linked to broader state-level dynamics that did not align with her own priorities. She noted, "Folks who politically support the ASD are almost diametrically opposed, politically and economically, on other social matters that impact the families we serve. Low-income folks, Black folks, and people of color like us are not single-issue voters. I think this has aligned us with people who, in other ways, negatively impact the families we serve, so we come across, politically and practically, as enemies."

There were, of course, those true believers, unequivocally pro- or anti-ASD, with little interest in compromise or more nuanced positions. But the comments of community members, organization leaders, district officials, and ASD staff suggest that hidden from view was the possibility of a broader coalition crossing boundaries and drawing from multiple constituencies. This coalition was attuned to local history, committed to collaboration with local teachers and leaders, and ready to confront the district's shortcomings and the entrenched interests that deter change. It is this type of broad-based coalition that underlies the concept of civic capacity as a political resource for tackling community-wide problems.

It would be naive to suggest that Memphis could easily muster the kind of civic capacity needed to sustain a broad, multiconstituent coalition for school reform. In contexts where communities have often been excluded from decision-making or pitted against one another, asking diverse stakeholders to align around a common agenda or cultivate the trust that enables collective action is far from straightforward. Moreover, just as instructional systems must be continuously refined, coalitions must be continuously nurtured and sustained. As the political scientist Eric Patashnik notes, the politics of sustaining a reform are no less daunting than the politics of initiating it.[13] Yet even in a city with as complicated a legacy as that of Memphis, reformers have little choice but to confront these challenges rather than presume they can be transcended by good intentions alone.

It would be equally naive to assume that such a coalition, were it to emerge, would automatically yield dramatic improvements in teaching and learning. Democratic localism has rarely proven to be hospitable terrain for the development and sustainment of effective, long-term educational reform.[14] Community ownership may lend legitimacy, but it holds limited value if it does not give rise to reforms marked by coherence and continuity and informed by professional knowledge. Civic capacity, in other words, is not an end in itself—it is a political resource that must be transformed into strategic action that leads to the development of a coherent, high-performing instructional system.

Still, if there is an overarching theme to this chapter, it is one of opportunity forgone. While the ASD did provide the spark that led to the creation of the iZone, and while the iZone saw some early success, one cannot help but wonder what might have been possible had their leaders coordinated their efforts, learned from shared experience, and aligned their strategies. More broadly, what might Memphis have accomplished if civic leaders, educators, and communities had come together around a unified vision for educational improvement? Building civic capacity in a city like Memphis is undeniably difficult, but not unlike the professional work of designing a robust instructional system, the political work of reform is incremental and plodding. It requires patience, negotiation, and a willingness to forgo shortcuts that promise quick fixes but undermine long-term progress.

CHAPTER FIVE

Politics, Systems, and Practice

The Fragile Architecture of School Improvement

The relationship between politics and system building can seem like a catch-22. On the one hand, it's difficult to generate a supportive political dynamic in the face of public concerns about the quality of teaching and learning, while on the other, it's nearly impossible to build effective educational systems in political environments that threaten their long-term survival and legitimacy. System building requires public support, but public support requires effective systems.

The implications of this dynamic for Innovation Zone (iZone) and Achievement School District (ASD) leaders were stark. ASD leaders, in particular, were in a precarious position. The political environment had degenerated to the point where a highly critical public openly contested the right of the ASD to take control of local schools, packed community meetings erupted in anger at the prospect of new takeovers, critics published strident op-ed pieces, and emboldened local politicians called for the dissolution of the agency. Academic outcomes that fell far short of earlier promises fueled a narrative that the ASD was motivated by power and money more than by concern for local children. Far from generating civic capacity, the ASD had become a lightning rod for dissent.

In July 2015, a chastened Chris Barbic announced his resignation. The official press release referenced health concerns (he had suffered a heart attack a year earlier), but a combination of private and public remarks made it evident that he was worn down from an experience that proved far more difficult than he had imagined. He remarked on hard lessons learned: "As a charter school founder, I did my fair share of chest pounding over great results. I've learned that getting these same results in a zoned neighborhood school environment is much harder."[1] Equally evident was that unrelenting attacks on the ASD had taken a toll: "I'm getting my ass kicked from every direction," he said. Past leaders who had tried to improve Memphis schools—Willie Herenton, Gerry House, Gates Foundation officials, and countless others—surely sympathized. On November 3 of that year, Tennessee Governor Bill Haslam appointed Barbic's deputy, Malika Anderson, as the ASD's new superintendent.[2]

While Anderson brought years of experience and a strong reputation to the position, much of what ailed the ASD was beyond her control. She could not change the law that established the ASD as a takeover apparatus that circumvented the local school board; only the state legislature could do that. Nor could she rewrite a history that had left Memphis's African American population highly suspicious of White outsiders promising to make things better. And while Anderson, herself African American, had a long track record of working to improve urban education, it was far from certain that new leadership would change the underlying political dynamics. For many Memphians, the ASD was "White," regardless of who was speaking on its behalf. But there was one thing that could reverse the ASD's downward spiral: improving educational outcomes. For that to happen, however, ASD leaders had to overcome two obstacles.

The first was that despite their statutory authority, Anderson and her central office team had little leverage over the school-level functions that contribute to student outcomes. If there was going to be any improvement in student achievement, it would need to come from the fourteen independent operators that the ASD had authorized to run its thirty-one schools.[3]

The ASD could make suggestions, implore operators to do better, and threaten to revoke contracts, but it could not tell operators how to run their schools.

This led to a second obstacle. For charter operators to achieve meaningful improvements in student learning, they would have to fundamentally redesign their systems, which in turn meant reexamining the core educational assumptions that informed those systems. On the surface, this may seem straightforward: If a strategy isn't working, change the strategy. But that sentiment greatly underestimates the difficulty of letting go of ideas and practices that leaders had spent entire careers developing, many of which had brought them prior success. Moreover, pinpointing where change is most needed is difficult because the interplay among curriculum, assessment, leadership, teacher knowledge, and professional learning is complex and often ambiguous. These challenges are magnified in high schools, where size and organizational complexity make the task all the more formidable.

It is remarkable, then, that most ASD charter operators we studied not only persisted but also made significant adaptations to their approach. Beyond minor fixes made at the margins, the changes reflected new understandings of how to construct and manage instructional systems commensurate with the challenges posed by Memphis and the ASD. In the first part of this chapter, we discuss the evolution of ASD operators' strategies and the implications for designing instructional systems in contemporary environments.

The ASD was not the only system to undergo fundamental change. The iZone, while basking in the glow of national attention and civic pride, was facing its own crisis. For all the political clout afforded by strong results, iZone leaders realized that their approach was unlikely to yield continued success. Hand-picking principals and providing them with nearly complete autonomy worked when the iZone was fewer than ten schools and when the state's assessment was rooted in low-level basic skills. But by the time Dr. Antonio Burt took over the iZone in the summer of 2017, neither of those conditions applied. Stretching from Frayser in the north to Whitehaven in the south, from the Mississippi River to southeast Memphis, the iZone's twenty-three schools now spread across the three-hundred-square-mile city (see fig. 5). Moreover, a new state assessment posed a far more formidable challenge, and as ASD leaders would attest, the pool of extraordinary teachers had reached its limits. Further, in a region with six suburban municipalities, fourteen independent ASD operators, and one large district, competition for qualified teachers was fierce.

As the new leader of the iZone, Dr. Burt instituted sweeping changes that transformed it into a system grounded in a shared vision of teaching and learning, common tools, and capacity-building processes designed to strengthen the expertise of teachers, principals, and district coaches. Later in this chapter, we discuss these changes to the iZone and what they tell us about the possibilities for reforming urban systems.

But designs alone do not ensure improvements to teaching and learning. Those improvements materialize only to the extent that school-level professionals use new resources to improve practice, accept the risk that comes with change, and stick around long enough to get better. Doing that is difficult in the best of circumstances, and Memphis—competitive, fractured, and politicized—was far from the best of circumstances. In the

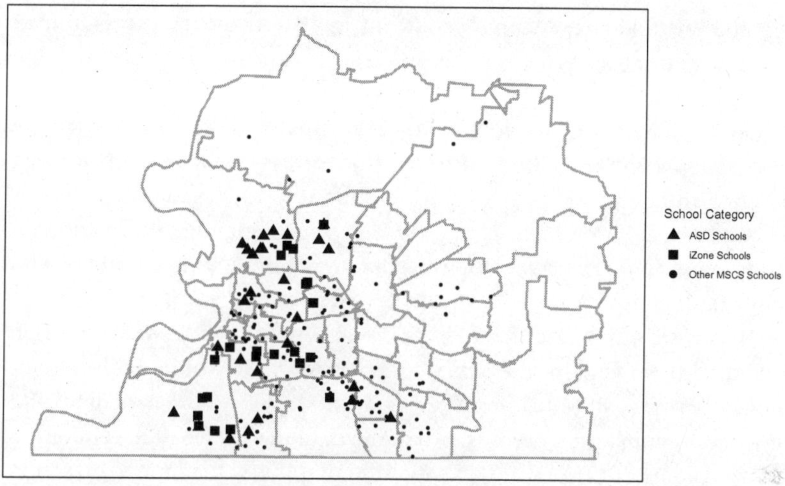

FIGURE 5. A map of Memphis depicting the location of all ASD schools within Shelby County, all iZone schools, and other Memphis–Shelby County Schools (MSCS) in 2017–18.

Note: Data points labeled "Other MSCS Schools" are included for context and may not reflect all physical school sites in 2017–18.

second half of this chapter, we examine the way in which fierce competition for students, teachers, and legitimacy complicated the effort to turn new designs into better practice. The analysis takes us directly into the intersection of politics, practice, and systems as we illustrate the way in which the political environment influenced the dynamics of implementation and, in doing so, the futures of the ASD and iZone.

The ASD's Turn Toward Robust Instructional Systems

Across the ASD, charter operators recognized the need to make fundamental changes to the design of their instructional systems. The experience and expertise that had led to impressive results elsewhere had not translated into success in the ASD. This was true in the aggregate, where assessment results revealed little if any across-the-board improvement, and it was true for the individual operators in our study, all of whom recognized the need to revamp their systems.

Despite Green Dot's impressive track record in other parts of the country, the 2016 state assessment results dispelled any remaining doubts about the need for change. As one leader put it: "We knew there was a need to do something, but [the release of the state assessment scores] was the moment of 'we can't wait.'" Chrystie Edwards, a Green Dot instructional leader, explained how the reliance on individual teachers led to troubling inconsistencies: "We realized through student data that we really weren't meeting the demands of rigor . . . We definitely had inconsistent results across schools and within schools. It really just depended on an individual teacher's experience, their understanding of the standards, and how to implement it."

They were not alone. Martin Luther King Jr. College Preparatory High School (MLK) leaders, despite their bravado, could not deny the sobering reality of weak outcomes. The organization's head of curriculum and instruction didn't mince words: "With the data that we've received for the first two years of the new test, we realized that this is the time to do something different. We have to change the way in which we present our information to our students. No more 'who's the author of this story?' No longer pulling out your calculator to calculate a particular mathematical problem. It's about the *why*. Why is this answer correct? We have to figure that out."

The problem was not just disappointing test scores but also an unsatisfactory level of classroom instruction. Katie Kling's exasperation with the quality of teaching in Aspire captured the sentiments expressed by several ASD operators: "My hair is definitely on fire about instruction right now because it's just not good enough for our kids." Kling's observation was echoed by one of Aspire's instructional coaches, who noted that teachers rarely "ask conceptual questions [or] provide scaffolds and models that help students understand content conceptually." A Green Dot leader expressed a similar sentiment: "What we would see when we went into classrooms was teaching some general topic but not actually what kids need to know." The director of teacher development at MLK arrived at a similar conclusion: "The autonomy in the classroom left teachers to utilize what they felt were best practices, but there was a gap in rigor."

Each charter operator's approach to redesigning its network was informed by its individual starting point, philosophy, and available resources. Those that ran high schools faced a different set of challenges from operators that managed elementary schools. Operators new to Memphis needed to adjust to their students' staggering level of poverty, whereas for local organizations, this was hardly a surprise. On the other hand, national organizations like Aspire and Green Dot could leverage the experience of their networks, whereas MLK had to rely on local organizations and community partnerships to support their educational missions. The details of each case were unique.

Stepping back, however, one sees a common effort to shift leadership and classroom teaching from individual pursuits to a collective endeavor. Charter operators did not address their challenges by searching for superhero teachers, gaming assessments, or diluting the curriculum but by integrating teachers and leaders into a shared technical enterprise that harnessed their collective capacities. What stands out in the cases that follow is how each operator transformed its system by linking curriculum, leadership practices, collegial interactions, and professional learning to a clearly specified vision of instruction. The challenges of student need, rigor, and accountability remained just as before, but the strategy for managing them was transformed. In each case, the process began with the adoption of a new curriculum.

Aspire, Green Dot, and MLK all transformed their approach to curriculum. Rather than providing a variety of curricular resources that teachers could choose from, assemble into lessons, or combine with other materials, these charter operators adopted a complete curriculum in English language arts (ELA) and math that included detailed lesson plans that teachers were expected to use. Aspire's instructional leaders saw an urgent need to move from what was a loose array of instructional materials to a comprehensive, well-specified curriculum. Katie Kling explained, "Teachers had a lot of choice in materials that they could pull from, so they weren't lacking in materials. But what we saw is that we were asking people to do too much. So we decided to go with a curriculum that shifts teachers away from a lot of choices and time spent gathering materials." Green Dot leaders, much like those of Aspire, recognized that offering a wide array of instructional resources, without more structured guidance, placed an unrealistic and often overwhelming burden on teachers to design high-quality lessons each day. As one leader explained: "With the suggested curriculum we had before, you not only had to figure out 'what do I teach?,' but also 'how do I design my lesson, how do I start, what type of practice questions am I giving my students, what type of assessment am I giving my students?' There were too many variables that teachers had to determine on their own."

MLK leaders initially attempted to improve instruction by establishing formal structures to support regular collaboration without integrating common curricular materials. They hoped that by providing teachers more time to work together and share ideas, the overall level of practice would improve. Yet absent a clear set of pedagogical principles and shared curriculum, collaboration revolved more around "storytelling" than collective work on problems of practice. Laura Groth, whose research included firsthand observations of these sessions, noted that "without shared resources or facilitated problem solving, these collaborative opportunities tended to consist more of story-sharing than productive professional discourse."[4] Moreover, teachers were still spending a lot of time simply creating daily lessons.

Absent observable changes in classroom practice, MLK leaders eventually concluded that their effort to build capacity required a shared set of classroom tools and a common pedagogical approach. MLK's instructional coach explained: "We're going to utilize a vetted curriculum that's used across the nation and that's closely aligned to all of the assessment platforms to ensure that it's all merged together."

Changes went beyond curriculum. Across the ASD, charter operators redesigned their instructional systems to provide teachers and leaders with robust guidance that transformed the challenges of classroom practice into a shared enterprise. At Aspire, leaders created new collegial structures in which teachers collaboratively dissected the curriculum before teaching it. They supplied teachers with lesson plans and complementary materials, along with opportunities to practice lesson delivery before colleagues who provided feedback. The new materials addressed questions such as, How are you going to extend learning for advanced learners? How do you plan to scaffold the text-dependent questions (TDQs)? What are your steps to meet the needs of your struggling learners? The provision of detailed lessons enabled teachers and leaders to redirect resources at the individual and organizational levels to engage in a deeper level of planning and preparation. "It was shifting our brains from lesson planning to lesson internalization and delivery," explained Allison Leslie, Aspire's regional director.

Similar changes were underway at Green Dot. These included planning documents that further elaborated instructional goals and pedagogical principles, and a suggested plan for each lesson. A common set of weekly assessments provided teachers with regular feedback on student learning while enabling network leaders to identify areas where teachers needed additional support. Teachers were still expected to adapt lessons to meet variable student needs, but they were now equipped with a far more elaborate and coordinated set of resources that was common across the network. A Green Dot instructional coach explained, "Our desire was to have some uniformity across the region so that we can have more consistent data, and so that we can support teachers in a more strategic manner. Having an external curriculum eliminates the question of what to teach, and it puts the focus on how to teach."

At MLK, the introduction of the curriculum and accompanying lesson plans enabled leaders to construct a system in which an array of supports and resources was tied to shared curriculum, lesson plans, assessments, and an overarching instructional vision. Bobby White and his team initially adopted a hands-off approach to instructional leadership, but they eventually recognized that formidable challenges required a robust instructional system grounded in a shared vision of teaching and learning and designed to build the professional capacity to enact it. White explained the transformation in thinking: "Having a real system is the one thing that I did not see as important as I do now. I was a teacher that didn't want the principal in my classroom, so I brought that spirit to being an administrator. [Now I realize] we have to be in the weeds around what we are doing every day to make teachers better. We have to figure out what works and put our stamp on it. That is so different from the old way."

Across the ASD, charter operators built new systems encompassing curriculum, leadership, coaching, professional development, lesson planning, collegial collaboration, and more. While the specifics varied, these strategies were guided by a shared logic rooted in common experiences, shared tools, and a unified vision of teaching and learning. The strategy shifted from hiring exceptional individuals to developing robust instructional systems that supported teachers in rethinking and transforming their practice.

As we discuss in the second half of this chapter, the new strategies and instructional designs that ASD operators devised did not always produce the hoped-for results. In part, this is because even the most robust systems do not change the fact that instructional improvement is a slow, arduous process. It is also because charter operators could do little to alter the contentious political environment, the fierce competition for teachers and students, staff turnover, and the intergenerational poverty that left students years behind grade level. These represented formidable obstacles that challenge even the most thoughtfully constructed designs. But if educational improvement rests on the ability of system leaders to demonstrate humility, learn from past mistakes, and reconsider deeply held beliefs, then the individuals who ran Green Dot, Aspire, MLK, and other ASD schools held up their end. That results did not always meet expectations does not detract from the extraordinary effort these leaders made to revamp their systems in the face of formidable obstacles.

From Autonomy and Isolation Toward Coherence and Collaboration: The iZone Reorganizes

A few blocks away, the iZone's new leadership was undertaking an equally profound redesign of its system. The iZone's initial success had been enabled by a combination of small scale, recruitment of highly accomplished principals and teachers, teaching to the test, and the fact that the state had not yet transitioned to rigorous standards and assessments. Moreover, much like their ASD counterparts, iZone leaders' internal assessment was that instruction was often at a low level and that few teachers had the professional knowledge or skill that the new standards demanded. iZone leaders knew that in too many cases, improved test scores did not reflect a high level of teaching and learning. Dr. Griffin summed up the iZone's predicament: "I have to keep reminding people not to rest on their laurels, because we're not where we're supposed to be. Growth is great, and we're doing better than ASD, but all that means is that you're on the top of the bottom . . . We are nowhere near where we need to be, and the new [state] test is going to be a rude awakening."

Complicating matters further, iZone leadership had yet to begin the most challenging aspects of building a coherent and high-capacity system. These included redesigning central office supports, building consensus around a common pedagogical approach, and confronting deeply entrenched but ineffective practices among leaders and teachers. A singular focus on raising test scores had masked these issues, but the rapid expansion of the iZone and the introduction of a more rigorous state assessment now forced iZone leaders to address them directly.

Under the leadership of Dr. Antonio Burt (who replaced Dr. Griffin in 2017), the iZone charted a new course. Rather than relying on the talents of individual educators, Burt and his colleagues assembled a multifaceted, integrated design in which the central office played a prominent role in guiding schools. This design included a codified theory of teaching and learning, a core curriculum and set of classroom tools (e.g., lesson plans, assessments), and an organizational blueprint for school leaders to monitor and support instruction. An elaborate system of coaching and professional learning supported capacity building and coordination across schools. The theory of teaching and learning rested on three core principles: (1) a commitment to grade-level instruction for all students; (2) a focus on the conceptual underpinnings of curricular content, such as math and English; and (3) providing students with structured opportunities to grapple with complex tasks. Dr. Alethea Henry, the director of the iZone's Instructional Support Team, described the vision:

> Students should be taking ownership of the work and be asking questions—not just surface-level questions, but questions that build their understanding of the concepts being taught. You should see the teacher acting as a facilitator and crafting lessons that put the responsibility of learning on the student. The teacher should not just be delivering information but constructing lessons so that students are the ones doing the discovery.

Central to the vision was that instruction would not be exclusively test driven. The iZone's lead math educator was unrelenting on this point: "When we speak about mathematical proficiency, we're not talking about scores on a test; we're talking about students who actually have conceptual understanding, who have procedural skills, who have adaptive reasoning, who have a productive disposition. Our job is to teach kids how to think, and if you can create kids with mathematical minds, they can think through any situation or test question, whether they've seen it before or not." Similar to their ASD counterparts, iZone leaders introduced a common curriculum for both math and ELA that embodied their approach to teaching and learning and that served as the cornerstone for the reorganization of schools, leadership, and professional development.

An expanded iZone central office now consisted of an enhanced and newly empowered Instructional Support Team responsible for content-specific instructional coaching and a Leadership Development Team charged with supervising and coaching school principals. The combination of a common curriculum and specified instructional vision enabled iZone coaches to link broad principles of instruction to specific problems of practice that teachers were struggling with in their classrooms. Previously, when schools selected their own materials and pursued their own ideas about teaching, coaches spent the majority of their time helping teachers simply get a lesson off the ground. Empowered by the shared curriculum, coaches began to host monthly learning collaboratives with teachers across schools to study upcoming modules and anticipate student misconceptions. Professional discourse shifted from general and abstract to granular and rooted in practice. One member of the iZone's leadership team explained the importance of common materials: "There needed to be some consistency in all the schools. Coaches need to be able to coach around the same curriculum . . . [and] the same lesson plan template and the same instructional expectations. If not, we can never really make a difference because we're flipping and flopping from school to school."

The common curriculum and instructional model provided a foundation for professional learning and instructionally focused leadership. Similar to the approach adopted by ASD providers, school leaders instituted rehearsal routines that called on teachers to practice unfamiliar lessons in front of colleagues. Newly formed instructional leadership teams used a common rubric for observing instruction, providing feedback to teachers, and identifying school-wide problems of practice that required sustained focus. Principal Latasha Harris, whom we introduced in chapter 3, used the iZone's classroom observation rubric to identify her teachers' struggle to pose the type of cognitively demanding questions that cultivate a conceptual understanding of mathematics. Recognizing this as a school-wide issue, she made questioning the focal point of a school-wide professional learning initiative.

The new iZone was not designed to generate the sensational but short-term gains of the early iZone. Rather, it was a long-term effort to make fundamental changes in schools' organization, leadership, professional culture, collegial structures, and professional capacity. It was decidedly not a quick fix and not immune to the challenges of implementation, but as an instructional system, it was designed to foster long-term, meaningful changes in students' educational experience.

In the historical context of Memphis, the effort of iZone leaders to create a coherent, coordinated, instructionally ambitious education system harkens back to the heroic efforts of Edward Shaw, Willie Herenton, Maxine Smith, and the other educators who came before them. Although the iZone could not put an end to the poverty that afflicted so many of its students, and although the iZone leaders had no way to break the nearly total racial segregation of these schools, they attempted to establish a level of intellectual and pedagogical rigor that few urban districts have accomplished. Their efforts can be seen as a blueprint for future attempts to redesign systems that aspire to intellectually ambitious teaching and learning in communities where decades of economic and social marginalization have left students far behind. Our point is not that the iZone was a perfectly constructed system (it wasn't), or that it catapulted outcomes to the top tier of performance (it didn't), but that its leaders took on the difficult but important work of building an instructional system that rests on principles of coherence, rigor, shared experience, and incremental improvement.

What the newly designed systems could not change, however, was the profound shifts in practice and mindset they demanded of teachers, as well as the risks teachers and leaders incurred in pursuing such changes in a high-stakes environment. These shifts represented an about-face for a region that had spent over a century teaching in a direct-instruction style, limiting content to basic skills, watering down lessons for those deemed incapable of rigorous work, defining professionalism as the right to teach according to personal style, and investing little in fostering expertise. One cannot help but recall the 1919 Bureau of Education report, mentioned in chapter 1, that castigated Memphis education as "too dependent upon rote memory." Even more risky was the notion that in a region where assessment results carried great weight, success amounted to more than test scores.

For these and other reasons, it was far from certain that the revamped ASD and iZone systems would lead to meaningful and consistent changes in teaching and learning, and it was virtually guaranteed that their implementation would be fraught with tension and dissent. In the second half of this chapter, we examine the clash that ensued as these new systems charged headfirst into a highly politicized and contentious environment, where legitimacy and survival depended on short-term gains, competition often prevailed over collaboration, and twenty-one independent systems vied for students and teachers.

Slow Gains in a Fast-Paced Fight: The Long Road to Instructional Change

Taken at face value, the changes instituted by ASD and iZone leaders seemed like a harbinger of improvements in teaching and learning, animated by gains on the state assessment. But the complexity of the improvement process means that little can be taken at face value. The reality is that the relationship between design, implementation, and outcomes is far more complicated than what is implied by easy predictions of change. Well-designed instructional systems establish the potential for improvements in teaching and learning, and are thus critical, but realizing that potential depends on several other factors that enable productive use of those systems.

In the remainder of this chapter, we illustrate how Memphis's political environment shaped and complicated the way the newly revised systems were interpreted and put into practice. The discussion makes three central points. First, the mutual support these systems were intended to foster was often undermined by an environment that prioritized competition over collegiality. The second is that political confrontation comes at an educational cost. The acrimony that the ASD engendered forced charter operators to devote scarce resources to shoring up public credibility; recruiting families, teachers, and principals; and bolstering their legitimacy. The third point is that the all-consuming, frenzied press to improve standardized measures of achievement delegitimized the incremental work of educationally meaningful and sustainable change. Cutting across these three points is a fourth one: The politics of competition and division exacted a steep price from the city of Memphis. It forced a short-term perspective on a problem that required a long-term solution, divided a community that desperately needed to work together, and limited the extent to which the newly designed iZone and ASD could fulfill their potential.

Readers will note that our discussion of implementation avoids terms such as *working*, *failing*, *effective*, and *ineffective* because these oversimplify the incremental nature of pedagogical change and the tumultuous political environment in which it unfolded. Instead, our aim is to illuminate the interaction between ambitious instructional systems, the teachers and leaders charged with turning ideas into practice, and the social and political contexts in which this work occurred. What follows is an account of progress and setbacks: of teachers who embraced new ideas and those who resisted them; of collegiality undermined by competition; of thoughtfully designed systems that produced only modest results; and of accountability measures that spurred change even as they undermined improvement. While this collection of paradoxes and contradictions may frustrate those searching for clear-cut paths to reform, our purpose is to underscore that well-conceived designs, although important, are never sufficient; real changes to teaching and learning emerge from the complex interplay of politics, practice, and system design.

In the years that followed the system design changes noted in the first half of this chapter, outcomes for both the ASD and iZone varied, and leaders of both organizations reported inconsistent levels of practice. In the ASD, charter operators were only partially successful in turning their revised instructional systems into better outcomes. The leaders of Aspire, Green Dot, and MLK reported progress, but results on the state assessment told a story of modest improvement, at best, and certainly nothing approaching the dramatic gains that Barbic had predicted years earlier. In the fourth, fifth, and sixth years, outside evaluators reported that the ASD had a negative impact on achievement outcomes, although the results were not statistically significant. The outcomes for iZone schools reflected modest and inconsistent improvement that was far from the extraordinary gains that had dominated headlines in the early years. A negative dip in year four of the iZone was followed by positive impacts in years five and six, although neither of these latter two was statistically significant.[5] The iZone's run of head-turning results had come to an end.

iZone and ASD leaders described a familiar combination of progress and struggle as teachers attempted to make sense of new materials and ambitious pedagogies that challenged their tried-and-true ways of working. Many teachers and leaders earnestly grappled with new ideas and practices, often taking meaningful steps forward, and we highlight some of these cases here. But overall, the work of transforming the way hundreds of teachers understood and performed the work of teaching proved to be a slow and arduous process. An Aspire leader's candid reflection about the complexities of integrating new materials and practices into Aspire's network of schools reveals the sobering reality of the work:

> When you talk about implementing a curriculum, it takes some time. You spend a year understanding the materials that are before you. Then you find out that there are some spots where the curriculum needs to be augmented, adapted in some way, and has holes in some way. And so those things have to be worked out over time. There is not an immediate jolt to the system like we would've thought. So, yes, progress, but slow and not meteoric, with challenges along the way. We underestimated the challenge.

This proved no less true in the iZone. Consider the words of Riverview Principal Latasha Harris, whose commitment to the iZone's core ideas and practices was unmatched by any of the iZone principals we encountered: "I think that eventually we will see an improvement. We just have to be consistent with it. It is going to take some time."

Chrystie Edwards of Green Dot noted that while a robust curriculum and system of guidance helped, they, too, were no magic bullet: "I attribute a lot to the high-quality instructional materials we added. But knowing what I know now, you can't just take curricular materials and say, 'this is the panacea, this is the end-all and be-all.' It must be accompanied with systems and multiple stakeholders working in concert." Thelma Perry, who directed the iZone's effort to revamp mathematics instruction, also emphasized the long-term learning trajectory that confronted teachers in learning to cultivate students' understanding of underlying concepts: "Teachers want to rely on the traditional, procedural way of teaching. We're helping them to see the why, and the damage that is caused when they're only teaching the shortcuts and the tricks. I think that we're headed in the right direction, but it's going to take time."

Perhaps less ambitious changes might have been implemented more quickly, but the instructional systems adopted by iZone schools and ASD operators challenged conventional assumptions about what it means to know content, how students learn, and what defines good instruction. These ambitions clashed with deeply entrenched ideas about how to teach in an urban context with students who are often multiple years below grade level. Many principals and teachers were incredulous that their students could grapple with complex tasks and grasp abstract concepts—and most of all, that this approach would lead to an increase in assessment results. None other than Rodney Rowan, who had played an instrumental role in helping the iZone best the ASD, expressed skepticism toward the idea that students far below grade level could productively grapple with big mathematical ideas: "Conceptual thinking for a child who does not have a grasp around the procedures is not happening. For a child who has a strong foundation, they're going to be able to comprehend conceptually, they're going to be able to analyze, they're going to be able to evaluate because they have those necessary tools. But this is an urban school district; we don't have many children who come to you on grade level."

Katie Kling reported a similar response among some Aspire teachers, lamenting the tendency to drop the level of intellectual rigor for students they deemed academically behind. "I don't want to hear about how our kids don't read at grade level," she said. "Our job is to keep the bar high." Echoing the attitudes that confounded Kling, some iZone educators saw little sense in asking their students to grapple with complex content, despite instructional leaders' assurances that productive struggle could be a powerful driver of learning. Said one principal: "It's never going to be productive for a child who does not have the chops to bite into it." An iZone high school principal chafed at the notion that the district's ambitious curriculum would meet the needs of his school's student body: "What sense is there in following the curriculum when [the student] lacks the skills to do the work?"

At the classroom level, teachers' doubts about teaching grade-level content to already-struggling students often led them to reduce the curriculum's complexity. In one case, an iZone high school teacher explained the decision to remove the negative numbers from a math problem, stating that "there was a big struggle in a problem where students have to create their own solutions, so I took out the negative numbers." Other teachers would skip over math lessons intended to help students grapple with underlying concepts, preferring to focus on routine problem-solving. As one teacher put it: "I would love for them to have a conceptual understanding, but overall, I go for procedural with the lower children before I go for conceptual."

iZone instructional coaches worked tirelessly to show teachers that students who lacked some foundational knowledge could still grapple with complex tasks and that reducing the level of rigor was ultimately self-defeating. And in several instances, these efforts led to inspiring changes. Jaron Carson, whom we profiled in chapter 3, recounted his realization that in reducing the complexity of the curriculum, he had undermined his own commitment to equity: "Hell, I've been killing my kids. I'm thinking I'm helping them by dropping down a level or taking components out, but actually I'm harming them. The child is going to live up to the expectations that you put in place for them." Other teachers came to understand that even students who had struggled in previous years and had gaps in their knowledge could still learn important conceptual ideas. One ninth-grade algebra teacher talked about the evolution of his own practice: "Even though the kids do not know their basic multiplication facts, they can pretty much work that problem out in a place value chart, and it helps them to understand the why and the how of things. When I was in school, we learned the regular standard algorithm; the teacher never taught me 'why are we doing this?'"

For seasoned observers of education reform, this pattern of incremental progress marked by a combination of success and setback is undoubtedly familiar. It fits within a larger educational story unfolding across the country, as the contemporary focus on rigor and equity has challenged the conventional organization of districts and schools, along with traditional classroom practices. That ambitious ideas for teaching and learning were adopted unevenly and met with resistance is unsurprising, if not inevitable. But if one part of this story is about the inherent challenges of instructional change, another part is about how those processes are shaped by the political and social environment. It is here that Memphis has a particular set of lessons to offer.

The Promise of Collaboration, the Reality of Competition: "There Was Just a Lack of Trust"

In theory, shared problems create an opportunity for the development of shared solutions. Indeed, the application of common solutions to common problems is at the core of all professional work, whether that's landing a commercial airliner, replacing a carburetor, or filing income taxes. Professions are, above all, systems of shared expertise. The potential for iZone and ASD practitioners to learn from one another while developing solutions to shared educational problems was substantial. Consider the ASD. All the charter operators were struggling to meet the academic and social needs of their student body, were under enormous pressure to produce results, and were coping with similar problems of system design. Nobody understood the potential for collaboration among operators better than Chris Barbic. As early as 2013, he stated: "The fact is that right now people are hopping on planes to visit each other's schools. But what if instead of hopping on a plane, you just drive down the street?"

The vision of operator collaboration was more than just talk. ASD officials established collaborative structures that brought operators together to discuss problems of practice, visit each other's schools, observe instruction, and provide feedback. These collegial structures seemed like promising opportunities for charter operators to discuss shared challenges, learn from one another, and turn improvement into a collective endeavor. For a profession known for leaving its practitioners to solve problems on their own, this was a remarkable opportunity.

But collegial structures are of little value in an environment where the incentives encourage protecting innovations more than sharing them.[6] Although charter operators met with each other, visited schools, and knew each other well, they were often reluctant to engage in the type of open conversation that fuels collaborative learning. A lack of trust hid just below the surface. Speaking about the school walkthroughs, one operator said, "It was like a verdict . . . It didn't feel formative," whereas another said that schools treated the visits more as a "dog and pony show" than as an opportunity to solicit productive feedback. Green Dot's Edwards summed it up as follows: "The ASD brought us together, but there was a lack of trust, and always an air of competition. And so even when we said, 'Hey, let's have this collaboration day. What are you all doing?' It just never really reached its potential."

The region's competitive environment also had a chilling effect on collaboration within the iZone, where principals were under extraordinary pressure to move their schools out of the bottom 10 percent in the state. Although some iZone principals described sharing strategies and collaborative work across schools, others described an atmosphere of interschool competition. If the ASD was going to take over a school, principals wanted to make sure that it wasn't theirs. As Thelma Perry explained, this left some iZone principals reluctant to collaborate with their colleagues: "The way the state ranks schools, as long as I'm above you, that pushes me up. So when I talk with the principals, they're like, 'I'm not sharing.' I say, 'But this is for the kids.' But there's a reality of, 'it's impacting my job. I'm in this race to get to the top,' and so you develop this competitive mentality."

The political environment also discouraged collaboration and joint problem-solving among the two most important educational leaders in Memphis: Shelby County Superintendent Dorsey Hopson and ASD Superintendent Chris Barbic (and then later Malika Anderson). Although leaders of both systems privately acknowledged their mutual respect and ability to work together behind closed doors, Hopson and other district officials had no choice but to maintain a degree of distance from the deeply unpopular ASD. Hopson put it this way: "I have to walk a tightrope, because quite frankly I have to make determinations about what kinds of things I want to put my credibility on the line for." Hopson's deputy, Bradley Leon, reiterated the point more bluntly: "What the ASD wanted was to go to community meetings and say the Shelby County School District is in favor of us taking this school . . . You actually want Dorsey Hopson from Memphis, who went to White Haven High School, to stand up and put his arm around you? That's ridiculous."

The lack of collaboration is not an indictment of ASD or iZone leaders, nor of the individuals who hesitated to open their schools to outside observers. Rather, it reflects an environment organized around the idea that competition drives improvement. Market-based systems may, in some cases, spur improvement, and there is evidence that competition contributed to a needed sense of urgency in Memphis. But a competitive environment does not encourage collaboration, even among organizations with much to gain from mutual support, and it does not encourage the kind of broad-based effort that leads to civic capacity and, in turn, collective action. That the many extraordinary educators working across the iZone and ASD were unable to work together, share experiences, and learn from one another was a wasted opportunity that the city could ill afford.

Recruitment at All Costs: The Battle for Students and Teachers

In a city already experiencing declining enrollment, the competition for students was a high-stakes effort for both Shelby County and the ASD. By the spring of 2015, Shelby County Schools had lost twenty-two schools to the ASD, resulting in a funding loss of over $23 million.[7] For ASD charter operators, whose financial viability was tied to growth projections, the consequences were even more dire. From 2016 to 2017, twenty-one of the thirty-two ASD schools experienced a decline in enrollment, while overall enrollment across the ASD declined from 11,763 to 11,060. MLK experienced a near 10 percent decline, Aspire had a drop of about 4 percent, and Green Dot lost over 10 percent of its student body. And while a handful of ASD schools experienced growth, nearly 75 percent were underenrolled.[8] Finding ways to boost student recruitment became an existential issue, requiring an outlay of time, people, and money. Green Dot's Edwards noted that despite the pressing demands of improving teaching and learning, student recruitment was often the foremost concern: "Butts in seats. That's what it came down to, unfortunately. A lot of conversation was devoted to what does it look like recruiting students? How do we ensure our enrollment? How do we ensure that we're not having to do layoffs and that we have a sustainable student population to support our staff?"

Across the ASD, charter operators had little choice but to allocate scarce resources to bolster student recruitment. The leader of one charter operator organization reported calling 1,800 families, knocking on hundreds of doors, attending dozens of public events, and walking families through the registration process. Allison Leslie recalled Aspire's all-encompassing effort to recruit new students: "We were visiting daycares and preschools, attending every fair that exists, advertising, and doing home visits." Another ASD charter operator reported that during the summer months, all organizational resources were allocated to recruitment: "We threw everything out in the summertime and just worked on recruitment. We went door to door. We had two town-hall meetings with pizza dinners. We did Saturday morning bounce houses and snow cones and music and just met as many people as we possibly could."

For charter school organizations, in general, the imperative of attracting and retaining families is recognized as the cost of doing business within a sector that values competition. But for ASD operators, taking on these challenges came at a particularly steep price. The time devoted to recruitment and retention was time not spent on supporting teachers, adapting materials and routines, and finding ways to advance student learning. Moreover, ASD operators invested considerable financial resources in attendance specialists, recruitment officers, and community liaisons—all toward the goal of bringing in more students.[9] For the district, the shrinking student population, the loss of schools to the ASD, the urgency of preventing additional takeovers, and the budget implications were equally taxing. The overall situation clearly required a comprehensive regional plan, but the life-and-death struggle for students between the ASD and iZone precluded that level of coordination.

In addition to the competition for students, the fractured teacher labor market, combined with the exhausting nature of the work, severely undermined the ASD's stability. A devastating rate of teacher turnover meant that the newly designed systems struggled to gain traction. As one charter operator put it: "We're losing great teachers because it's not a sustainable work environment. Our turnover number this year is going to be around 40 percent." The tight teacher labor market and competitive environment took a toll on the iZone as well. A senior district official described the region's fierce competition over teachers: "We just have so much competition with other teacher employers. Because you've got your [non-ASD] charter schools, you've got your ASD charters, you've got all of your municipal schools. When I started, there were two games in town—if you weren't in Legacy Shelby, you were in Legacy Memphis, and there really wasn't a lot of pressure on the district."

Dr. Burt acknowledged the challenges this posed to his effort to transform the iZone: "One of the major issues we've had to deal with at the district is teacher shortage, and we're already dealing with the most fragile schools." The effect of the teacher shortage rippled across the iZone. Not only were there not enough experienced teachers, but now the district needed to assign instructional coaches to classrooms rather than having them support other teachers. The iZone system that Dr. Burt and his colleagues designed was remarkably integrated and cohesive, but those very same qualities also made it fragile and vulnerable to disruption.

Memphis is not the only region where teacher recruitment and retention pose a serious challenge. Nationwide, urban districts have historically struggled to recruit and retain effective teachers.[10] However, neither demographic changes nor national trends fully explain the competition for students and teachers that diverted valuable resources and undermined improvement efforts in Memphis. Rather, these dynamics must be understood within the context of policies, both old and new, that created a fractured educational landscape in which one large district, six suburban districts, and fourteen ASD charter operators competed in a zero-sum battle for students and teachers.

In addition to the fierce competition for teachers and students, a churn of relatively inexperienced school leaders challenged the ability of schools to enact newly designed systems. In the ASD, the proportion of new principals peaked at a remarkable 70 percent in years five and six of its existence. So great was principal turnover that by year six, the average ASD principal had a meager 1.8 years of leadership experience.[11] The combination of pressure to increase results, public scrutiny, thinly staffed organizations, and the enormous educational challenges simply wore principals down. The director of one operator organization put it this way: "The work is very, very demanding. I just don't really see a point in which we won't always be at risk of losing a school leader. I just don't know that we have gotten to a place where you can comfortably do this work for five or six years without it really taking a toll on you. It's just exhausting."

Allison Leslie offered a similar analysis: "It comes down to how can you do this job. It's pretty insane. Principals are at a place where they need to just step back for their own physical, mental and emotional health and engage in a work that's a little less grinding. They're burning out at a rate that's too fast." The combination of turnover, burnout, and competition led to a situation in which incoming ASD principals often lacked even a minimum level of experience and expertise. The leader of one charter organization admitted that four of the principals in their network lacked the qualifications to tackle a job of extraordinary difficulty. "None of them had ever been a principal anywhere before, let alone a principal in a turnaround network. I don't know how prepared they are to do this work."

The ASD has no monopoly on the problem of principal turnover. Nationally, the turnover rate for principals in urban, high-need schools hovers around 27 percent annually, and as noted, the iZone also endured its share of principal turnover.[12] Yet even when placed in a national context or when compared with other priority schools in Memphis, the rate of turnover among ASD principals was staggering. It is little wonder that so few teachers remained in schools with constantly changing leadership or that newly designed instructional systems failed to produce desired results.

Proving Versus Improving: The Dilemma of High-Stakes Accountability

There is no denying that the competitive environment pressed Shelby County Schools to make long-overdue changes that would have otherwise proved politically unpalatable. This view was voiced not just by ASD advocates but also by numerous officials inside the district. But the high-stakes environment was not without unintended consequences.

One was that it turned assessment outcomes into a fight for survival that undermined commitment to loftier instructional principles. For iZone principals and teachers, the threat of ASD takeover and the overall battle for legitimacy placed a premium on quick test score gains. As much as iZone leaders implored principals and teachers to eschew pedagogically unsound practices that artificially drove up scores, many were reluctant to take the risk. In math, for example, the iZone's instructional leaders argued tirelessly that once students understood the conceptual underpinnings, they would be able to adapt to a variety of test questions. But for principals and teachers worried about reputations, jobs, and the fate of their school, this was a risky proposition. Jaron Carson expressed his doubts: "The district thinks that somehow, by osmosis, these kids are going to learn this Eureka Math and then apply it to that test question. For my kids, I know it doesn't work that way. Understanding the content is one thing; applying that within a timed test is another. Somehow, the district doesn't think that's important."

Rodney Rowan made it clear that he had no intention of experimenting with practices that risked even a temporary decline in test scores. "If you don't have children pass the test, then people don't have jobs. Schools close. Or they're taken over by charter networks," he said, referring to the ASD. The anxiety about test scores manifested itself in myriad ways. Some principals tossed out the iZone's classroom observation rubric in favor of tools they saw as explicitly aligned with the state assessment, while another principal made the extraordinary decision to reteach the entire curriculum in the months leading up to the state assessment. Many teachers relied on an alternative and more traditional curriculum that they thought better prepared students for the assessment. So great was the pressure to realize assessment gains that improved outcomes often became synonymous with effective practice. No one exhibited this perspective more clearly than Principal Rowan: "At the beginning of the year, I had a conversation with the teachers where I said, 'This child scored 55 percent on a test. This child scored 70 percent on a test. If our end game is 80 percent, do you have 15 percent in you? Can you add 15 percent? Is your value added 15 percent to this child this year?'" Teachers in the school heard the message loud and clear. As one put it, "I like the conceptual [part of the lesson], but sometimes you have to forfeit the conceptual so that we can get to how you're going to be tested on it."

A similar dynamic unfolded in the ASD, where test results carried even greater consequences. Like their iZone counterparts, charter operators attempted to walk a tightrope, acknowledging the political importance of strong test performance without abandoning their core pedagogical principles. Aspire's Allison Leslie explained the dilemma: "Kids take tests in school, and they need to perform well. But we can't stop focusing on mastery of standards, and teaching and learning, and we can't make our focus the test. That's not our intention." Yet with the future of their schools, jobs, and the overall legitimacy of the ASD on the line, it was impossible to prevent concern over test results from creeping into their instructional systems. Aspire's Katie Kling conceded that as much as she tried to keep the focus on quality practice, the pull of explicit test-prep practices was impossible to overcome: "It forces everyone to think about end-of-year assessment, as opposed to just thinking about the kind of kids we have in our building, the kind of learners and thinkers we are building, and whether we are growing. That's what I'd really like to think about, and instead I still find myself saying, 'But what about that question on TNReady?'"

Other ASD operators similarly reported the way in which anxiety over assessment results influenced their practices and allocation of instructional resources. At MLK, teachers were told to design the opening of their lessons to mimic the format of the state assessment. Another charter operator, whose approach was rooted in problem-based learning, spent the months leading up to the assessment explicitly focusing on discrete skills they thought would improve scores, even though such an approach was antithetical to the charter operator's instructional philosophy. At Green Dot, test anxiety grew to the point where leaders relied on previous state tests to construct curriculum materials in the hope that this would boost assessment results. "This is the last opportunity that we have to get in front of teachers before the actual exams," said one leader.

Some readers might argue that by forcing schools to align curriculum with intellectually rigorous standards, the state's policy was having the intended effect. After all, what's wrong with teaching to the test if that test is based on high-status knowledge and skill? Indeed, were it not for the state's accountability regime, there is little reason to believe that concern over the quality and future of public education in Memphis would have been at the center of public discourse. Moreover, decades of experience have shown that in the absence of standards and accountability, schools frequently reduce the intellectual rigor for low-income and minority students, whereas schools serving more affluent communities expose students to creative and challenging content.[13] There is little sense in returning to that era.

What we see in the previously described examples, however, is that test performance displaced student learning as the goal, and a high-stakes environment undermined attention to core pedagogical principles and long-term capacity building. Practices that reflected commitment to conceptual understanding and opportunity to struggle were often cast aside for ones directly tied to the state's assessment. Forced to choose between investing in meaningful but long-term shifts in instruction and practices that drive short-term gains in tested outcomes, many teachers and leaders (although not all) opted for the latter. Daniel Koretz, among the country's leading psychometricians, who has written extensively on the effects of high-stakes testing, put it this way: "We have to start by saying, what do we really want to see when we walk into a classroom? I want to see kids who show a high level of cognitive engagement and who are not turned off. If you had an inspection system, you could tell the inspectors that we want to see teaching that engages kids. And if the teacher is doing that, and the test score increases are not as high as the teacher next door who's drilling them on test prep materials, the one who should get credit is the first one."

Many instructional leaders whom we encountered in the ASD and iZone would wholeheartedly agree with Koretz's statement, but with jobs and reputations on the line, not all were willing to take that risk.

Conclusion

It is easy to find fault with the teachers and principals who found ways to circumvent a curriculum and pedagogy meant to expose students to the type of intellectual rigor and classroom environment too often reserved for more privileged students. Some readers will interpret these attitudes as putting adult interests over the needs of students or as a lack of commitment to equitable educational practices. But there is little surprise about this pattern of implementation. In part, this reflects the fact that the iZone and ASD leaders sought to displace ideas and practices that have dominated schools since the emergence of mass education in the mid-nineteenth century. The fact that some teachers and leaders embraced the changes while others selectively adopted some new practices, or even rejected them altogether, is part and parcel of large-scale, ambitious instructional change, whether that be in Memphis or elsewhere.

Our point, then, is not that the second generation of iZone leaders failed to maintain the rapid gains of the first three years, or that ASD charter operators failed to live up to Barbic's lofty top-quartile goals. Those types of miraculous improvement stories were never in the cards. If there is a finger to be pointed, it is at the policies that fractured public education in Shelby County, that pitted two systems against each other, that exacerbated a tight teacher labor market, that turned competition for students and outcomes into a life-and-death battle, and that threw salt on the region's historic wounds. The competition and division that characterized the environment penetrated deep into the organizations of the ASD and iZone, shaped practice and the allocation of resources, and in doing so, undermined the educational aspirations of both systems.

The history of US education does offer some telling examples of system building that unfolded in more stable environments. Comprehensive School Reform (CSR), as we stated in chapter 1, was a concerted effort to replace piecemeal reforms with a comprehensive design aimed at improving instruction. Even while effects varied, CSRs showed how coherent systems could provide practitioners with a common vocabulary, a shared mission, and a collective approach to solving complex problems of practice. Similarly, Advanced Placement (AP), Montessori schools, and International Baccalaureate (IB)—large-scale systems that aim to elevate the rigor of teaching and learning in thousands of classrooms—are rooted in central organizations that develop and deploy professional development, curriculum materials, and other instructional supports. As instructional systems, they are far from perfect, but they share core characteristics with the systems that iZone leaders and ASD operators attempted to construct.[14]

Yet similarities in the design of these instructional systems are offset by differences in political context. What distinguishes CSR, AP, Montessori, and IB from the efforts of the ASD and iZone is that they are *niche reforms* that function as subsystems serving specialized clienteles that actively opt into them.[15] In doing so, they avoid the contentious political environments that both the iZone and ASD—place-based systems tied to a specific region and its history—were required to navigate. They illustrate the educational potential of coherent systems tied to a shared vision and designed to build the requisite professional capacity, but they have less to teach us about building such systems in less insulated and more turbulent environments. For that, we must turn to places like Memphis, whose accomplishments and setbacks offer many lessons in designing instructional systems in contested and historically divided spaces.

There is, then, a bittersweet flavor to Memphis's decade and a half of reform in which the ASD and iZone have been the central players. Across both systems, significant efforts were undertaken to put forward educationally ambitious visions, to embrace the grit and the grind that inheres in putting ideas into practice, and to adopt long-term perspectives while under enormous political pressure and intense public scrutiny. The fact that the leaders of the iZone and ASD learned how to construct coherent, integrated, capacity-building systems while simultaneously navigating the torrential waters of educational politics in a postindustrial, Southern city is a worthy entry into this chapter of Memphis's long history of public education.

Moreover, the fact that progress was halting and uneven does not mean that it was nonexistent. Out of public view, positive changes transpired in myriad classrooms across the ASD and iZone. We say this in part to recognize the heroic efforts of these educators, school leaders, and system designers. We also say it because their experiences illuminate critical lessons from the ASD and iZone. Those lessons inspired a gradual shift from instructional systems organized around individual teachers solving the most difficult educational problems on their own, to ones in which those same problems were tackled collectively by practitioners empowered by a common set of tools and a shared vision of teaching and learning. Systems that are informed by these principles are the sin qua non of educational improvement, and the lessons learned by the iZone and the ASD apply to all those who share in these ambitions for public education.

Yet even as we acknowledge the relentless effort of ASD operators and iZone leaders, the final analysis must recognize that policies fostering competition and division prevented these redesigned systems from reaching their full potential. Educational improvement is a technical challenge requiring a high level of expert knowledge and experience, but it is also a public—and therefore political—enterprise that demands policies capable of uniting multiple interest groups around a common goal. The politics and pedagogy of school improvement go hand in hand.

CHAPTER SIX

School Improvement as a Partnership Between the Profession and the Public

If there is one thing the previous chapters make clear, it is that politics and pedagogy can tug in contrary directions. But how might they work in mutually reinforcing ways?

It's a tenuous proposition, because in some ways the professional part of education fits uncomfortably with the political. As much scholarship attests, education demands as high a level of knowledge and skill as professions like dentistry, nursing, and psychiatry.[1] But even in an era of public attacks on science, the targeting of law firms and universities, and a decades-long decline in the power of the professions, it remains the case that the majority of other professions work at arm's length from the public and are at least somewhat buffered from societal debates and controversies.[2] They can, in comparison to teaching, refine their practices and technology over time with relatively minimal concern that shifting political winds or changing public sentiment will force them to abruptly change course. One would be hard-pressed to find organizations such as Moms for Liberty that target the work of actuaries or accountants.

But educators' work is more tied to public values, history, and politics than that of most other professions. As such, school improvement cannot advance by removing politics from the educational equation but rather by fostering a more productive partnership between its professional and political sides. Such is the reality for a "public profession" like teaching. What might a constructive partnership between the public and the profession look like, and what are the roles and responsibilities of the partners? The Memphis experience offers some clues.

The Professional Side of the Partnership: Building a Coherent System

Educators' side of the professional–political partnership hinges on the design of educationally coherent systems that communicate a vision and a system for realizing it. A clear vision of teaching and learning, paired with mechanisms for building capacity and learning from experience, not only drives improvement (even if incremental) but also shows the public that schools can confront their toughest challenges. Coherent systems, in short, are the cornerstone of both the professional and political work of meaningful school improvement.

Consider this from the perspective of the two initiatives discussed in this book. Initially, the Achievement School District (ASD) and Innovation Zone (iZone) were built on what reformers call "talent." This focus led early iZone leaders to handpick a small group of principals (who then handpicked their own teachers) capable of producing results with minimal support. No new curriculum would need to be purchased, learned, or adapted; no changes made to professional learning; no new training for school leaders; and most importantly, no consensus brokered on controversial issues. All that was needed was to put the right people in the right place and, as Malika Anderson once put it, "let the magic happen." Some might see the glowing evaluations of the early iZone as an indication that the strategy worked to perfection (at least for the iZone), but if that's true, it's only in the narrowest sense of what *working* means. If *working* means building an instructional system that develops professional capacity, sustains grade-level content, and fosters dynamic classroom discourse, then it would be hard to classify that version of the iZone as a success.

Some ASD operators also placed an emphasis on talent that proved equally self-defeating. The leaders of Martin Luther King Jr. College Preparatory High School (MLK) gambled that the district's finest educators would flock to their school to be free of district bureaucracy and red tape. But when those talented teachers failed to materialize, MLK had few organizational processes to elevate the performance of a largely inexperienced staff. As the leader of another charter operator organization put it: "How can we expect teachers to solve educational problems that have been unsolvable nationally without support beyond what's in their building? That's just a really bad idea." While *talent* and *autonomy* are seductive terms, for the education reformer, they amount to little more than fool's gold.

If a talent-based system is a bad educational idea, it's not a politically great one either. As Andrew Abbott showed in his landmark book *The System of Professions*, professions acquire cultural legitimacy and political muscle from their ability to demonstrate a system for identifying, reasoning about, and remedying problems. Such a system, Abbott wrote, "reinforces legitimacy by showing how, in simple cases, the professional knowledge system leads ineluctably from diagnosis to treatment."[3] The point is critical for education. Abbott provides the example of early approaches to psychotherapy that, while often effective, were eventually vanquished by the Freudian system, which was rooted in a more consistent and transparent logic while being less dependent on the God-given talent of individual practitioners. Lawyers, doctors, social workers, accountants, and other professionals cannot remedy every problem they encounter, are not immune to the powers of the market and the state, and are not entirely sealed off from societal controversies, but through systems of practice that convey occupational competence, they can better hold their own amid powerful institutional forces.[4]

The implication for education is that legitimacy lies not just in student learning outcomes and not just in the ability to recruit and retain a handful of talented teachers but also in the design of instructional systems that communicate a coherent and compelling approach to solving educational problems. Writing over a decade before Abbott, Dan Lortie made a similar point: "Teachers," Lortie argued, "have not developed codified and systematic bodies of professional knowledge; lacking that knowledge, their stance vis-à-vis laymen is, in turn, weakened."[5] The sociologist Robert Dreeben has similarly argued that teaching has historically failed to present the public with a persuasive theory of practice and thus is highly vulnerable to outside interference.[6] The overarching point is that when educational systems fail to project a problem-solving apparatus tied to a pedagogical vision, they also fail to create a compelling narrative that can stand out in the marketplace of educational ideas. They communicate that some teachers are competent and a few are outstanding, but the profession as a whole cannot be trusted.

In the initial version of the iZone, for example, the educational vision was tied strictly to increases in student learning outcomes, and as such, state assessment results were critical to its legitimacy. There were no common practices or tools, no common language, and no working theory of teaching and learning. The iZone's claim to fame was that it outperformed the ASD, but how it accomplished that was largely a mystery to outsiders (as well as to district leaders). Once its spectacular performance on state assessments tailed off—as it inevitably would—the rationale for continued public support weakened. The iZone's early results led to a surge in credibility and civic pride, but they did less to set the stage for long-term success.

It is a credit to Dr. Antonio Burt that, at considerable risk to the district and his own reputation, he constructed a robust instructional design, or *educational infrastructure*, as some call it, that encompassed a compelling vision of teaching and learning, elaborate and well-specified materials, a shared set of practices, system-wide collaboration, and a working theory of organizational change. He and his colleagues created teams of instructional coaches (mini-systems in and of themselves), reorganized the structure of school leadership, and established more opportunities for collegial work and collective problem-solving both within and across iZone schools. Legitimacy was still tied to outcomes, but the iZone's vision and system of practice provided it with a larger narrative with which to draw in the public and build support.

If this later generation of iZone leaders erred, it was in failing to communicate to the public that this version of the iZone was not designed to generate eye-popping results but to advance a conception of teaching and learning that placed it alongside previous efforts to expand opportunity for the city's historically marginalized students.

If the initial focus on short-term gains proved a mixed bag for the iZone, it was an unmitigated disaster for the ASD. Lacking the imprimatur of the local district, the ASD based its claim to legitimacy and right to operate local schools not on a vision of teaching and learning or a conception of practice tied to the region's history and culture but on its ability to drive test scores to largely unattainable levels. In setting unrealistic expectations, ASD leaders deprived operators of the time needed to learn a new context, refine their approach, and make incremental improvements. The desperate need to demonstrate impact created near-impossible dilemmas for school leaders, caught between ambitious visions of teaching and learning, building the capacity of inexperienced teachers, cultivating community buy-in, and delivering instant gains in student achievement.

That said, it is equally to the credit of ASD operators that in the face of insurmountable obstacles, they persisted in their efforts to learn from experience and improve their strategies. In fact, we would go so far as to say that those early reports pointing to the iZone's superior performance were of little long-term educational significance. They showed simply that the iZone played a better short-term game whose political implications were far more consequential than its educational ones. Once ASD and iZone leaders got down to the work of building coherent instructional systems, they found themselves in the same educational boat. Like their iZone counterparts, ASD operators discovered that designing (and continuously refining) these systems while building the capacity of teachers and leaders to use them is a grueling and incremental process. In an environment that encouraged collaboration, the leaders and teachers of the iZone and ASD would have been natural colleagues with much to learn from one another.

For the ASD, however, these changes came too late. By the time charter operators understood the need to shift their strategies, the damage of poor results had done irreversible harm to the ASD's reputation and morale. And even after they established more robust designs, instability and turnover impeded progress. In truth, it is unlikely that charter operators who were new to Memphis, new to school turnaround, new to managing a network of schools, or new to some combination of these factors could have rapidly produced the type of transformative results that would have silenced critics. ASD operators' fate was sealed before they even started.

One lesson from this account of the iZone and the ASD is that relying exclusively on improved test scores for legitimacy is a risky business for system leaders. Not only does this place extraordinary pressure on schools to make unrealistic and unsustainable gains, but it also weakens the incentive to redesign core school functions, such as leadership, curriculum, and professional learning, that, while critical, do not always lead to quick gains in test scores. At the end of the day, betting on short-term outcomes to legitimize improvement efforts is a game that public education cannot win.

The Public Side of the Partnership: Building Civic Capacity

A second lesson that the ASD and iZone have to offer is that teachers, principals, and administrators cannot do this work alone. They need not just the support but the active involvement of the communities that claim a stake in the ownership of local schools. With that ownership, however, comes the public's obligation to hold up its side of this partnership. This includes putting aside past divisions to work together on issues of shared concern, crafting policies that equitably distribute the risk of adopting challenging and unfamiliar practices, putting expertise before patronage, and adopting a long-term approach to reform without sliding into the complacency of the past. It is a community's ability to coalesce around common goals that we, following Clarence Stone, refer to as *civic capacity*, or what Susan Moffitt and her colleagues refer to as *political infrastructure*.[7]

But civic capacity and political infrastructure require more than a spirit of collaboration. They require policies that engender support across multiple interest groups and that are designed to forge common ground. Another way to put this is that just as there is a political element to educational systems, so is there an educational side to policy. If learners are not empty vessels into which can be poured new knowledge, neither are communities blank canvases onto which can be painted new policies. The work of policymaking would be considerably easier if policymakers were granted a clean historical slate, but this is rarely the case, and in cities like Memphis, it is far from reality. Instead, reforms enter into an "inherited terrain" in which past policies live on, as do the social and political histories that shape the way that communities interpret and enact policies.[8]

Indeed, if there is one message that the last decade of Memphis delivers, it is that social and historical context shape the normative frames and interpretive lenses through which communities interpret reforms and ascribe them meaning. The problem with the ASD was not that its critique of Memphis education was entirely wrong (it wasn't) or that it was political (that was inevitable); it was that its problem definition and theory of change were easily interpreted as a combination of intimidation and arrogance, regardless of its leaders' intentions. Rather than offering an opportunity to bridge past differences in pursuit of shared goals, it aggravated the city's most painful divisions and threw salt on old wounds. In cities like Memphis, civic capacity is difficult to generate in the best of circumstances; ASD-like policies make it nearly impossible.

As we write in 2025, it is fair to ask whether civic capacity is a relic of a bygone era—if such an era ever truly existed—and if so, what value there is in speaking of a partnership between the public and the profession. Yet an important body of scholarship has shown that the ideologically driven politics that dominate the national stage can obscure the more pragmatic and collaborative approaches often found at the local level.[9] In *Deliberative Policymaking*, Elizabeth Grant argues that "policymaking can serve democracy through deliberative processes that are inclusive and build a collective capacity to solve public problems." Likewise, Susan DeJarnatt and Barbara Ferman frame inclusive policies as platforms for "shared learning and critique."[10] James and Deborah Fallows, in their portrait of American towns and cities, document striking examples of civic capacity that stand in contrast to the partisan rancor of national politics.[11] Similarly,

Beth Schueler's account of the Massachusetts Department of Education's partnership with the town of Lawrence illustrates how state agencies can work collaboratively with local districts to support school improvement.[12]

Even in Memphis, with all its history and anguish, one can find the fortitude and resolve to forge a partnership rooted in a shared vision for public education. Indeed, one need look no further than the iZone to see the power of diverse stakeholders committed to the pursuit of a common goal. As we write, the iZone has grown to include thirty-four schools, with no indications of decline. It is easy to forget, however, the skepticism and resistance that iZone leaders encountered from a community that looked askance at the replacement of school staff and the curtailing of community control. But those early conflicts eventually gave way to the collective pursuit of a common goal. Perhaps this is the iZone's most important political accomplishment, less visible but more meaningful than its victory over the ASD.

There are, however, caveats.

One is that even the broadest coalition is no magic bullet for tackling educational inequity or fostering improvement. Entrenched interests, counterproductive practices, risk aversion, and an overall reluctance to make hard changes are not simply the invention of education reformers looking to dismantle the old system. Reform would be easier were this the case, but as numerous voices inside Shelby County made clear, it is not. One question, then, is whether a determined coalition of citizens, interest groups, and leaders can catalyze change absent the threat of a state takeover. Superintendent Dorsey Hopson lamented that among the many competing interests vying for priority and resources, kids were often "*third or fourth on the list.*" If local leaders, community members, and system managers are going to advance meaningful reform absent the pressure of a state takeover apparatus or a market-based system, they will need to confront this reality. Some contemporary reformers doubt the ability of traditional districts to drive change; it will be up to the profession and the public to form partnerships that prove them wrong.

A second caveat is that neither the iZone nor the concept of civic capacity should be understood as an unconditional embrace of localism or a return to previous eras defined by a lack of common standards, shared tools, and systems of measurement. Because while it is tempting to see the iZone as a locally born David vanquishing the state-sponsored Goliath, such a portrayal masks the constellation of policies, resources, and ideas that sustained the iZone as an educational and political enterprise.

Financially, the iZone was the product of state, federal, and private funds that supported its extended learning time and salary bonuses. And while some readers might bemoan the role of private capital in education reform or prefer a smaller federal role, the reality is that at $600,000 per school, the cost of the iZone far surpassed what a cash-strapped city could afford. Without investment from the state, federal government, and private donors, there would have been no iZone.[13]

Similarly, the ideas, materials, and theories that animated the iZone as an educational system originated among disparate organizations, agencies, and individuals. The iZone's math curriculum, Eureka Math, was developed outside the state and first adopted by the New York Department of Education. The instructional experts who breathed life into the iZone's vision were themselves products of professional learning seminars run by the University of Pittsburgh and paid for by the Tennessee State Department of Education. Nonprofit organizations like New Leaders and Memphis Teacher Residency trained scores of iZone principals and teachers. What makes the iZone local, therefore, is how district leaders drew on a wide range of intellectual and material resources to craft a system that was informed by professional knowledge yet rooted in local culture and animated by a vision of community empowerment. The iZone, in other words, exemplifies the interaction between the agency of determined local actors and the "subtle webs" of national organizations and entities that provide a complex brew of resources and ideas to local schools and districts.[14]

The task for local leaders, therefore, is not to invent new materials and ideas out of whole cloth (scarcely any iZone materials were local inventions) but to assemble these resources into a meaningful educational vision, construct an educational infrastructure designed to realize that vision, coalesce local support, and persevere in the face of centrifugal forces that can derail progress. If the iZone is a success story, it is because it represents a coming together of local leadership, high-level policies, and environmental resources in ways that encompass current ideas about teaching and learning while grounding that system in local history and culture.

Partnerships between the public and the profession are not easy to construct or maintain, do not lead to instant improvement, and do not vanquish public education's historic inequities. What they can do, however, is enable the politics of education and the profession of education to inch closer together toward a common vision and, in doing so, to embrace the long-term challenge of building more equitable education systems. This is the most important lesson that the iZone has to offer.

Conclusion

We began this book with a lengthy discussion of the history of Memphis, emphasizing the deep connection between the educational system and over a century of civil rights struggles. We noted that the ASD's implicit message that the local district was incapable of educating its own students harkened back to the words of Northern philanthropists during Reconstruction who belittled the notion that the formerly enslaved African Americans could run their own schools. We also showed that neither the iZone nor ASD materialized from thin air but were in fact the product of decades of school reform efforts both in Memphis and nationally.

We return to that past now to argue that the iZone—with all its politics, instability, and imperfections—speaks to the inextricable and historical ties between education and civil rights. In putting core educational questions about content, pedagogy, leadership, professional capacity, and system building at the center of the educational conversation, Dr. Sharon Griffin, Dr. Antonio Burt, and their many colleagues sit alongside past Black educators who, despite working in segregated and underresourced schools, exemplified an ethos of caring, high expectations, expertise, and unwavering professionalism.[15]

The iZone, however, is more than an example of high-quality Black schools. Its historical and contemporary importance lies in the design of a multischool system that puts forth a theory of improvement rooted in collective action; embraces the complexity of large-scale change; and tackles unproductive yet entrenched norms, politics, and practices. While some reformers are captivated by the breezy rhetoric of imagining new systems cut from whole cloth, iZone leaders were afforded no such luxury. Their task was to reform an existing system with all its pitfalls and pathologies. In this way, the iZone takes its place within the long history of Black organizing and collective action in the pursuit of shared educational goals. In the Jim Crow South, Black educators formed professional associations such as the Georgia Teachers and Education Association, the Alabama State Teachers Association, and the cross-state National Association for Teachers in Colored Schools.[16] These groups not only fought for equal funding, facilities, and teacher pay but also served as channels through which Black educators could share and disseminate curricula, textbooks, and ideas. As Jarvis Givens notes in his book on famed educator Carter G. Woodson, the "work of reimagining Black education was a shared endeavor."[17]

The iZone, of course, is a different type of shared endeavor. Cultivating changes in practice in a politicized, bureaucratic, and large public system involves complexities that volunteer associations are less likely to encounter. Still, as an instructional system built on the interdependence of practitioners, collective expertise, and shared goals, the iZone represents a return to the idea that providing a rigorous and equitable education in the face of formidable challenges exceeds the capacity of any one individual. Givens wrote that Woodson, Mary McLeod Bethune, and other Black education leaders understood that the "teaching of black life and history could not be by happenstance and sporadic; it was worthy of coordinated and intentional action." iZone leaders would surely agree.[18]

* * *

In closing, we return to the scores of individuals who, through their grit and their grind, created more meaningful learning opportunities for the students of Memphis. On the occasions when we caught a glimpse of their work, be it in the ASD or iZone, we often saw extraordinary dedication and determination. For those who teach and lead in Shelby County Schools, the job is far from over and, in many ways, has just begun. Because even if the ASD has lost the battle for public education in Memphis, the iZone and Shelby County Schools have not won. Winning does not mean besting the ASD through short-term gains or reveling in the community pride that those gains once generated. Nor is winning achieved by simply sticking around as the ASD fades from sight. Winning, rather, lies in the dogged determination to rebuild instructional systems in ways that expose all students to intellectually rigorous, grade-level content and dynamic classroom discourse. It lies in systems that continuously cultivate and reward teachers' and leaders' knowledge and skill and that embed the capacity to learn from mistakes and continuously improve. The administrators, principals, and teachers discussed in these chapters have made an admirable start to this work, constructing a system whose core principles depart from traditional yet ineffective ways of doing business. But as we have seen, to maintain this work into the future, they will need to contend with numerous countervailing forces, inevitable leadership turnover, and the allure of past practices. Like all reformers who take on this challenge, they have their work cut out for them.

Technical Appendix: Methodological Procedures

The data that inform this book come from two independent studies into the Achievement School District (ASD) and Innovation Zone (iZone) that were conducted between 2013 and 2020. Although the studies shared similar overarching questions and theoretical perspectives, there were noteworthy methodological differences between them. In this appendix, we outline the research methods that we employed in each study.

The Achievement School District

The findings and analysis related to the ASD are supported by longitudinal case studies that we conducted from 2013 until 2017 and that sought to examine the educational strategies, evolution, and political dynamics of the ASD and the operators that managed its schools. Sampling strategies, data collection, and analytic procedures are discussed in the following subsections.[1]

Sampling Techniques

Our questions and theoretical frames motivated three broad domains of data: the ASD leadership team, the operator organizations that managed schools, and the community and state environment. For each of these, a distinct strategy informed our sampling decisions.

STATE AND LOCAL REPRESENTATIVES. On the local and state level, we adopted a strategy that enabled us to understand the underlying values and perspectives regarding the purpose of and motivations behind the ASD. Toward this end, we included members of the state legislature, current and former commissioners from the Tennessee Department of Education, and state education officials with direct responsibility for or involvement with the ASD. We also sampled school district officials, school board members, and local legislators.

ASD MANAGEMENT. Our sampling strategy at the level of the ASD management was threefold. First, to help us understand the ASD's organizational blueprint, we spoke with ASD leaders who played an instrumental role in setting the ASD's policy and overarching vision. Second, to better grasp the ASD's understanding of the community and its local needs, we included ASD staff members who were involved in community outreach activities. Third, we included ASD personnel who were local to Memphis, and typically African American, in order to see if their perspective differed from those of nonlocal ASD officials.

For operators, our sample included a combination of high schools and elementary schools, as well as varying degrees of experience, network size, and pedagogical approach. We also included national networks that came from out of state and networks local to Memphis. We started with nine independent operators authorized by the ASD in its first two years, but this sample was reduced to six operators after our first year of fieldwork. Within these individual operator organizations, we sampled top-level network staff, including organizational executives, instructional managers, program developers, and community liaisons. Because of our focus on the evolution of the network and its overarching strategy, and in consideration of resource constraints, we did not include school-level staff in our sample.

COMMUNITY. From the community, we included Memphis-based nonprofit educational organizations, neighborhood associations, local philanthropies, school board members, and reporters who have been involved in communal work around educational problems or had a good understanding of the neighborhoods and districts most directly affected by the ASD. This group provided a perspective on how the ASD approach was perceived by those embedded in neighborhood contexts and attuned to local history.

Data Collection Procedures

We employed a combination of interviews, observations, and document analysis to capture diverse interpretations of the ASD.

INTERVIEWS. Overall, we conducted 181 interviews with 93 people between 2013 and 2017 (some respondents were interviewed multiple times). Interviews were organized in a semistructured manner that sought a balance between consistency and flexibility for follow-up questions. We developed "master protocols" for the different role groups we interviewed (e.g., operator leaders, local community members), and based on those, we developed protocols tailored to each respondent. This approach allowed us to elicit answers that shed light on respondents' backgrounds, their perception of underlying problems, their understanding of the ASD's strategy and intentions, and the values and experiences that framed their perspectives. We conducted multiple interviews with key respondents and typically administered them a few months apart, often drawing connections to comments made in earlier interviews. After data collection, we transcribed the interviews and uploaded them to a digital data-analysis software program.

State and Local Representatives' Protocol. For state and local representatives, our interview protocols were developed to explore the values and perspectives that informed their degree of political support for the ASD.

ASD Management Protocol. For ASD leaders and upper staff, our interview protocols were focused on formal ASD policies, such as operator authorization and accountability, student enrollment policy, timing of student entry, building location and facilities, and special education services. We also inquired into the overarching ASD improvement strategy and the way in which ASD officials thought that improvement would unfold over several years. As the ASD gained experience, we queried ASD staff about the lack of strong outcomes and community backlash. In the final year of the study, we focused on the primary lessons that leaders took from their ASD experience.

Operator Protocol. For ASD operators, our interview protocols iteratively focused on four central themes: (1) school-level turnaround strategies, including the instructional vision, the school leadership model, teacher learning strategies, data and information use, and key problems of practice; (2) interpretations of their environments, including the ASD central office, other ASD operators, the Shelby County district, market pressures, and community demands; (3) their investment in community outreach and extracurricular activities; and (4) strategic adaptations made in response to experience and outcomes.

Community Protocol. For community members, our interview protocols elicited their interpretation of the city's educational problems, the solutions they saw as most promising, and their perception of the ASD's improvement strategy and underlying agenda.

OBSERVATIONS. A second source of data stemmed from observations of meetings between ASD staff and school operators, school performance reviews, professional development sessions, school walkthroughs, and community meetings in Memphis. These observations, numbering over two dozen, enabled us to triangulate data and confirm themes that emerged from other sources. Operator-specific events (e.g., school walkthroughs) provided further insight into operators' strategies and challenges. Observing the interactions between local citizens, ASD representatives, and district leaders at community meetings shed additional light on local political dynamics that were unfolding around the ASD. These meetings afforded an opportunity to account for public views that were represented in local media and public communication channels and to understand the depth of resistance toward the ASD. They also illuminated the extent of parental involvement and the attempts of ASD leaders to counter the opposition and explain their intentions to the public. We took comprehensive notes during these events, identified key leaders in the community, and took note of the signs and posters held by attendees.

SECONDARY DATA. Secondary data in the form of print and digital documents represented a final source of information. We examined documents accessed directly through the ASD, legal documents accessed through the state legislature, material resources distributed by the community, and articles published in local media outlets. We also collected curriculum and policy documents that ASD operators agreed to share with us. These secondary data allowed us to supplement our findings from interviews and confirm participant interpretations that were expressed in interviews and observed at meetings. To keep track of ASD-related updates, we conducted a daily scan of Tennessee's two leading newspapers and created a daily Google alert using *ASD* as a keyword. We also drew on other scholarship written about the ASD to supplement our interpretation.

Analytic Procedures

We analyzed the data using a set of descriptive and analytic codes aligned with the study's theoretical framework and its primary research questions. This coding system was amended iteratively in advance of each round of data collection as our interpretations evolved (e.g., political discord) and events on the ground changed (e.g., state leadership turnover). Our research team strived to ensure high levels of intercoder reliability by having several norming sessions to help ensure consistent interpretation and application of codes across members. This process was facilitated by using computer software to calculate interrater reliability. The analytic process began with researchers using the software to extract data sorted under relevant codes. After the extraction of data, researchers drafted interim reports that organized interview and field-note excerpts into an emergent narrative. As part of this process, researchers highlighted portions of the text that pertained to the specific components of our theoretical framework.

Once that stage was completed, a project-wide Excel spreadsheet was created, with one column designated to excerpts entered by code, a second for entries summarizing the main points of these excerpts, and a third for a succinct interpretation. Out of this process emerged central themes that informed a new set of analytic memos that outlined a coherent narrative analysis. We member checked our interpretations by showing quoted participants drafts of our manuscripts, through peer review, and by regularly discussing our interpretations among each other and revising them accordingly.

The iZone

The findings and analysis of the iZone are informed by data collected from a longitudinal, mixed-methods study that we conducted from 2017 to 2019. The details pertaining to the methods undertaken for these studies are summarized in the following subsection.[2]

Sampling Techniques

To construct a sample of iZone schools, we met with three district leaders to identify schools with varying levels of leadership experience, collegial structures and cultures, and content area expertise—all school-level attributes theoretically salient for school improvement.[3] This conversation produced an initial list of seven schools, but two were later eliminated for convenience and practicality purposes. This left us with three elementary schools and two high schools. In each of the five schools, we focused on school leaders and third- to fifth-grade math teachers. The reason for our choice of subject matter was twofold. First, selecting a single content area allowed us to delve into the details and complexities of fostering instructional improvement. Second, the selection of mathematics proved opportune because the district had recently adopted a new curriculum that was to be used by teachers across the district. The selection of grades three to five was motivated by the importance of the state assessment for these grades and the consequent high-stakes nature of school performance.

To better grasp the organizational structure of the iZone, we constructed a sample that included original and subsequent district leaders who were involved in establishing the iZone and articulating its vision. To gain an understanding of the iZone's approach to pedagogy and leadership, we interviewed instructional and leadership coaching teams that were supporting our case-study schools. We also interviewed district leadership, including the superintendent and members of his cabinet. This allowed us to understand the iZone in relation to the larger district, as well as to the state department of education, the ASD, and the local community.

Data Collection Procedures

At the school level, our primary methods of data collection were interviews and focus groups with iZone leaders, principals, assistant principals, and math teachers.[4] We collected data from schools twice a year for the 2017–18 and 2018–19 academic years and once in 2020. We conducted a total of 150 interviews with 70 participants, such that we interviewed most participants at least twice and principals four times. Our interview protocols were designed according to role group. For example, our principal-interview protocol comprised questions pertaining to instructional leadership practices, continuous improvement strategies, views about math instruction, the Eureka Math curriculum, and support from the iZone.

Focus groups were conducted with school leadership teams and math departments and focused on instructional practices, problems of practice encountered by leaders and teachers, and strategies for improvement. After every interview and focus group, a summary memo capturing the central themes was drafted, typically on the same day. All summary memos were analyzed by the research team to produce school-level memos (one per school) representing leaders' and teachers' accounts of the improvement process. We administered surveys across iZone and non-iZone priority schools, targeting school leaders and teachers. We do not draw on survey data in this book.

Analytic Procedures

Our analytic process for the iZone studies was guided by a codebook of descriptive and structural codes. Our attention was initially directed toward the key technical elements in an improvement model for driving instructional changes. However, during the course of our fieldwork, we revised our research questions to incorporate some of the challenges imposed by the environment. At the end of the first year, we homed in on three main challenges: the conceptual and pedagogical rigor of the iZone's vision for math instruction; the pressure of a high-stakes accountability environment; and the formidable academic, social, and emotional needs of many iZone students.

At the end of the second year, we refined our theory to distinguish between the iZone as an instructional system, on the one hand, and a system of professional learning and support, on the other. This led to several procedural adjustments. We constructed a revised set of analytical domains and developed a more refined set of subquestions. From there, we used our original codebook as a guide to extract a subset of excerpts that could be recoded through pattern coding with our new domains. We downloaded these excerpts from our data-analysis software into an Excel spreadsheet and designated columns for the actual excerpts, their identifying attributes, summaries, their relation to each subquestion, and analytic notes that could inform our memo-writing process.

The end result of this (massive) spreadsheet was a set of themes that enabled us to better understand, sort, and make claims about problems of practice faced in the iZone in a coherent, well-informed narrative analysis.

To check the validity of our claims, we met weekly as a research team so that we could contest, refine, and supplement our initial claims with additional sources of data so that they would more accurately represent the analyzed data. We engaged in a thorough member-checking process that involved a two-day set of meetings with iZone leaders, instructional coaches, and leadership coaches.

Notes

Introduction

1. Unless otherwise noted, all quotes come from interviews conducted by the authors. Methodological details can be found in the technical appendix.

2. William R. Penuel and Vanessa Roberts, "The Theory and Practice of Democracy and Community," in *The Foundational Handbook on Improvement Research in Education*, ed. Donald J. Peurach et al. (Rowman & Littlefield, 2022), 111–30.

3. Barry Fishman and Leslie R. Herrenkohl, "Equitable Learning," in *The Foundational Handbook on Improvement Research in Education*, ed. Donald J. Peurach et al. (Rowman & Littlefield, 2022), 47–66; Eve L. Ewing, *Ghosts in the Schoolyard* (University of Chicago Press, 2018); Hava R. Gordon, *This Is Our School!: Race and Community Resistance to School Reform* (New York University Press, 2021).

4. Michael J. Feuer, "Fighting Racism with Mathematics," *EdFix* (podcast), May 12, 2023, accessed October 25, 2024, https://gsehd.gwu.edu/edfix-ts-ep23.

5. Fishman and Herrenkohl, "Equitable Learning," 53.

6. Janelle T. Scott, "A Rosa Parks Moment? School Choice and the Marketization of Civil Rights," *Critical Studies in Education* 54, no. 1 (2013): 9, https://doi.org/10.1080/17508487.2013.739570.

7. Domingo Morel and Sally Nuamah, "Who Governs? How Shifts in Political Power Shape Perceptions of Local Government Services," *Urban Affairs Review* 56, no. 5 (2019): 1503–28, https://doi.org/10.1177/1078087419855675; Huriya Jabbar and Joshua Childs, "Critical Perspectives on the Contexts of Improvement Research in Education," in *The Foundational Handbook on Improvement Research in Education*, ed. Donald J. Peurach et al. (Rowman & Littlefield, 2022), 241–61; Scott, "A Rosa Parks Moment?," 5–18.

8. In their technical report, Harris and Larsen found that the range of reform effect on high school graduation for the ninth- and tenth-grade cohorts was 3–9

percentage points, the effect for college attendance was 15 percentage points for on-time enrollment and 8 percentage points for any type of enrollment, the effect for college persistence was 4–7 percentage points, and the effect on college completion within 5 years of completion of the twelfth grade was 3–5 percentage points. Douglass N. Harris and Matthew F. Larsen, *The Effects of the New Orleans Post-Katrina Market-Based School Reforms on Medium-Term Student Outcomes* (Education Research Alliance for New Orleans, 2019), https://educationresearchalliancenola.org/files/publications/Harris-Larsen-Reform-Effects-2019-08-01.pdf.

9. Adam Gamoran and Cristina M. Fernandez, "Do Charter Schools Strengthen Education in High-Poverty Urban Districts?" in *Choosing Charters: Better Schools or More Segregation?*, ed. Iris C. Rotberg and Joshua L. Glazer (Teachers College Press, 2018), 133–52.

10. Morel and Nuamah, "Who Governs?"; Huriya Jabbar, "'Drenched in the Past': The Evolution of Market-Oriented Reforms in New Orleans," *Journal of Education Policy* 30, no. 6 (2015): 751–72, https://doi.org/10.1080/02680939.2015.1047409.

11. Adrienne D. Dixson et al., "The Color of Reform: Race, Education Reform, and Charter Schools in Post-Katrina New Orleans," *Qualitative Inquiry* 21, no. 3 (2015): 288–99, https://doi.org/10.1177/1077800414557826.

12. David K. Cohen et al., *Improvement by Design* (University of Chicago Press, 2014); James P. Spillane et al., "Striving for Coherence, Struggling with Incoherence: A Comparative Study of Six Educational Systems Organizing for Instruction," *Educational Evaluation and Policy Analysis* 44, no. 4 (2022): 567–92, https://doi.org/10.3102/01623737221093382.

13. For a discussion of an "instructionally focused" system, see Donald J. Peurach et al., "From Mass Schooling to Education Systems: Changing Patterns in the Organization and Management of Instruction," *Review of Research in Education* 43, no. 1 (2019): 32–67.

Chapter One

1. Tennessee State Government, "Tennessee Hires First Superintendent for Achievement School District," TN.gov, May 10, 2011, https://www.tn.gov/news/2011/5/10/tennessee-hires-first-superintendent-for-achievement-school-district.html.

2. A CMO is a nonprofit organization that operates and manages multiple charter schools under a centralized structure, providing services such as curriculum development, staffing, budgeting, and instructional support.

3. "Tennessee Charter School Incubator Launches Fellowship," *Business Wire*, September 20, 2012.

4. In January 2022, Shelby County Schools changed its name to Memphis-Shelby County Schools. We refer to the district as Shelby County Schools, its name during the time of our research studies.

5. Kids Count Data Center, *Children in Poverty in Memphis* (Annie E. Casey Foundation, 2024), https://datacenter.aecf.org/data/tables/43-children-in-poverty#detailed/3/72/false/1095,2048,1729,37,871,870,573,869,36,868/any/321,322.

6. Beverly Bond, "Educating the 'Common Man': Developing Public School Systems in Memphis and Shelby County, 1820 to 1954," in *Race, Economics, and the Politics of Educational Change: The Dynamics of School District Consolidation in Shelby County, Tennessee*, ed. John M. Amis and Paul M. Wright (University of Tennessee Press, 2018), 29; Lester C. Lamon, *Blacks in Tennessee, 1791–1970* (University of Tennessee Press, 1981), 37–38.

7. University of Memphis, "Civil War and Reconstruction," accessed February 19, 2024, https://www.memphis.edu/benhooks/mapping-civil-rights/civil-war-reconstruction.php; Robin Hardin and Marcie Hinton, "The Squelching of Free Speech in Memphis: The Life of a Black Post-Reconstruction Newspaper," *Race, Gender, and Class* 8, no. 4 (2001): 78–95, https://www.jstor.org/stable/41674996.

8. In 1869, two years after the passage of the original school law, Tennessee's state superintendent of public instruction reported that 446 schoolhouses for Whites had been built, whereas only 172 schoolhouses for Black children had been built. Yet Superintendent Eaton also admitted that many of the Black schoolhouses would not have been built had it not been for the financial assistance rendered by the Freedmen's Bureau. Thus, from the very outset, Tennessee school officials seemed reluctant to commit a fair share of state financial resources to the cause of Black education. Cynthia Griggs Fleming, "The Development of Black Education in Tennessee, 1865–1920" (PhD diss., Duke University, 1977), 47.

9. James D. Anderson, *The Education of Blacks in the South, 1860–1935* (University of North Carolina Press, 1988), 19.

10. Anderson, *The Education of Blacks*, 18.

11. Kathleen Berkeley, "The Politics of Black Education in Memphis, Tennessee, 1868–1881," in *Southern Cities, Southern Schools: Public Education in the Urban South*, ed. David N. Plank and Rick Ginsberg (Greenwood Press, 1990), 199–236; Marcus D. Pohlmann and Michael P. Kirby, *Racial Politics at the Crossroads: Memphis Elects Dr. W. W. Herenton* (University of Tennessee Press, 1996).

12. Marcus D. Pohlmann, *Opportunity Lost: Race and Poverty in Memphis City Schools* (University of Tennessee Press, 2008).

13. Berkeley, "The Politics of Black Education," 199–236; Lynette Boney Wrenn, "The Politics of Memphis School Reform, 1883–1927," in *Southern Cities, Southern Schools: Public Education in the Urban South* (Bloomsbury Academic, 1990), 38; Pohlmann and Kirby, *Racial Politics at the Crossroads*.

14. Bond, "Educating the 'Common Man,'" 30.

15. Berkeley, "The Politics of Black Education," 206; Bond, "Educating the 'Common Man.'"

16. Bond, "Educating the 'Common Man,'" 33.

17. Fleming, "The Development of Black Education," 363.

18. Anderson, *The Education of Blacks*.

19. W. E. B. Du Bois, "The Talented Tenth," in *The Negro Problem: A Series of Articles by Representative Negroes of Today*, ed. Booker T. Washington (James Pott, 1903), 33–75.

20. Frederick Dunn, "The Educational Philosophies of Washington, DuBois, and Houston: Laying the Foundations for Afrocentrism and Multiculturalism," *Journal of Negro Education* 62, no. 1 (1993): 25, https://doi.org/10.2307/2295397.

21. Fleming, "The Development of Black Education," 146–47.

22. Fleming, "The Development of Black Education," 155.

23. Wrenn, "The Politics of Memphis School Reform," XX.

24. Memphis Tech High, "Early Educators, Memphis City Schools," accessed April 26, 2024, https://www.memphistechhigh.com/blackeducation.html.

25. Pohlmann and Kirby, *Racial Politics at the Crossroads*, 66.

26. Fleming, "The Development of Black Education," 357.

27. Berkeley, "The Politics of Black Education," 221.

28. Berkeley, "The Politics of Black Education," 199–236.

29. David R. Goldfield, *Cotton Fields and Skyscrapers: Southern City and Region, 1607–1980* (Louisiana State University Press, 1982).

30. Bond, "Educating the 'Common Man,'" 42.

31. Ida B. Wells, *Crusade for Justice: The Autobiography of Ida B. Wells* (University of Chicago Press, 2020).

32. Carl A. Grant et al., *Black Intellectual Thought in Education: The Missing Traditions of Anna Julia Cooper, Carter G. Woodson, and Alain LeRoy Locke* (Routledge, 2016).

33. Jarvis R. Givens, *Fugitive Pedagogy: Carter G. Woodson and the Art of Black Teaching* (Harvard University Press, 2021).

34. Givens, *Fugitive Pedagogy*; Grant et al., *Black Intellectual Thought*; Gloria Ladson-Billings, "From the Achievement Gap to the Education Debt: Understanding Achievement in US School," *Educational Researcher* 35, no. 7 (2006): 3–12.

35. Beverly G. Bond and Jannan Sherman, *Memphis: In Black and White* (Arcadia, 2003); Pohlmann and Kirby, *Racial Politics at the Crossroads*, 11–12.

36. Bond and Sherman, *Memphis: In Black and White*, 78.

37. Berkeley, "The Politics of Black Education," 201–11; Wrenn, "The Politics of Memphis School Reform," 38.

38. Wanda Rushing, "Memphis and Durable Inequality," in *Race, Economics, and the Politics of Educational Change: The Dynamics of School District Consolidation*

in Shelby County, Tennessee, ed. John M. Amis and Paul M. Wright (University of Tennessee Press, 2018), 33.

39. Roger Biles, "The Persistence of the Past: Memphis in the Great Depression," *Journal of Southern History* 52, no. 2 (May 1986): 185, https://doi.org/10.2307/2209667.

40. Goldfield, *Cotton Fields and Skyscrapers*, 173.

41. Goldfield, *Cotton Fields and Skyscrapers*, 173.

42. Daniel Kiel, "A Memphis Dilemma: A Half-Century of Public Education Reform in Memphis and Shelby County from Desegregation to Consolidation," *University of Memphis Law Review* 41 (2010): 787.

43. Wrenn, "The Politics of Memphis School Reform," 38.

44. Wrenn, "The Politics of Memphis School Reform," 38, 92.

45. Roger Biles, "A Bittersweet Victory: Public School Desegregation in Memphis," *Journal of Negro Education* 55, no. 4 (1986): 470–83; Wrenn, "The Politics of Memphis School Reform," 38.

46. Wrenn, "The Politics of Memphis School Reform," 38, 93.

47. Wrenn, "The Politics of Memphis School Reform," 38.

48. Wrenn, "The Politics of Memphis School Reform," 93.

49. Kira Virginia Duke, "To Disturb the People as Little as Possible: The Desegregation of Memphis City Schools" (Master's thesis, University of Tennessee, 2005), https://trace.tennessee.edu/cgi/viewcontent.cgi?article=3224&context=utk_gradthes.

50. Daniel Kiel, "A Memphis Dilemma: A Half-Century of Public Education Reform in Memphis and Shelby County from Desegregation to Consolidation," *University of Memphis Law Review* 41 (2010): 787.

51. Kiel, "A Memphis Dilemma," 61.

52. Frankenberg, Erica, Genevieve Siegel-Hawley, and Sarah Diem. "Segregation by district boundary line: The fragmentation of Memphis area schools,"- *Educational Researcher* 46, no. 8 (2017): 449–63.

53. Pohlmann, *Opportunity Lost*, 77.

54. Kiel, "A Memphis Dilemma."

55. Pohlmann, *Opportunity Lost*, 82.

56. David Dawson, "Charade on Wheels: The Tragedy of Busing," *Memphis Magazine*, May 31, 2018, https://memphismagazine.com/features/longform/charade-on-wheels-the-tragedy-of-busing/.

57. Biles, "A Bittersweet Victory."

58. Pohlmann and Kirby, *Racial Politics at the Crossroads*, 166–67.

59. Goldfield, *Cotton Fields and Skyscrapers*; Pohlmann and Kirby, *Racial Politics at the Crossroads*.

60. Charles A. Santos, "Urban-Suburban Disparity and Geographic Stratification: A Context for Fiscal Conflict," in *Race, Economics, and the Politics of Educational Change: The Dynamics of School District Consolidation in Shelby*

County, Tennessee, ed. John M. Amis and Paul M. Wright (University of Tennessee Press, 2018), 156–89.

61. For a discussion of the racial undertones of suburban notions of local control, see Genevieve Siegel-Hawley et al., "The Disintegration of Memphis-Shelby County, Tennessee: School District Secession and Local Control in the 21st Century," *American Educational Research Journal* 55, no. 4 (2018): 651–92, https://doi.org/10.3102/0002831217748880.

62. Zach McMillin et al., "Schools Dazed—Shelby County System Begins Preparations for Crafting Mega District," *Commercial Appeal*, December 22, 2010.

63. John M. Amis and Paul M. Wright, "The Antecedents and Mechanism of School District Consolidation," in *Race, Economics, and the Politics of Educational Change: The Dynamics of School District Consolidation in Shelby County, Tennessee*, ed. John M. Amis and Paul M. Wright (University of Tennessee Press, 2018), 1–20.

64. A 2008 report commissioned by SCS and MCS, conducted by researchers from the University of Memphis, found that were SCS to achieve special-district status, it would have potentially dire economic consequences for MCS and the city overall. Regional Economic Development Center, *Impact of a Special School District on Memphis and Shelby County* (University of Memphis, 2008), http://s3.documentcloud.org/documents/25614/impact-spec-school-districtlr.pdf.

65. Tony Jones, "Voters Decide City Schools' Fate," *Tri-State Defender* 1, no. 8 (December 23, 2010).

66. Goldfield, *Cotton Fields and Skyscrapers*, 177.

67. Amis and Wright, "The Antecedents and Mechanism of School District Consolidation"; Erica Frankenberg et al., "Segregation by District Boundary Line: The Fragmentation of Memphis Area Schools," *Educational Researcher* 46, no. 8 (2017): 449–63, https://doi.org/10.3102/0013189X17732752; Kiel, "A Memphis Dilemma."

68. Santos, "Urban-Suburban Disparity," 184.

69. Siegel-Hawley et al., "The Disintegration of Memphis-Shelby County," 671.

70. Siegel-Hawley et al., "The Disintegration of Memphis-Shelby County," 653.

71. Goldfield, *Cotton Fields and Skyscrapers*, 11.

72. Santos, "Urban-Suburban Disparity."

73. Santos, "Urban-Suburban Disparity."

74. Siegel-Hawley et. al., "The Disintegration of Memphis-Shelby County"; Rushing, "Memphis and Durable Inequality."

75. Pohlmann and Kirby, *Racial Politics at the Crossroads*, 79.

76. Pohlmann and Kirby, *Racial Politics at the Crossroads*; Willie W. Herenton, "Memphis Inner-City School Improvement Project: A Holistic Approach for Developing Academic Excellence," *Urban League Review* 11 (1988): 209–16.

77. David K. Cohen et al., "Resources, Instruction, and Research," *Educational Evaluation and Policy Analysis* 25, no. 2 (Summer 2003): 119–42, http://www.jstor.org/stable/3699546.

78. Pohlmann and Kirby, *Racial Politics at the Crossroads*.

79. David K. Cohen et al., *Improvement by Design* (University of Chicago Press, 2014).

80. Dan C. Lortie, *Schoolteacher: A Sociological Study* (University of Chicago Press, 1975); David K. Cohen, "2: Politics and Research: Evaluation of Social Action Programs in Education," *Review of Educational Research* 40, no. 2 (1970): 213–38, https://doi.org/10.3102/00346543040002213; James S. Coleman et al., *Equality of Educational Opportunity* (US Department of Health, Education, and Welfare, Office of Education, 1966); John W. Meyer and Brian Rowan, "The Structure of Educational Organizations," in *Environments and Organizations*, ed. M. W. Meyer (Jossey-Bass, 1978), 217–25; Milbrey W. McLaughlin, "Implementation as Mutual Adaptation: Change in Classroom Organization," *Teachers College Record: The Voice of Scholarship in Education* 77, no. 3 (1976): 1–9, https://doi.org/10.1177/016146817607700304.

81. Reagan Walker, "Bush: Capturing the 'Education' Moment?" *Education Week*, October 19, 1988, quoting George H. W. Bush: "I want to be the Education President. I want to lead a renaissance of quality in our schools."

82. For a detailed explanation of US education policy during this era, see Donald J. Peurach et al., "From Mass Schooling to Education Systems: Changing Patterns in the Organization and Management of Instruction," *Review of Research in Education* 43, no. 1(2019): 32–67.

83. Harvey Kantor and Robert Lowe, "From New Deal to No Deal: No Child Left Behind and the Devolution of Responsibility for Equal Opportunity," *Harvard Educational Review* 76, no. 4 (Winter 2006): 490.

84. US Chamber of Commerce, *Leaders and Laggards: A State-by-State Report Card on Educational Effectiveness* (US Chamber of Commerce, 2007), 53, https://www.uschamber.com/assets/archived/images/2007-_us-chamber-leaders-and-laggards.pdf.

85. First to the Top passed with votes of 29-3 in the Senate and 83-10 in the House of Representatives.

86. Will Pinkston, "How Bad Actors Tried to Destroy Public Education," Race to the Bottom, February 2019, https://racetothebottom.us/race.html.

87. Bradley Leon, "Race to the Top and the Future of Memphis City Schools," *Smart City Memphis*, April 19, 2010, https://www.smartcitymemphis.com/2010/04/race-to-the-top-and-the-future-of-memphis-city-schools/.

88. Priority schools were those that had reached their fifth year of improvement status, otherwise known as the *Restructuring II phase*, or the lowest-performing 5 percent of Title I schools in the state. Tennessee Parents: Reclaiming Public Education for Our Children, "Is the State Manipulating Data to Give Our Public Schools to Charter Operators?" last modified November 24, 2013, http://www.tnparents.com/our-voicesblog/is-the-state-manipulating-data-to-give-our-public-schools-to-charter-operators; Marta W. Aldrich, "In Memphis and Nashville,

Here Are the Schools Eligible—and No Longer Eligible—for State Intervention," *Chalkbeat*, August 11, 2015, https://www.chalkbeat.org/tennessee/2015/8/11/21092359/in-memphis-and-nashville-here-are-the-schools-eligible-and-no-longer-eligible-for-state-intervention/.

Chapter Two

1. Clarence N. Stone, *Changing Urban Education* (University Press of Kansas, 1998); Clarence N. Stone et al., *Building Civic Capacity: The Politics of Reforming Urban Schools* (University Press of Kansas, 2001); Domingo Morel, *Takeover: Race, Education, and American Democracy* (Oxford University Press, 2018); Joshua L. Glazer and Cori Egan, "The Ties That Bind: Building Civic Capacity for the Tennessee Achievement School District," *American Educational Research Journal* 55, no. 5 (October 2018): 928–64, https://doi.org/10.3102/0002831218763088; Peter Burns, "Regime Theory, State Government, and a Takeover of Urban Education," *Journal of Urban Affairs* 25, no. 3 (2003): 285–303, https://doi.org/10.1111/1467-9906.00163.

2. Stone et al., *Building Civic Capacity*, 8.

3. Peter B. Dow, *Schoolhouse Politics: Lessons from the Sputnik Era* (Harvard University Press, 1991).

4. For a review of the literature on organizational legitimacy, see David L. Deephouse et al., "Organizational Legitimacy: Six Key Questions," in *The SAGE Handbook of Organizational Institutionalism*, ed. Royston Greenwood et al. (SAGE, 2017), 27–52.

5. John W. Meyer and Brian Rowan, "The Structure of Educational Organizations," in *Environments and Organizations*, ed. M. W. Meyer (Jossey-Bass, 1978), 217–25.

6. Heinz-Dieter Meyer and Brian Rowan, "Institutional Analysis and the Study of Education," in *The New Institutionalism in Education*, ed. Heinz-Dieter Meyer and Brian Rowan (State University of New York Press, 2007), 5.

7. Joshua L. Glazer et al., "Networked Improvement in the US and England: A New Role for the Middle Tier," in *The Foundational Handbook on Improvement Research in Education*, ed. Donald J. Peurach et al. (Rowman & Littlefield, 2022), 165–87.

8. US Tennessee General Assembly, Tennessee First to the Top Act of 2010, HB 7010, SB 7005, 106th General Assembly, introduced in House and Senate on January, 12, 2010, https://wapp.capitol.tn.gov/apps/BillInfo/default.aspx?BillNumber=HB7010&GA=106.

9. Burns, "Regime Theory"; Morel, *Takeover*; Beth E. Schueler, "A Third Way: The Politics of School District Takeover and Turnaround in Lawrence, Massachusetts," *Educational Administration Quarterly* 55, no. 1 (2019): 116–53.

10. Tennessee Department of Education, "Tennessee Hires First Superintendent for Achievement School District," press release, May 10, 2011, TN.gov, https://www.tn.gov/news/2011/5/10/tennessee-hires-first-superintendent-for-achievement-school-district.html.

11. Nelson Smith, *Redefining the School District in Tennessee* (Thomas Fordham Institute, 2013), https://fordhaminstitute.org/national/research/redefining-school-district-america.

12. From national philanthropies such as the Walton Family Foundation and the Laura and John Arnold Foundation, the ASD received $204,000 in 2015 and $1,046,420 in the 2015–2018 term, respectively. Local philanthropies such as the Hyde Family, Poplar, and Pyramid Peak Foundations collectively poured multimillion-dollar investments per year into Memphis's turnaround initiative involving both the ASD and the iZone. One ASD elementary school received $26,667 from the Poplar Foundation alone. Further, significant amounts were allocated by both national and local foundations to the Tennessee Charter School Association (TCSA) and the Tennessee Charter School Incubator (TCSI) more generally. The TCSA received $812,000 from the Walton Family Foundation in 2010 and $75,000 from the Poplar Foundation from 2010 to 2012. As for the TCSI, it received $375,000 from the Poplar Foundation in 2013 and $187,500 in 2014. Betsy Doyle and Mike Perigo, "Investing in 'Teacher Town,' USA," *Stanford Social Innovation Review*, September 18, 2014, https://ssir.org/articles/entry/investing_in_teacher_town_usa#; Mary L. Mason and Sarah Reckhow, "Rootless Reforms? State Takeovers and School Governance in Detroit and Memphis," *Peabody Journal of Education* 92, no. 1 (2017): 64–75, https://doi.org/10.1080/0161956X.2016.1264813; Smith, *Redefining the School District*; Walton Family Foundation, "2015 Walton Family Foundation Grants," accessed December 7, 2023, https://www.waltonfamilyfoundation.org/about-us/reports-financials/2015-walton-family-foundation-grants.

13. Smith, *Redefining the School District*, 2.

14. Jeffrey R. Henig, "The Politics of Localism in an Era of Centralization, Privatization, and Choice," *Teachers College Record: The Voice of Scholarship in Education* 111, no. 13 (December 2009): 112–29, https://doi.org/10.1177/016146810911110130.

15. Stone, *Changing Urban Education*, 2.

16. Eric M. Patashnik, *Reforms at Risk: What Happens after Major Policy Changes Are Enacted* (Princeton University Press, 2008).

17. Dale Russakoff, *The Prize: Who's in Charge of America's Schools?* (Houghton Mifflin Harcourt, 2015); Jeffrey R. Henig et al., *The Color of School Reform: Race, Politics, and the Challenge of Urban Education* (Princeton University Press, 2001); Douglas N. Harris, *Charter School City: What the End of Traditional Public Schools in New Orleans Means for American Education* (University of Chicago Press, 2020); Jeffrey R. Henig, "Washington DC: Race, Issue Definition, and School Board Restructuring," in *Mayors in the Middle: Politics, Race, and Mayoral Control*

of Urban Schools, ed. Jeffrey R. Henig and Wilbur C. Rich (Princeton University Press, 2004), 209–10.

18. Henig, "Washington DC."

19. Claudia Goldin and Lawrence F. Katz, *The Race between Education and Technology* (Harvard University Press, 2009).

20. Marcus D. Pohlmann, *Opportunity Lost: Race and Poverty in Memphis City Schools* (University of Tennessee Press, 2008).

21. Beverly G. Bond and Jannan Sherman, *Memphis: In Black and White* (Arcadia, 2003).

22. Jason Bolton, "Largest Memphis-Area Employers," *Memphis Business Journal*, July 16, 2021, https://www.bizjournals.com/memphis/subscriber-only/2021/07/16/largest-memphis-area-employers.html#footnote4.

23. Meili Powell, "Orange Mound, Memphis (1890–)," Black Past, July 30, 2018, https://www.blackpast.org/African American-history/orange-mound-memphis-1890/.

24. Daniel Kiel, "A Memphis Dilemma: A Half-Century of Public Education Reform in Memphis and Shelby County from Desegregation to Consolidation," *University of Memphis Law Review* 41 (2010): 787.

25. John A. Amis and Paul M. Wright, "The Antecedents and Mechanism of School District Consolidation," in *Race, Economics, and the Politics of Educational Change: The Dynamics of School District Consolidation in Shelby County, Tennessee*, ed. John M. Amis and Paul M. Wright (University of Tennessee Press, 2018); Kiel, "A Memphis Dilemma"; Wanda Rushing, "Memphis and Durable Inequality," in *Race, Economics, and the Politics of Educational Change: The Dynamics of School District Consolidation in Shelby County, Tennessee*, ed. John M. Amis and Paul M. Wright (University of Tennessee Press, 2018).

26. Tennessee Department of Education, "Assessment Files: District-Level 2014," https://www.tn.gov/education/districts/federal-programs-and-oversight/data/data-downloads.html.

27. Daniel Kiel, "Two Attempts, One Fate," in *Race, Economics, and the Politics of Educational Change: The Dynamics of School District Consolidation in Shelby County, Tennessee*, ed. John M. Amis and Paul M. Wright (University of Tennessee Press, 2018), 57–79.

28. New Leaders, formerly New Leaders for New Schools, is a nonprofit organization based in New York City that aims to cultivate educational leaders who are committed to bringing about educational equity. It is driven by a philosophy that schools perform best when their leaders collaborate with local communities to create the conditions that are conducive for all students to succeed. To that end, it launched its first-ever principal preparation program with a cohort of only fourteen educators in 2001. Since then, it has grown to develop more than eight thousand educational leaders in over forty-five cities across the nation. Through its adopted professional learning model, participants get to benefit from cohort-based learning, one-on-one coaching, and competency-based modules in an authentic setting and

with the support of fellow colleagues in professional learning communities. New Leaders, "Our Story," accessed January 19, 2024, https://www.newleaders.org/about/story; New Leaders, "Our Why," accessed January 19, 2024, https://www.newleaders.org/about/why; New Leaders, "Our Approach," accessed January 19, 2024, https://www.newleaders.org/about/approach.

29. Anthony S. Bryk et al., "Policy Lessons from Chicago's Experience with Decentralization," *Brookings Papers on Education Policy*, no. 2 (1999): 67–127, https://www.jstor.org/stable/20067207.

30. Luis A. Huerta and Andrew Zuckerman, "An Institutional Theory Analysis of Charter Schools: Addressing Institutional Challenges to Scale," *Peabody Journal of Education* 84, no. 3 (July 2009): 414–31, https://doi.org/10.1080/01619560902973621.

31. Iris C. Rotberg, "Charter Schools and the Risk of Increased Segregation," *Phi Delta Kappan* 95, no. 4 (2014): 26–31, https://doi.org/10.1177/003172171409500507; Natalie Lacireno-Paquet et al., "Creaming Versus Cropping: Charter School Enrollment Practices in Response to Market Incentives," *Educational Evaluation and Policy Analysis* 24, no. 2 (Summer 2002): 145–58, https://doi.org/10.3102/01623737024002145; Wagma Mommandi and Kevin Welner, "Shaping Charter Enrollment and Access: Practices, Responses, and Ramifications," in *Choosing Charters: Better Schools or More Segregation?*, ed. Iris C. Rotberg and Joshua L. Glazer (Teachers College Press, 2018), 61–81.

32. Twenty-five percent of students could be recruited from other low-income areas.

33. Gary T. Henry et al., *Teacher and Student Migration in and out of Tennessee's Achievement School District* (Tennessee Consortium on Research, Evaluation, and Development, 2014), https://cdn.vanderbilt.edu/vu-sub/wp-content/uploads/sites/280/2023/07/ASD_Teacher_Student_Migration.pdf.

34. Arne Duncan, "Secretary Duncan Urges Charters to Turn Around Schools, Improve Accountability," transcript of speech delivered at the National Charter Schools Conference, Washington, DC, June 22, 2009, https://tea.texas.gov/student-assessment/monitoring-and-interventions/school-improvement/title-i-priority-schools-grant/ttipsmodule2-transcript.pdf.

35. The notion of the problem turning into the solution is elaborated in David K. Cohen et al., "Policy and Practice: The Dilemma," *American Journal of Education* 113, no. 4 (2007): 515–48.

36. Shelby County Schools, *Fiscal Year 2014–15: Strategic Budget* (Shelby County Schools, 2014), https://shelbycountytn.gov/DocumentCenter/View/17399/Shelby-County-Schools-2014-2015-Strategic-Budget?bidId=.

37. Research from Zimmer et al. found that while non-iZone teachers received a 5 percent increase in pay, teachers who stayed in or transferred into an iZone school received an 11 percent and a 19 percent increase in pay, respectively. Ron Zimmer et al., "The Effects of School Turnaround in Tennessee's Achievement School District and Innovation Zones," *Educational Evaluation and Policy Analysis* 39, no. 4 (December 2017): 676.

Chapter Three

1. David K. Cohen et al., "Resources, Instruction, and Research," *Educational Evaluation and Policy Analysis* 25, no. 2 (Summer 2003): 119–42, http://www.jstor.org/stable/3699546.

2. Green Dot Public Schools, "About Us," accessed December 14, 2023, https://greendot.org/about/; Susan Colby and Kimberly Wicoff, *Aspire Public Schools: From 10 Schools to 6-Million Kids* (Bridgespan, 2006), https://files.eric.ed.gov/fulltext/ED535864.pdf.

3. Tennessee Department of Education, "Accountability Files: School-Level 2014," https://www.tn.gov/education/districts/federal-programs-and-oversight/data/data-downloads.html.

4. Jaclyn Zubrzycki, "Green Dot Prepares to 'Transform' First School in Memphis," *Chalkbeat*, January 14, 2014, https://www.chalkbeat.org/tennessee/2014/1/14/21100186/green-dot-prepares-to-transform-first-school-in-memphis/.

5. Research conducted by Dixon and colleagues found that in its first year, the iZone retained those principals whose schools experienced student growth in the previous years, whereas the principals whose schools experienced weak growth transitioned out. This was in contrast to the ASD, where it was the principals who led higher-performing schools who left for other schools. Latanya L. Dixon et al., "Who Leads Turnaround Schools? Characteristics of Principals in Tennessee's Achievement School District and Innovation Zones," *Educational Administration Quarterly* 58, no. 2 (December 2021): 258n99, https://doi.org/10.1177/0013161X211055702.

6. Caroline Bauman, "How Westhaven Elementary—Which Combined Three Schools in a New Building—May Be the New Model for Closing Schools in Memphis," *Chalkbeat*, December 19, 2016, https://www.chalkbeat.org/tennessee/2016/12/19/21100154/how-westhaven-elementary-which-combined-three-schools-in-a-new-building-may-be-the-new-model-for-clo/.

7. Philissa Cramer, "Strong iZone Scores Viewed as Chance to Grow Shelby County's Turnaround Initiative," *Chalkbeat*, August 3, 2015, https://tn.chalkbeat.org/2015/8/3/21094849/strong-izone-scores-viewed-as-chance-to-grow-shelby-county-s-turnaround-initiative.

8. Daarel Burnette II, "School Operations, Enrichment Cut 'to the Bone,' Says Shelby County's State Funding Lawsuit," *Chalkbeat*, September 2, 2015, https://www.chalkbeat.org/tennessee/2015/9/2/21092512/school-operations-enrichment-cut-to-the-bone-says-shelby-county-s-state-funding-lawsuit/.

9. Gary T. Henry et al., *Evaluating the Impact of Tennessee's Achievement School District: 1st Annual Report to the Walton Family Foundation* (Vanderbilt University, 2015), https://cdn.vanderbilt.edu/vu-sub/wp-content/uploads/sites/280/2023/07/HenryZimmer_Walton_Y1.pdf. Because of the nature of the study, the

results included the state's three iZones, which, in addition to Shelby County, also included Nashville and Hamilton County. Thus, the measures are not a precise measure of the Shelby County iZone. However, the research team also disaggregated iZone results by the three locations. The brief suggests that Memphis had the largest and most robust improvements in student test scores of the three. However, the brief acknowledges sample-size limitations when the data are disaggregated in this manner.

10. Gary T. Henry et al., "Peeking into the Black Box of School Turnaround: A Formal Test of Mediators and Suppressors," *Educational Evaluation and Policy Analysis* 42, no. 2 (April 2020): 232–56, https://doi.org/10.3102/0162373720908600.

11. Micaela Watts, "D.C. Public Schools Officials Tour Memphis iZone," *Chalkbeat*, January 13, 2016, https://tn.chalkbeat.org/2016/1/13/21098227/d-c-public-schools-officials-tour-memphis-izone.

12. Jason Gonzales, "Memphis iZone Schools Outpaced State-Run Turnaround Efforts," *Tennessean*, February 17, 2016, https://www.tennessean.com/story/news/education/2016/02/17/memphis-izone-schools-outpace-state-run-turnaround-efforts/78693182/.

13. See the March 2012 report of the State Collaborative on Reforming Education for details on this process. State Collaborative on Reforming Education, *The State of Education in Tennessee 2011–12* (State Collaborative on Reforming Education, 2012), https://tnscore.org/wp-content/uploads/2017/02/2011-12-State-of-Education-in-TN.pdf.

14. Andrew Ujifusa, "Common Core Supporters Firing Back," *Education Week*, May 14, 2013, https://www.edweek.org/teaching-learning/common-core-supporters-firing-back/2013/05; Tom Humphrey, "Common Core Controversy Heats Up," *Tennessean*, January 17, 2014, https://www.tennessean.com/story/news/politics/2014/01/12/common-core-controversy-heats-up/4425847/.

15. For example, one national organization that reviewed all state standards gave Tennessee a grade of A for the quality of its performance standards. American Legislative Exchange Council, *Report Card on American Education: Ranking State K–12 Performance, Progress, and Reform* (American Legislative Exchange Council, 2019), https://www.alecreportcard.org/app/uploads/2019/09/2019-ALEC-Report-Card.pdf.

16. Henry et al., "Peeking into the Black Box," 232–56.

17. Dixon et al., "Who Leads Turnaround Schools?"

18. John E. Chubb and Terry M. Moe, *Politics, Markets, and America's Schools* (Brookings Institution Press, 1991).

19. Gonzales, "Memphis iZone Schools."

20. Laura Faith Kebede and Marta W. Aldrich, "Schools in Tennessee's Achievement School District Won't Start Returning to Local Control until 2024," *Chalkbeat*, September 30, 2020, https://tn.chalkbeat.org/2020/9/30/21496121/tennessee-delays-schools-exiting-asd-after-nearly-a-decade-of-no-plan.

21. Donald J. Peurach and Christine M. Neumerski, "Mixing Metaphors: Building Infrastructure for Large Scale School Turnaround," *Journal of Educational Change* 16, no. 4 (November 2015): 379–420, https://doi.org/10.1007/s10833-015-9259-z.

22. Daarel Burnette II, "Philanthropic Grant for $10 Million Ensures Memphis iZone Expansion," Chalkbeat, September 16, 2015.

23. Research by Dixon et al. noted that in year four of the iZone, the number of principals who were new to their schools was roughly equivalent to the number of new principals in year one of the iZone, when the replacement of ineffective pre-iZone school principals was a key aspect of the iZone's theory of action. Dixon et al., "Who Leads Turnaround Schools?"

24. Henry et al., "Peeking into the Black Box," 243.

25. Richard F. Elmore, *Building a New Structure for School Leadership* (Albert Shanker Institute, 2000), 8, https://files.eric.ed.gov/fulltext/ED546618.pdf.

Chapter Four

1. Beth E. Schueler, "A Third Way: The Politics of School District Takeover and Turnaround in Lawrence, Massachusetts," *Educational Administration Quarterly* 55, no. 1 (2019): 116–53.

2. Beth E. Schueler and Martin R. West, "Federalism, Race, and the Politics of Turnaround: US Public Opinion on Improving Low-Performing Schools and Districts," *Educational Researcher* 51, no. 2 (2022): 122–33; Peter Burns, "Regime Theory, State Government, and a Takeover of Urban Education," *Journal of Urban Affairs* 25, no. 3 (2003): 285–303, https://doi.org/10.1177/0042085908322653; Steven L. Nelson, "'They're Destabilizing a Community of People': State Takeovers of Public Schools and Districts as Political Regime Change," *Washburn Law Journal* 64, no. 2 (2025): 211–48; Eve L. Ewing, "The Fight for Dyett: How a Community in Chicago Saved Its Public School," *American Educator* 43, no. 1 (2019): 30; Kristen Buras, "Race, Charter Schools, and Conscious Capitalism: On the Spatial Politics of Whiteness as Property (and the Unconscionable Assault on Black New Orleans)," *Harvard Educational Review* 81, no. 2 (2011): 296–331; Domingo Morel, *Takeover: Race, Education, and American Democracy* (Oxford University Press, 2018); Noah De Lissovoy, "Pedagogy in Common: Democratic Education in the Global Era," *Educational Philosophy and Theory* 43, no. 10 (2011): 1119–34; Noliwe Rooks, *Cutting School: Privatization, Segregation, and the End of Public Education* (New Press, 2017); Jeffrey R. Henig et al., *The Color of School Reform: Race, Politics, and the Challenge of Urban Education* (Princeton University Press, 2001); Peter Burns, "Race and Support for State Takeovers of Local School Districts," *Urban Education* 45, no. 3 (2010): 274–92, https://doi.org/10.1177/0042085908322653.

3. Lorraine M. McDonnell and Stephen M. Weatherford, "Organized Interests and the Common Core," *Educational Researcher* 42, no. 9 (2013): 488–97.

4. David M. Houston, "Polarization, Partisan Sorting, and the Politics of Education," *American Educational Research Journal* 61, no. 3 (2024): 508–40, https://doi.org/10.3102/00028312241228280; Jeffrey R. Henig, "Charter Schools in a Changing Political Landscape," in *Choosing Charters: Better Schools or More Segregation*, ed. I. Rotberg and Joshua L. Glazer (Teachers College Press, 2018), 6–23.

5. Gloria Ladson-Billings, "From the Achievement Gap to the Education Debt: Understanding Achievement in U.S. Schools," *Educational Researcher* 35, no. 7 (2006): 5, https://doi.org/10.3102/0013189X035007003.

6. Shelby County Board of Education, *Fiscal Year 2013–2014: District Budget*, May 16, 2013, https://www.scsk12.org/finance/files/2013/FY14%20PROPOSED%20v3_WEB.pdf.

7. The financial motives associated with urban school reform have been discussed in the literature. See, for example, Rooks, *Cutting School*; Brian Rowan, "The Ecology of School Improvement: Notes on the School Improvement Industry in the United States," *Journal of Educational Change* 3, no. 3 (2002): 283–314.

8. Michael T. Hartney, *How Policies Make Interest Groups: Governments, Unions, and American Education* (University of Chicago Press, 2022).

9. Jason Gonzales, "Memphis iZone Schools Outpaced State-Run Turnaround Efforts," *Tennessean*, February 17, 2016, https://www.tennessean.com/story/news/education/2016/02/17/memphis-izone-schools-outpace-state-run-turnaround-efforts/78693182/.

10. Grace Tatter, "Vanderbilt Study: iZone More Effective Than ASD in Turning around Struggling Schools Thus Far," *Chalkbeat*, December 8, 2015, https://www.chalkbeat.org/tennessee/2015/12/8/21092459/vanderbilt-study-izone-more-effective-than-asd-in-turning-around-struggling-schools-thus-far/.

11. Joshua L. Glazer et al., "Beyond Boundary Spanning: Theory and Learning in Research-Practice Partnerships," *American Journal of Education* 129, no. 2 (2023): 265–95.

12. Thanks to Clarence Stone for helping us uncover this point.

13. Eric M. Patashnik, *Reforms at Risk: What Happens after Major Policy Changes Are Enacted* (Princeton University Press, 2008).

14. David K. Cohen and James P. Spillane, "Chapter 1: Policy and Practice: The Relations between Governance and Instruction," *Review of Research in Education* 18, no. 1 (January 1992): 3–49, https://doi.org/10.3102/0091732X018001003.

Chapter Five

1. Philissa Cramer, "Seven Lessons Chris Barbic Says He Learned from Trying to Turn Around Tennessee's Lowest-Performing Schools," *Chalkbeat*, July 17, 2015, https://www.chalkbeat.org/tennessee/2015/7/17/21092295/seven-lessons-chris-barbic-says-he-learned-from-trying-to-turn-around-tennessee-s-lowest-performing/.

2. Laura Faith Kebede, "Memphis' New iZone Chief Shares His Data-Driven Plan for Fixing Struggling Schools," *Chalkbeat*, September 13, 2017, https://www.chalkbeat.org/tennessee/2017/9/13/21100925/memphis-new-izone-chief-shares-his-data-driven-plan-for-fixing-struggling-schools/.

3. This includes the five "direct-run" schools that were operated directly by the ASD.

4. Laura M. Groth, "'This Is Not a Lifetime Story': A Case Study of Organizational Growth and Learning in School Improvement" (EdD diss., The George Washington University, 2020), 133.

5. Lam D. Pham et al., *School Turnaround in Tennessee: Insights after Six Years of Reform* (Tennessee Education Research Alliance, 2019); Lam D. Pham et al., "Do the Effects Persist? An Examination of Long-Term Effects after Students Leave Turnaround Schools," *American Educational Research Journal* 62, no. 1 (2024): 180–213, https://doi.org/10.3102/00028312241284026. Pham, Lam D., Gary T. Henry, Adam Kho, and Ron Zimmer. "Sustainability and Maturation of School Turnaround: A Multiyear Evaluation of Tennessee's Achievement School District and Local Innovation Zones." AERA Open 6, no. 2 (2020): 2. https://doi.org/10.1177/2332858420922841.

6. For an excellent discussion of the potential of teacher collaboration to spur instructional improvement, see Adam Lefstein et al., "Taking Stock of Research on Teacher Collaborative Discourse: Theory and Method in a Nascent Field," *Teaching and Teacher Education* 88 (February 2020): 102954. https://doi.org/10.1016/j.tate.2019.102954.

7. Daarel Burnette II, "Shelby County Expands Education Reform Efforts amid $125 Million Shortfall," *Chalkbeat*, April 8, 2015, https://tn.chalkbeat.org/2015/4/8/21094484/shelby-county-expands-education-reform-efforts-amid-125-million-shortfall.

8. Caroline Bauman, "Lagging Enrollment Fuels Tennessee Charter Schools' Push for Student Contact Data," *Chalkbeat*, September 15, 2017, https://tn.chalkbeat.org/2017/9/15/21100928/lagging-enrollment-fuels-tennessee-charter-schools-push-for-student-contact-data.

9. Gary T. Henry et al., "Peeking into the Black Box: A Formal Test of Mediators and Suppressors," *Educational Evaluation and Policy Analysis* 42, no. 2 (April 2020): 232–56, https://doi.org/10.3102/0162373720908600.

10. Half of all urban teachers leave the profession within the first three to five years, and half of the highest-performing 20 percent leave within five years. Hamilton Lankford et al., "Teacher Sorting and the Plight of Urban Schools: A Descriptive Analysis," *Educational Evaluation and Policy Analysis* 24, no.1 (Spring 2002): 37–62, https://www.jstor.org/stable/3594146; Paul Bland et al., "Strategies for Attracting and Retaining Teachers," *Administrative Issues Journal* 4, no. 1 (April 2014): 9–18, https://dc.swosu.edu/aij/vol4/iss1/4?utm_source=dc.swosu.edu%2Faij%2Fvol4%2Fiss1%2F4&utm_medium=PDF&utm_campaign=PDFCoverPages.

11. Latanya L. Dixon et al., "Who Leads Turnaround Schools? Characteristics of Principals in Tennessee's Achievement School District and Innovation Zones," *Educational Administration Quarterly* 58, no. 2 (December 2021): 258–99, https://doi.org/10.1177/0013161X211055702.

12. Denisa R. Superville, "Principal Turnover Takes Costly Toll on Students and Districts, Report Says," *Education Week*, November 5, 2014, https://www.edweek.org/leadership/principal-turnover-takes-costly-toll-on-students-and-districts-report-says/2014/11; Rebecca Goldring and Soheyla Taie, *Principal Attrition and Mobility: Results from the 2016–17 Principal Follow-Up Survey* (National Center for Education Statistics, 2018), https://files.eric.ed.gov/fulltext/ED585933.pdf.

13. Arthur G. Powell et al., *The Shopping Mall High School: Winners and Losers in the Educational Marketplace* (Houghton Mifflin Harcourt, 1985); Jeannie Oakes, *Keeping Track: How Schools Structure Inequality* (Yale University Press, 1985), 3–14; Ray Rist, "Student Social Class and Teacher Expectations: The Self-Fulfilling Prophecy in Ghetto Education," *Harvard Educational Review* 70, no. 3 (Fall 2000): 257–301, https://faculty.washington.edu/rsoder/EDUC305/310RistHarvardEdReview.pdf; Robert Rosenthal and Lenore Jacobson, "Pygmalion in the Classroom," *Urban Review* 3 (September 1968): 16–20, https://doi.org/10.1007/BF02322211.

14. David K. Cohen and Jal D. Mehta, "Why Reform Sometimes Succeeds: Understanding the Conditions That Produce Reforms That Last," *American Educational Research Journal* 54, no. 4 (2017): 644–90, https://www.jstor.org/stable/26641619.

15. Dakid K. Cohen et al., *Improvement by Design* (University of Chicago Press, 2014); Joshua L. Glazer and Donald J. Peurach, "Occupational Control in Education: The Logic and Leverage of Epistemic Communities," *Harvard Educational Review* 85, no. 2 (2015): 172–202, https://doi.org/10.17763/0017-8055.85.2.172; Whitney M. Hegseth, "Teaching and Learning for Mutual Respect: A Framework for Disrupting Pervasive Power Asymmetries," *Educational Researcher* 53, no. 3 (2024): 175–83, https://doi.org/10.3102/0013189X241227445.

Chapter Six

1. Deborah L. Ball and David K. Cohen, "Developing Practice, Developing Practitioners: Toward a Practice-Based Theory of Professional Development," in *Teaching as the Learning Profession: Handbook of Policy and Practice*, ed. G. Sykes and L. Darling-Hammond (Jossey Bass, 1999), 30–32; Lee S. Shulman, "Those Who Understand: Knowledge Growth in Teaching," *Educational Researcher* 15, no. 2 (1986): 4–14, https://doi.org/10.2307/1175860.

2. Elliott A. Krause, *Death of the Guilds: Professions, States, and the Advance of Capitalism, 1930 to the Present* (Yale University Press, 1996); Gil Eyal, *The Crisis of Expertise* (Polity Press, 2019).

3. Andrew Abbott, *The System of the Professions: An Essay on the Division of Expert Labor* (University of Chicago Press, 1988), 51.

4. Joshua L. Glazer and Donald J. Peurach, "Occupational Control in Education: The Logic and Leverage of Epistemic Communities," *Harvard Educational Review* 85, no. 2 (2015): 172–202, https://doi.org/10.17763/0017-8055.85.2.172; Joshua L. Glazer, "Educational Professionalism: An Inside-Out View," American Journal of Education 114, no. 2 (February 2008): 169–189.

5. Dan Lortie, "The Balance of Control and Autonomy in Elementary School Teaching," in *The Semi-Professions and Their Organization: Teachers, Nurses, Social Workers*, ed. Amitai Etzioni (Free Press, 1969), 24.

6. Robert Dreeben, "Teaching and the Competence of Occupations," in *The Social Organization of Schooling*, ed. Larry V. Hedges and Barbara Schneider (Russell Sage Foundation, 2005), 51–71. See also Jal Mehta, *The Allure of Order: High Hopes, Dashed Expectations, and the Troubled Quest to Remake American Schooling* (Harvard University Press, 2013).

7. Susan L. Moffitt et al., *Reforming the Reform: Problems of Public Schooling in the American Welfare State* (University of Chicago Press, 2023), 192.

8. Moffitt et al., *Reforming the Reform*.

9. Jeffrey R. Henig and Clarence N. Stone, "Rethinking School Reform: The Distractions of Dogma and the Potential for a New Politics of Progressive Pragmatism," *American Journal of Education* 114, no. 3 (2008): 191–218; Melissa Arnold Lyon and Jeffrey R. Henig, "Blurring Lines? How Locally Based Collaborations Handle the Redistribution/Development Tradeoff," *Urban Affairs Review* 55, no. 4 (2019): 1100–24.

10. Elizabeth Grant, *Deliberative Policymaking: Redesigning How We Make Education Policy* (Harvard Education Press, 2024), 130; Susan DeJarnatt and Barbara Ferman, "Preserving Education as a Collective Good," in *The Fight for America's Schools*, ed. Barbara Ferman (Harvard Education Press, 2017), 131–46.

11. James Fallows and Deborah Fallows, *Our Towns: A 100,000-Mile Journey into the Heart of America* (Pantheon Books, 2018).

12. Beth E. Schueler, "A Third Way: The Politics of School District Takeover and Turnaround in Lawrence, Massachusetts," *Educational Administration Quarterly* 55, no. 1 (2019): 116–53.

13. Daarel Burnette II, "Philanthropic Grant for $10 Million Ensures Memphis iZone Expansion," *Chalkbeat*, September 16, 2015.

14. Jose Eos Trinidad, *Subtle Webs: How Local Organizations Shape US Education* (Oxford University Press, 2025).

15. See, for example, Faustine C. Jones-Wilson, "Race, Realities, and American Education: Two Sides of the Coin," *Journal of Negro Education* 59, no. 2 (1990): 119–28; Thomas Sowell, "Black Excellence: The Case of Dunbar High School," *Public Interest* 35 (1974): 3; Vanessa Siddle Walker, *Their Highest Potential: An African American School Community in the Segregated South* (University of

North Carolina Press, 1996); Vanessa Siddle Walker, "Valued Segregated Schools for African American Children in the South, 1935–1969: A Review of Common Themes and Characteristics," *Review of Educational Research* 70, no. 3 (2000): 253–85.

16. Vanessa Siddle Walker, "Tolerated Tokenism, or the Injustice in Justice: Black Teacher Associations and Their Forgotten Struggle for Educational Justice, 1921–1954," *Equity & Excellence in Education* 46, no. 1 (2013): 64–80; Vanessa Siddle Walker, "Ninth Annual Brown Lecture in Education Research: Black Educators as Educational Advocates in the Decades before *Brown v. Board of Education*," *Educational Researcher* 42, no. 4 (2013): 207–22.

17. Jarvis R. Givens, *Fugitive Pedagogy: Carter G. Woodson and the Art of Black Teaching* (Harvard University Press, 2021), 165.

18. Givens, *Fugitive Pedagogy*, 172.

Technical Appendix

1. This section has been synthesized from the following sources: Joshua L. Glazer and Cori Egan, "The Ties That Bind: Building Civic Capacity for the Tennessee Achievement School District," *American Educational Research Journal* 55, no. 5 (October 2018): 928–64, https://doi.org/10.3102/0002831218763088; Joshua L. Glazer et al., "Charter Schools in Turnaround: Competing Institutional Logics in the Tennessee Achievement School District," *Educational Evaluation and Policy Analysis* 41, no. 1 (March 2019): 5–33, https://doi.org/10.3102/0162373718795051; Joshua L. Glazer et al., "Opportunities and Challenges for NGOs amid Competing Institutional Logics," *Journal of Educational Administration* 57, no. 4 (May 2019): 376–92, https://doi.org/10.1108/JEA-10-2018-0191; Laura Groth et al., "Autonomy and Accountability in Turnaround Work: The Myth of Portfolio Districts and Organizational Learning," in *Enduring Myths That Inhibit School Turnaround*, ed. Coby V. Meyers and Marlene J. Darwin (Information Age, 2017), 153–71; Matthew R. Malone et al., "Leading in Complex Environments: The Role of Leadership in Multi-School Organization Improvement," *School Leadership and Management* 41, no. 4–5 (2021): 352–69, https://doi.org/10.1080/13632434.2021.1948397.

2. This section has been synthesized from the following sources: Adrian Larbi-Cherif et al., "Continuous Improvement in Urban Districts: Bringing Environments Back In," *American Journal of Education* 130, no. 3 (2024); Adrian Larbi-Cherif et al., "Emergent Analysis: Strategies for Making Sense of an Evolving Longitudinal Study," in *Analyzing and Interpreting Qualitative Data: After the Interview*, ed. Charles Vanover et al. (Sage, 2021), 295–312; Joshua L. Glazer et al., *District-Led School Turnaround: Aiming for Ambitious and Equitable Instruction in Shelby County's iZone* (Consortium for Policy Research in Education, 2020).

3. Keith Leithwood et al., "Testing a Conception of How Leadership Influences Student Learning," *Educational Administration Quarterly* 46, no. 5 (2010): 671–706; Ilana S. Horn and Judith W. Little, "Attending to Problems of Practice: Routines and Resources for Professional Learning in Teachers' Workplace Interactions," *American Educational Research Journal* 47, no. 1 (2010): 181–217; Paul Cobb et al., *Systems for Instructional Improvement: Creating Coherence from the Classroom to the District Office* (Harvard Education Press, 2018).

4. Data collection at the school and classroom level represents a significant methodological difference between the ASD and iZone studies.

Bibliography

Abbott, Andrew. *The System of Professions: An Essay on the Division of Expert Labor (Institutions). University of Chicago, 1988.*

Aldrich, Marta W. "In Memphis and Nashville, Here Are the Schools Eligible—and No Longer Eligible—for State Intervention." *Chalkbeat*, August 11, 2015. https://www.chalkbeat.org/tennessee/2015/8/11/21092359/in-memphis-and-nashville-here-are-the-schools-eligible-and-no-longer-eligible-for-state-intervention/.

American Legislative Exchange Council. *Report Card on American Education: Ranking State K-12 Performance, Progress, and Reform*. American Legislative Exchange Council, 2019. https://www.alecreportcard.org/app/uploads/2019/09/2019-ALEC-Report-Card.pdf.

Amis, John A., and Paul M. Wright. "The Antecedents and Mechanism of School District Consolidation." In *Race, Economics, and the Politics of Educational Change: The Dynamics of School District Consolidation in Shelby County, Tennessee*, edited by John M. Amis and Paul M. Wright. University of Tennessee Press, 2018.

Anderson, James D. *The Education of Blacks in the South, 1860–1935*. University of North Carolina Press, 1988.

Ball, Deborah L., and David K. Cohen. "Developing Practice, Developing Practitioners: Toward a Practice-Based Theory of Professional Development." In *Teaching as the Learning Profession: Handbook of Policy and Practice*, edited by G. Sykes and L. Darling-Hammond. Jossey-Bass, 1999.

Bauman, Caroline. "How Westhaven Elementary—Which Combined Three Schools in a New Building—May Be the New Model for Closing Schools in Memphis." *Chalkbeat*, December 19, 2016. https://www.chalkbeat.org/tennessee/2016/12/19/21100154/how-westhaven-elementary-which-combined-three-schools-in-a-new-building-may-be-the-new-model-for-clo/.

Bauman, Caroline. "Lagging Enrollment Fuels Tennessee Charter Schools' Push for Student Contact Data." *Chalkbeat*, September 15, 2017. https://tn.chalkbeat.org/2017/9/15/21100928/lagging-enrollment-fuels-tennessee-charter-schools-push-for-student-contact-data.

Berkeley, Kathleen. "The Politics of Black Education in Memphis, Tennessee, 1868–1881." In *Southern Cities, Southern Schools: Public Education in the Urban South*, edited by David N. Plank and Rick Ginsberg. Greenwood Press, 1990.

Biles, Roger. "A Bittersweet Victory: Public School Desegregation in Memphis." *Journal of Negro Education* 55, no. 4 (1986): 470–83.

Biles, Roger. "The Persistence of the Past: Memphis in the Great Depression." *Journal of Southern History* 52, no. 2 (May 1986): 183–212. https://doi.org/10.2307/2209667.

Bland, Paul, Edwin Church, and Mingchu Luo. "Strategies for Attracting and Retaining Teachers." *Administrative Issues Journal* 4, no. 1 (April 2014): 9–18. https://dc.swosu.edu/aij/vol4/iss1/4?utm_source=dc.swosu.edu%2Faij%2Fvol4%2Fiss1%2F4&utm_medium=PDF&utm_campaign=PDFCoverPages.

Bolton, Jason. "Largest Memphis-Area Employers." *Memphis Business Journal*, July 16, 2021. https://www.bizjournals.com/memphis/subscriber-only/2021/07/16/largest-memphis-area-employers.html#footnote4.

Bond, Beverly. "Educating the 'Common Man': Developing Public School Systems in Memphis and Shelby County, 1820 to 1954." In *Race, Economics, and the Politics of Educational Change: The Dynamics of School District Consolidation in Shelby County, Tennessee*, edited by John M. Amis and Paul M. Wright. University of Tennessee Press, 2018.

Bond, Beverly G., and Jannan Sherman. *Memphis: In Black and White*. Arcadia, 2003.

Bryk, Anthony S., G. Alfred Hess Jr., Jeffrey Mirel, and Kenneth Wong. "Policy Lessons from Chicago's Experience with Decentralization." *Brookings Papers on Education Policy*, no. 2 (1999): 67–127. https://www.jstor.org/stable/20067207.

Buras, Kristen. "Race, Charter Schools, and Conscious Capitalism: On the Spatial Politics of Whiteness as Property (and the Unconscionable Assault on Black New Orleans)." *Harvard Educational Review* 81, no. 2 (2011): 296–331.

Burnette, Daarel, II. "Philanthropic Grant for $10 Million Ensures Memphis iZone Expansion." *Chalkbeat*, September 16, 2015. https://www.chalkbeat.org/tennessee/2015/9/16/21092441/philanthropic-grant-for-10-million-ensures-memphis-izone-expansion/.

Burnette, Daarel, II. "School Operations, Enrichment Cut 'to the Bone,' Says Shelby County's State Funding Lawsuit." *Chalkbeat*, September 2, 2015. https://www.chalkbeat.org/tennessee/2015/9/2/21092512/school-operations-enrichment-cut-to-the-bone-says-shelby-county-s-state-funding-lawsuit/.

Burnette, Daarel, II. "Shelby County Expands Education Reform Efforts amid $125 Million Shortfall." *Chalkbeat*, April 8, 2015. https://tn.chalkbeat.org/2015/4/8/21094484/shelby-county-expands-education-reform-efforts-amid-125-million-shortfall.

Burns, Peter. "Race and Support for State Takeovers of Local School Districts." *Urban Education* 45, no. 3 (2010): 274–92. https://doi.org/10.1177/0042085908322653.

Burns, Peter. "Regime Theory, State Government, and a Takeover of Urban Education." *Journal of Urban Affairs* 25, no. 3 (2003): 285–303. https://doi.org/10.1111/1467-9906.00163.

Chubb, John E., and Terry M. Moe. *Politics, Markets, and America's Schools*. Brookings Institution Press, 1991.

Cobb, Paul, Kara Jackson, Erin Henrick, and Thomas M. Smith. *Systems for Instructional Improvement: Creating Coherence from the Classroom to the District Office*. Harvard Education Press, 2018.

Cohen, David K. "2: Politics and Research: Evaluation of Social Action Programs in Education." *Review of Educational Research* 40, no. 2 (1970): 213–38. https://doi.org/10.3102/00346543040002213.

Cohen, David K., and Jal D. Mehta. "Why Reform Sometimes Succeeds: Understanding the Conditions That Produce Reforms That Last." *American Educational Research Journal* 54, no. 4 (2017): 644–90. https://www.jstor.org/stable/26641619.

Cohen, David K., Susan L. Moffitt, and Simona Goldin. "Policy and Practice: The Dilemma," *American Journal of Education* 113, no. 4 (2007): 515–48.

Cohen, David K., Donald J. Peurach, Joshua L. Glazer, Karen E. Gates, and Simona Goldin. *Improvement by Design*. University of Chicago Press, 2014.

Cohen, David K., Stephen W. Raudenbush, and Deborah Loewenberg Ball. "Resources, Instruction, and Research." *Educational Evaluation and Policy Analysis* 25, no. 2 (Summer 2003): 119–42. http://www.jstor.org/stable/3699546.

Cohen, David K., and James P. Spillane. "Chapter 1: Policy and Practice: The Relations between Governance and Instruction." *Review of Research in Education* 18, no. 1 (January 1992): 3–49. https://doi.org/10.3102/0091732X018001003.

Colby, Susan, and Kimberly Wicoff. *Aspire Public Schools: From 10 Schools to 6-Million Kids*. Bridgespan Group, 2006. https://files.eric.ed.gov/fulltext/ED535864.pdf.

Coleman, James S., Ernest Q. Campbell, Carol J. Hobson, James McPartland, Alexander M. Mood, Frederic D. Weinfeld, and Robert L. York. *Equality of Educational Opportunity*. US Department of Health, Education, and Welfare, Office of Education, 1966.

Cramer, Philissa. "Seven Lessons Chris Barbic Says He Learned from Trying to Turn Around Tennessee's Lowest-Performing Schools." *Chalkbeat*, July 17, 2015. https://www.chalkbeat.org/tennessee/2015/7/17/21092295/seven-lessons-chris-barbic-says-he-learned-from-trying-to-turn-around-tennessee-s-lowest-performing/.

Cramer, Philissa. "Strong iZone Scores Viewed as Chance to Grow Shelby County's Turnaround Initiative." *Chalkbeat*, August 3, 2015. https://tn.chalkbeat.org/2015/8/3/21094849/strong-izone-scores-viewed-as-chance-to-grow-shelby-county-s-turnaround-initiative.

Dawson, David. "Charade on Wheels: The Tragedy of Busing." *Memphis Magazine*, May 31, 2018. https://memphismagazine.com/features/longform/charade-on-wheels-the-tragedy-of-busing/.

De Lissovoy, Noah. "Pedagogy in Common: Democratic Education in the Global Era." *Educational Philosophy and Theory* 43, no. 10 (2011): 1119–34.

Deephouse, David L., Jonathan Bundy, Leigh P. Tost, and Mark C. Suchman. "Organizational Legitimacy: Six Key Questions." In *The SAGE Handbook of Organizational Institutionalism*, edited by Royston Greenwood, Christine Oliver, Thomas B. Lawrence, and Renate E. Meyer. SAGE, 2017.

DeJarnatt, Susan, and Barbara Ferman. "Preserving Education as a Collective Good." In *The Fight for America's Schools*, edited by Barbara Ferman. Harvard Education Press, 2017.

Dixon, Latanya L., Lam D. Pham, Gary T. Henry, Sean P. Corcoran, and Ron Zimmer. "Who Leads Turnaround Schools? Characteristics of Principals in Tennessee's Achievement School District and Innovation Zones." *Educational Administration Quarterly* 58, no. 2 (December 2021): 258–99. https://doi.org/10.1177/0013161X211055702.

Dixson, Adrienne D., Kristen L. Buras, and Elizabeth K. Jeffers. "The Color of Reform: Race, Education Reform, and Charter Schools in Post-Katrina New Orleans." *Qualitative Inquiry* 21, no. 3 (2015): 288–99. https://doi.org/10.1177/1077800414557826.

Dow, Peter B. *Schoolhouse Politics: Lessons from the Sputnik Era*. Harvard University Press, 1991.

Doyle, Betsy, and Mike Perigo. "Investing in 'Teacher Town,' USA." *Stanford Social Innovation Review*, September 18, 2014. https://ssir.org/articles/entry/investing_in_teacher_town_usa#.

Dreeben, Robert. "Teaching and the Competence of Occupations." In *The Social Organization of Schooling*, edited by Larry V. Hedges and Barbara Schneider. Russell Sage Foundation, 2005.

Du Bois, W. E. B. "The Talented Tenth." In *The Negro Problem: A Series of Articles by Representative Negroes of Today*, edited by Booker T. Washington. James Pott, 1903.

Duke, Kira Virginia. "To Disturb the People as Little as Possible: The Desegregation of Memphis City Schools." Master's thesis, University of Tennessee, 2005.

Duncan, Arne. "Secretary Duncan Urges Charters to Turn Around Schools, Improve Accountability." Transcript of speech delivered at the National Charter Schools Conference, Washington, DC, June 22, 2009. https://tea.texas.gov/student-assessment/monitoring-and-interventions/school-improvement/title-i-priority-schools-grant/ttipsmodule2-transcript.pdf.

Dunn, Frederick. "The Educational Philosophies of Washington, DuBois, and Houston: Laying the Foundations for Afrocentrism and Multiculturalism." *Journal of Negro Education* 62, no. 1 (1993): 25. https://doi.org/10.2307/2295397.

Elmore, Richard F. *Building a New Structure for School Leadership*. Albert Shanker Institute, 2000. https://files.eric.ed.gov/fulltext/ED546618.pdf.

Ewing, Eve L. "The Fight for Dyett: How a Community in Chicago Saved Its Public School." *American Educator* 43, no. 1 (2019): 30–40. https://files.eric.ed.gov/fulltext/EJ1213136.pdf.

Ewing, Eve L. *Ghosts in the Schoolyard*. University of Chicago Press, 2018.

Eyal, Gil. *The Crisis of Expertise*. Polity Press, 2019.

Fallows, James, and Deborah Fallows. *Our Towns: A 100,000-Mile Journey into the Heart of America*. Pantheon Books, 2018.

Feuer, Michael J. "Fighting Racism with Mathematics." *EdFix* (podcast), May 12, 2023. Accessed October 25, 2024. https://gsehd.gwu.edu/edfix-ts-ep23.

Fishman, Barry, and Leslie R. Herrenkohl. "Equitable Learning." In *The Foundational Handbook on Improvement Research in Education*, edited by Donald J. Peurach, Jennifer Lin Russell, Lora Cohen-Vogel, and William R. Penuel. Rowman & Littlefield, 2022.

Fleming, Cynthia Griggs. "The Development of Black Education in Tennessee, 1865–1920." PhD diss., Duke University, 1977.

Frankenberg, Erica, Genevieve Siegel-Hawley, and Sarah Diem. "Segregation by District Boundary Line: The Fragmentation of Memphis Area Schools." *Educational Researcher* 46, no. 8 (2017): 449–63. https://doi.org/10.3102/0013189X17732752.

Gamoran, Adam, and Cristina M. Fernandez. "Do Charter Schools Strengthen Education in High-Poverty Urban Districts?" In *Choosing Charters: Better Schools or More Segregation?*, edited by Iris C. Rotberg and Joshua L. Glazer, 133–52. Teachers College Press, 2018.

Givens, Jarvis R. *Fugitive Pedagogy: Carter G. Woodson and the Art of Black Teaching*. Harvard University Press, 2021.

Glazer, Joshua L. "Educational Professionalism: An Inside-Out View." *American Journal of Education* 114, no. 2 (2008): 169–89. http://dx.doi.org/10.1086/524314.

Glazer, Joshua L., and Cori Egan. "The Ties That Bind: Building Civic Capacity for the Tennessee Achievement School District." *American Educational Research Journal* 55, no. 5 (October 2018): 928–64. https://doi.org/10.3102/0002831218763088.

Glazer, Joshua L., Toby Greany, Megan Duff, and William Berry. "Networked Improvement in the US and England: A New Role for the Middle Tier." In *The Foundational Handbook on Improvement Research in Education*, edited by Donald J. Peurach, Jennifer Lin Russell, Lora Cohen-Vogel, and William Penuel. Rowman & Littlefield, 2022.

Glazer, Joshua L., Laura Groth, and Blair Beuche. "Opportunities and Challenges for NGOs amid Competing Institutional Logics." *Journal of Educational Administration* 57, no. 4 (May 2019): 376–92. https://doi.org/10.1108/JEA-10-2018-0191.

Glazer, Joshua L., Diane Massell, and Matthew Malone. "Charter Schools in Turnaround: Competing Institutional Logics in the Tennessee Achievement School District." *Educational Evaluation and Policy Analysis* 41, no. 1 (March 2019): 5–33. https://doi.org/10.3102/0162373718795051.

Glazer, Joshua L., Diane Massell, Sarah Winchell Lenhoff, Adrian Larbi-Cherif, Cori Egan, James E. Taylor, Ashley Ison, Joelle Deleveaux, and Zachary Millington. *District-Led School Turnaround: Aiming for Ambitious and Equitable Instruction in Shelby County's iZone*. Consortium for Policy Research in Education, 2020.

Glazer, Joshua L., and Donald J. Peurach. "Occupational Control in Education: The Logic and Leverage of Epistemic Communities." *Harvard Educational Review* 85, no. 2 (2015): 172–202. https://doi.org/10.17763/0017-8055.85.2.172.

Glazer, Joshua L., Matthew Shirrell, Megan Duff, and Dryw Freed. "Beyond Boundary Spanning: Theory and Learning in Research-Practice Partnerships." *American Journal of Education* 129, no. 2 (2023): 265–95.

Goldfeld, Michael. "The Decline of Organized Labor: NLRB Union Certification Election Results." *Politics and Society* 11, no. 2 (June 1982): 167–205. https://doi.org/10.1177/003232928201100202.

Goldfield, David R. *Cotton Fields and Skyscrapers: Southern City and Region, 1607–1980*. Louisiana State University Press, 1982.

Goldin, Claudia, and Lawrence F. Katz. *The Race between Education and Technology*. Harvard University Press, 2009.

Goldring, Rebecca, and Soheyla Taie. *Principal Attrition and Mobility: Results from the 2016–17 Principal Follow-Up Survey*. National Center for Education Statistics, 2018. https://files.eric.ed.gov/fulltext/ED585933.pdf.

Gonzales, Jason. "Memphis iZone Schools Outpaced State-Run Turnaround Efforts." *Tennessean*, February 17, 2016. https://www.tennessean.com/story/news/education/2016/02/17/memphis-izone-schools-outpace-state-run-turnaround-efforts/78693182/.

Gordon, Hava R. *This Is Our School!: Race and Community Resistance to School Reform*. New York University Press, 2021.

Grant, Carl A., Keffrelyn D. Brown, and Anthony L. Brown. *Black Intellectual Thought in Education: The Missing Traditions of Anna Julia Cooper, Carter G. Woodson, and Alain LeRoy Locke*. Routledge, 2016.

Grant, Elizabeth. *Deliberative Policymaking: Redesigning How We Make Education Policy*. Harvard Education Press, 2024.

Green Dot Public Schools. "About Us." Accessed December 14, 2023. https://greendot.org/about/.

Groth, Laura M. "'This Is Not a Lifetime Story': A Case Study of Organizational Growth and Learning in School Improvement." EdD diss., George Washington University, 2020.

Groth, Laura M., Matthew Malone, and Joshua L. Glazer. "Autonomy and Accountability in Turnaround Work: The Myth of Portfolio Districts and Organizational Learning." In *Enduring Myths that Inhibit School Turnaround*, edited by Coby V. Meyers and Marlene J. Darwin, 153–71. Information Age, 2017.

Hardin, Robin, and Marcie Hinton. "The Squelching of Free Speech in Memphis: The Life of a Black Post-Reconstruction Newspaper." *Race, Gender, and Class* 8, no. 4 (2001): 78–95. https://www.jstor.org/stable/41674996.

Harris, Douglas N. *Charter School City: What the End of Traditional Public Schools in New Orleans Means for American Education*. University of Chicago Press, 2020.

Harris, Douglas N., and Matthew F. Larsen. *The Effects of the New Orleans Post-Katrina Market-Based School Reforms on Medium-Term Student Outcomes*. Education Research Alliance for New Orleans, 2019. https://educationresearchalliancenola.org/files/publications/Harris-Larsen-Reform-Effects-2019-08-01.pdf.

Hartney, Michael T. *How Policies Make Interest Groups: Governments, Unions, and American Education*. University of Chicago Press, 2022.

Hegseth, Whitney M. "Teaching and Learning for Mutual Respect: A Framework for Disrupting Pervasive Power Asymmetries." *Educational Researcher* 53, no. 3 (2024): 175–83. https://doi.org/10.3102/0013189X241227445.

Henig, Jeffrey R. "Charter Schools in a Changing Political Landscape." In *Choosing Charters: Better Schools or More Segregation*, edited by Iris Rotberg and Joshua L. Glazer. Teachers College Press, 2018.

Henig, Jeffrey R. "The Politics of Localism in an Era of Centralization, Privatization, and Choice." *Teachers College Record: The Voice of Scholarship in Education* 111, no. 13 (December 2009): 112–29. https://doi.org/10.1177/016146810911101130.

Henig, Jeffrey R. "Washington DC: Race, Issue Definition, and School Board Restructuring." In *Mayors in the Middle: Politics, Race, and Mayoral Control of Urban Schools*, edited by Jeffrey R. Henig and Wilbur C. Rich. Princeton University Press, 2004.

Henig, Jeffrey R., Richard C. Hula, Marion Orr, and Desiree S. Pedescleaux. *The Color of School Reform: Race, Politics, and the Challenge of Urban Education*. Princeton University Press, 2001.

Henig, Jeffrey R., and Clarence N. Stone. "Rethinking School Reform: The Distractions of Dogma and the Potential for a New Politics of Progressive Pragmatism." *American Journal of Education* 114, no. 3 (2008): 191–218.

Henry, Gary T., Lam D. Pham, Adam Kho, and Ron Zimmer. "Peeking into the Black Box of School Turnaround: A Formal Test of Mediators and Suppressors." *Educational Evaluation and Policy Analysis* 42, no. 2 (April 2020): 232–56. https://doi.org/10.3102/0162373720908600.

Henry, Gary T., Ron Zimmer, Johnathan Attridge, Adam Kho, and Samantha Viano. *Teacher and Student Migration in and out of Tennessee's Achievement School*

District. Tennessee Consortium on Research, Evaluation, and Development, 2014. https://cdn.vanderbilt.edu/vu-sub/wp-content/uploads/sites/280/2023/07/ASD_Teacher_Student_Migration.pdf.

Henry, Gary T., Ron Zimmer, Adam Kho, and Samantha Viano. *Evaluating the Impact of Tennessee's Achievement School District: 1st Annual Report to the Walton Family Foundation*. Vanderbilt University, 2015. https://cdn.vanderbilt.edu/vu-sub/wp-content/uploads/sites/280/2023/07/HenryZimmer_Walton_Y1.pdf.

Herenton, Willie W. "Memphis Inner-City School Improvement Project: A Holistic Approach for Developing Academic Excellence." *Urban League Review* 11 (1988): 209–16.

Horn, Ilana S., and Judith W. Little. "Attending to Problems of Practice: Routines and Resources for Professional Learning in Teachers' Workplace Interactions." *American Educational Research Journal* 47, no. 1 (2010): 181–217. https://trace.tennessee.edu/cgi/viewcontent.cgi?article=3224&context=utk_gradthes.

Houston, David M. "Polarization, Partisan Sorting, and the Politics of Education." *American Educational Research* 61, no. 3 (2024): 508–40. https://doi.org/10.3102/00028312241228280.

Huerta, Luis A., and Andrew Zuckerman. "An Institutional Theory Analysis of Charter Schools: Addressing Institutional Challenges to Scale." *Peabody Journal of Education* 84, no. 3 (July 2009): 414–31. https://doi.org/10.1080/01619560902973621.

Humphrey, Tom. "Common Core Controversy Heats Up." *Tennessean*, January 17, 2014. https://www.tennessean.com/story/news/politics/2014/01/12/common-core-controversy-heats-up/4425847/.

Jabbar, Huriya. "'Drenched in the Past': The Evolution of Market-Oriented Reforms in New Orleans." *Journal of Education Policy* 30, no. 6 (2015): 751–72. https://doi.org/10.1080/02680939.2015.1047409.

Jabbar, Huriya, and Joshua Childs. "Critical Perspectives on the Contexts of Improvement Research in Education." In *The Foundational Handbook on Improvement Research in Education*, edited by Donald J. Peurach, Jennifer Lin Russell, Lora Cohen-Vogel, and William R. Penuel, 241–61. Rowman & Littlefield, 2022.

Jones, Tony. "Voters Decide City Schools' Fate." *Tri-State Defender* 1, no. 8 (December 23, 2010).

Jones-Wilson, Faustine C. "Race, Realities, and American Education: Two Sides of the coin." *Journal of Negro Education* 59, no. 2 (1990): 119–28.

Kantor, Harvey, and Robert Lowe. "From New Deal to No Deal: No Child Left Behind and the Devolution of Responsibility for Equal Opportunity." *Harvard Educational Review* 76, no. 4 (2006): 474–502.

Kebede, Laura Faith. "Memphis' New iZone Chief Shares His Data-Driven Plan for Fixing Struggling Schools." *Chalkbeat*, September 13, 2017. https://www.chalkbeat.org/tennessee/2017/9/13/21100925/memphis-new-izone-chief-shares-his-data-driven-plan-for-fixing-struggling-schools/.

Kebede, Laura Faith, and Marta W. Aldrich. "Schools in Tennessee's Achievement School District Won't Start Returning to Local Control until 2024." *Chalkbeat*, September 30, 2020. https://tn.chalkbeat.org/2020/9/30/21496121/tennessee-delays-schools-exiting-asd-after-nearly-a-decade-of-no-plan.

Kebede, Laura Faith, and Marta W. Aldrich. "Tennessee's Turnaround District Gets New Leadership Team for a New Chapter." *Chalkbeat*, July 22, 2017. https://www.chalkbeat.org/tennessee/2017/7/21/21100843/tennessee-s-turnaround-district-gets-new-leadership-team-for-a-new-chapter/.

Kids Count Data Center. *Children in Poverty in Memphis*. Annie E. Casey Foundation, 2024. https://datacenter.aecf.org/data/tables/43-children-in-poverty#detailed/3/72/false/1095,2048,1729,37,871,870,573,869,36,868/any/321,322.

Kiel, Daniel. "A Memphis Dilemma: A Half-Century of Public Education Reform in Memphis and Shelby County from Desegregation to Consolidation." *University of Memphis Law Review* 41 (2010): 787.

Kiel, Daniel. *The Transition: Interpreting Justice from Thurgood Marshall to Clarence Thomas*. Stanford University Press, 2023.

Kiel, Daniel. "Two Attempts, One Fate." In *Race, Economics, and the Politics of Educational Change: The Dynamics of School District Consolidation in Shelby County, Tennessee*, edited by John M. Amis and Paul M. Wright. University of Tennessee Press, 2018.

Krause, Elliott A. *Death of the Guilds: Professions, States, and the Advance of Capitalism, 1930 to the Present*. Yale University Press, 1996.

Lacireno-Paquet, Natalie, Thomas T. Holyoke, Michele Moser, and Jeffrey R. Henig. "Creaming versus Cropping: Charter School Enrollment Practices in Response to Market Incentives." *Educational Evaluation and Policy Analysis* 24, no. 2 (Summer 2002): 145–58. https://doi.org/10.3102/01623737024002145.

Ladson-Billings, Gloria. "From the Achievement Gap to the Education Debt: Understanding Achievement in US School." *Educational Researcher* 35, no. 7 (2006): 3–12.

Lamon, Lester C. *Blacks in Tennessee, 1791–1970*. University of Tennessee Press, 1981.

Lankford, Hamilton, Susanna Loeb, and James Wyckoff. "Teacher Sorting and the Plight of Urban Schools: A Descriptive Analysis." *Educational Evaluation and Policy Analysis* 24, no.1 (Spring 2002): 37–62. https://www.jstor.org/stable/3594146.

Larbi-Cherif, Adrian, Cori Egan, and Joshua L. Glazer. "Emergent Analysis: Strategies for Making Sense of an Evolving Longitudinal Study." In *Analyzing and Interpreting Qualitative Data: After the Interview*, edited by Charles Vanover, Paul Mihas, and Johnny Saldaña. Sage, 2021.

Larbi-Cherif, Adrian, Joshua L. Glazer, and Ashley Ison. "Continuous Improvement in Urban Districts: Bringing Environments Back In." *American Journal of Education* 130, no. 3 (2024).

Lefstein, Adam, Nicole Louie, Aliza Segal, and Ayelet Becher. 2020. "Taking Stock of Research on Teacher Collaborative Discourse: Theory and Method in a Nascent Field." *Teaching and Teacher Education* 88 (February): 102954. https://doi.org/10.1016/j.tate.2019.102954.

Leithwood, Keith, Sarah Patten, and Doris Jantzi. "Testing a Conception of How Leadership Influences Student Learning." *Educational Administration Quarterly* 46, no. 5 (2010): 671–706.

Leon, Bradley. "Race to the Top and the Future of Memphis City Schools." *Smart City Memphis*, April 19, 2010. https://www.smartcitymemphis.com/2010/04/race-to-the-top-and-the-future-of-memphis-city-schools/.

Lortie, Dan C. "The Balance of Control and Autonomy in Elementary School Teaching." In *The Semi-Professions and Their Organization: Teachers, Nurses, Social Workers*, edited by Amitai Etzioni. Free Press, 1969.

Lortie, Dan C. *Schoolteacher: A Sociological Study*. University of Chicago Press, 1975.

Lyon, Melissa Arnold, and Jeffrey R. Henig. "Blurring Lines? How Locally Based Collaborations Handle the Redistribution/Development Tradeoff." *Urban Affairs Review* 55, no. 4 (2019): 1100–24.

Malone, Matthew R., Laura M. Groth, and Joshua L. Glazer. "Leading in Complex Environments: The Role of Leadership in Multi-School Organization Improvement." *School Leadership and Management* 41, no. 4–5 (2021): 352–69. https://doi.org/10.1080/13632434.2021.1948397.

Mason, Mary L., and Sarah Reckhow. "Rootless Reforms? State Takeovers and School Governance in Detroit and Memphis." *Peabody Journal of Education* 92, no. 1 (2017): 64–75. https://doi.org/10.1080/0161956X.2016.1264813.

McDonnell, Lorraine M., and Stephen M. Weatherford. "Organized Interests and the Common Core." *Educational Researcher* 42, no. 9 (2013): 488–97.

McLaughlin, Milbrey W. "Implementation as Mutual Adaptation: Change in Classroom Organization." *Teachers College Record: The Voice of Scholarship in Education* 77, no. 3 (1976): 1–9. https://doi.org/10.1177/016146817607700304.

McMillin, Zach, Jane Roberts, and Sherri Drake Silence. "Schools Dazed—Shelby County System Begins Preparations for Crafting Mega District." *Commercial Appeal*, December 22, 2010.

Mehta, Jal. *The Allure of Order: High Hopes, Dashed Expectations, and the Troubled Quest to Remake American Schooling*. Harvard University Press, 2013.

Memphis Data Hub. *Shelby County Schools Shapefile*. EGIS, 2023. https://data.memphistn.gov/dataset/Shelby-County-Schools-Shapefile/xhgg-d4u5/about_data.

Memphis Data Hub. *Shelby County Zip Codes*. EGIS, 2018. https://data.memphistn.gov/dataset/Shelby-County-Zip-Codes/98jk-gvpk/about_data.

Memphis Tech High. "Early Educators, Memphis City Schools." Accessed April 26, 2024. https://www.memphistechhigh.com/blackeducation.html.

Meyer, Heinz-Dieter, and Brian Rowan. "Institutional Analysis and the Study of Education." In *The New Institutionalism in Education*, edited by Heinz-Dieter Meyer and Brian Rowan. State University of New York Press, 2007.

Meyer, John W., and Brian Rowan. "The Structure of Educational Organizations." In *Environments and Organizations*, edited by M. W. Meyer. Jossey-Bass, 1978.

Moffitt, Susan L., Michaela Krug O'Neill, and David K. Cohen. *Reforming the Reform: Problems of Public Schooling in the American Welfare State*. University of Chicago Press, 2023.

Mommandi, Wagma, and Kevin Welner. "Shaping Charter Enrollment and Access: Practices, Responses, and Ramifications." In *Choosing Charters: Better Schools or More Segregation?*, edited by Iris C. Rotberg and Joshua L. Glazer. Teachers College Press, 2018.

Morel, Domingo. *Takeover: Race, Education, and American Democracy*. Oxford University Press, 2018.

Morel, Domingo, and Sally Nuamah. "Who Governs? How Shifts in Political Power Shape Perceptions of Local Government Services." *Urban Affairs Review* 56, no. 5(2019): 1503–28. https://doi.org/10.1177/1078087419855675.

Nelson, Steven L. "'They're Destabilizing a Community of People': State Takeovers of Public Schools and Districts as Political Regime Change," *Washburn Law Journal* 64, no. 2 (2025): 211–48.

New Leaders. "Our Approach." Accessed January 19, 2024. https://www.newleaders.org/about/approach.

New Leaders. "Our Story." Accessed January 19, 2024. https://www.newleaders.org/about/story.

New Leaders. "Our Why." Accessed January 19, 2024. https://www.newleaders.org/about/why.

Oakes, Jeannie. *Keeping Track: How Schools Structure Inequality*. Yale University Press, 1985.

Patashnik, Eric M. *Reforms at Risk: What Happens after Major Policy Changes Are Enacted*. Princeton University Press, 2008.

Penuel, William R., and Vanessa Roberts. "The Theory and Practice of Democracy and Community." In *The Foundational Handbook on Improvement Research in Education*, edited by Donald J. Peurach, Jennifer Lin Russell, Lora Cohen-Vogel, and William R. Penuel. Rowman & Littlefield, 2022.

Peurach, Donald J., David K. Cohen, Maxwell M. Yurkofsky, and James P. Spillane. "From Mass Schooling to Education Systems: Changing Patterns in the Organization and Management of Instruction." *Review of Research in Education* 43, no. 1 (2019): 32–67.

Peurach, Donald J., and Christine M. Neumerski. "Mixing Metaphors: Building Infrastructure for Large Scale School Turnaround." *Journal of Educational Change* 16, no. 4 (November 2015): 379–420. https://doi.org/10.1007/s10833-015-9259-z.

Pham, Lam D., Sean P. Corcoran, Gary T. Henry, and Ron Zimmer. "Do the Effects Persist? An Examination of Long-Term Effects after Students Leave Turnaround Schools." *American Educational Research Journal* 62, no. 1 (2024): 180–213. https://doi.org/10.3102/00028312241284026.

Pham, Lam D., Gary T. Henry, Adam Kho, and Ron Zimmer. *School Turnaround in Tennessee: Insights after Six Years of Reform*. Tennessee Education Research Alliance, 2019. https://cdn.vanderbilt.edu/vu-sub/wp-content/uploads/sites/280/2023/07/School_Turnaround_After_Six_Years.pdf.

Pham, Lam D., Gary T. Henry, Adam Kho, and Ron Zimmer. "Sustainability and Maturation of School Turnaround: A Multiyear Evaluation of Tennessee's Achievement School District and Local Innovation Zones." *AERA Open* 6, no. 2 (2020): 2. https://doi.org/10.1177/2332858420922841.

Pinkston, Will. "How Bad Actors Tried to Destroy Public Education." *Race to the Bottom*, February 2019. https://racetothebottom.us/race.html.

Pohlmann, Marcus D. *Opportunity Lost: Race and Poverty in Memphis City Schools*. University of Tennessee Press, 2008.

Pohlmann, Marcus D., and Michael P. Kirby. *Racial Politics at the Crossroads: Memphis Elects Dr. W. W. Herenton*. University of Tennessee Press, 1996.

Powell, Arthur G., Eleanor Farrar, David K. Cohen, National Association of Secondary School Principals, and National Association of Independent Schools. *The Shopping Mall High School: Winners and Losers in the Educational Marketplace*. Houghton Mifflin Harcourt, 1985.

Powell, Meili. "Orange Mound, Memphis (1890–)." *Black Past*, July 30, 2018. https://www.blackpast.org/African American-history/orange-mound-memphis-1890/.

Regional Economic Development Center. *Impact of a Special School District on Memphis and Shelby County*. University of Memphis, 2008. http://s3.documentcloud.org/documents/25614/impact-spec-school-districtlr.pdf.

Rist, Ray. "Student Social Class and Teacher Expectations: The Self-Fulfilling Prophecy in Ghetto Education." *Harvard Educational Review* 70, no. 3 (Fall 2000): 257–301. https://faculty.washington.edu/rsoder/EDUC305/310RistHarvardEdReview.pdf.

Rooks, Noliwe. *Cutting School: Privatization, Segregation, and the End of Public Education*. New Press, 2017.

Rosenthal, Robert, and Lenore Jacobson. "Pygmalion in the Classroom." *Urban Review* 3 (September 1968): 16–20. https://doi.org/10.1007/BF02322211.

Rotberg, Iris C. "Charter Schools and the Risk of Increased Segregation." *Phi Delta Kappan* 95, no. 4 (2014): 26–31. https://doi.org/10.1177/003172171409500507.

Rowan, Brian. "The Ecology of School Improvement: Notes on the School Improvement Industry in the United States." *Journal of Educational Change* 3, no. 3 (2002): 283–314.

Rushing, Wanda. "Memphis and Durable Inequality." In *Race, Economics, and the Politics of Educational Change: The Dynamics of School District Consolidation in Shelby County, Tennessee*, edited by John M. Amis and Paul M. Wright. University of Tennessee Press, 2018.

Russakoff, Dale. *The Prize: Who's in Charge of America's Schools?* Houghton Mifflin Harcourt, 2015.

Santos, Charles A. "Urban-Suburban Disparity and Geographic Stratification: A Context for Fiscal Conflict." In *Race, Economics, and the Politics of Educational Change: The Dynamics of School District Consolidation in Shelby County, Tennessee*, edited by John M. Amis and Paul M. Wright. University of Tennessee Press, 2018.

Schueler, Beth E. "A Third Way: The Politics of School District Takeover and Turnaround in Lawrence, Massachusetts." *Educational Administration Quarterly* 55, no. 1 (2019): 116–53.

Schueler, Beth E., and Martin R. West. "Federalism, Race, and the Politics of Turnaround: US Public Opinion on Improving Low-Performing Schools and Districts." *Educational Researcher* 51, no. 2 (2022): 122–33.

Scott, Janelle T. "A Rosa Parks Moment? School Choice and the Marketization of Civil Rights." *Critical Studies in Education* 54, no. 1 (2013): 5–18. https://doi.org/10.1080/17508487.2013.739570.

Shelby County Board of Education. *Fiscal Year 2013–2014: District Budget*. May 16, 2013. https://www.scsk12.org/finance/files/2013/FY14%20PROPOSED%20v3_WEB.pdf.

Shelby County Schools. *Fiscal Year 2014–15: Strategic Budget*. 2014. https://shelbycountytn.gov/DocumentCenter/View/17399/Shelby-County-Schools-2014-2015-Strategic-Budget?bidId=.

Shulman, Lee S. "Those Who Understand: Knowledge Growth in Teaching." *Educational Researcher* 15, no. 2 (1986): 4–14. https://doi.org/10.2307/1175860.

Siegel-Hawley, Genevieve, Sarah Diem, and Erica Frankenberg. "The Disintegration of Memphis-Shelby County, Tennessee: School District Secession and Local Control in the 21st Century." *American Educational Research Journal* 55, no. 4 (2018). https://doi.org/10.3102/0002831217748880.

Smith, Nelson. *Redefining the School District in Tennessee*. Thomas B. Fordham Institute, 2013.

Sowell, Thomas. "Black Excellence: The Case of Dunbar High School." *Public Interest* 35 (Spring 1974): 3–21.

Spillane, James P., Naomi L. Blaushild, Christine M. Neumerski, Jennifer L. Seelig, and Donald J. Peurach. "Striving for Coherence, Struggling with Incoherence: A Comparative Study of Six Educational Systems Organizing for Instruction." *Educational Evaluation and Policy Analysis* 44, no. 4 (2022): 567–92. https://doi.org/10.3102/01623737221093382.

State Collaborative on Reforming Education. *The State of Education in Tennessee 2011–12*. State Collaborative on Reforming Education, 2012. https://tnscore.org/wp-content/uploads/2017/02/2011-12-State-of-Education-in-TN.pdf.

Stone, Clarence N. *Changing Urban Education*. University Press of Kansas, 1998.

Stone, Clarence N., Jeffrey R. Henig, Bryan D. Jones, and Carol Pierannunzi. *Building Civic Capacity: The Politics of Reforming Urban Schools*. University Press of Kansas, 2001.

Superville, Denisa R. "Principal Turnover Takes Costly Toll on Students and Districts, Report Says." *Education Week*, November 5, 2014. https://www.edweek.org/leadership/principal-turnover-takes-costly-toll-on-students-and-districts-report-says/2014/11.

Tatter, Grace. "Vanderbilt Study: iZone More Effective Than ASD in Turning Around Struggling Schools Thus Far." *Chalkbeat*, December 8, 2015. https://www.chalkbeat.org/tennessee/2015/12/8/21092459/vanderbilt-study-izone-more-effective-than-asd-in-turning-around-struggling-schools-thus-far/.

"Tennessee Charter School Incubator Launches Fellowship." *Business Wire*, September 20, 2012.

Tennessee Department of Education. "Accountability Files: School-Level 2014." https://www.tn.gov/education/districts/federal-programs-and-oversight/data/data-downloads.html.

Tennessee Department of Education. "Assessment Files: District-Level 2014." https://www.tn.gov/education/districts/federal-programs-and-oversight/data/data-downloads.html.

Tennessee Department of Education. "Assessment Files: School-Level 2013." https://www.tn.gov/education/districts/federal-programs-and-oversight/data/data-downloads.html.

Tennessee Parents: Reclaiming Public Education for Our Children. "Is the State Manipulating Data to Give Our Public Schools to Charter Operators?" Last modified November 24, 2013. http://www.tnparents.com/our-voicesblog/is-the-state-manipulating-data-to-give-our-public-schools-to-charter-operators.

Tennessee State Government. "Tennessee Hires First Superintendent for Achievement School District." TN.gov, May 10, 2011. https://www.tn.gov/news/2011/5/10/tennessee-hires-first-superintendent-for-achievement-school-district.html.

Trinidad, Jose Eos. *Subtle Webs: How Local Organizations Shape US Education*. Oxford University Press, 2025.

Ujifusa, Andrew. "Common Core Supporters Firing Back." *Education Week*, May 14, 2013. https://www.edweek.org/teaching-learning/common-core-supporters-firing-back/2013/05.

University of Memphis. "Civil War and Reconstruction." Accessed February 19, 2024. https://www.memphis.edu/benhooks/mapping-civil-rights/civil-war-reconstruction.php.

US Chamber of Commerce. *Leaders and Laggards: A State-by-State Report Card on Educational Effectiveness*. US Chamber of Commerce, 2007. https://www.uschamber.com/assets/archived/images/2007-_us-chamber-leaders-and-laggards.pdf.

US Tennessee General Assembly. Tennessee First to the Top Act of 2010. HB 7010, SB 7005, 106th General Assembly. Introduced in House and Senate on January 12, 2010. https://wapp.capitol.tn.gov/apps/BillInfo/default.aspx?BillNumber=HB7010&GA=106.

Walker, Reagan. "Bush: Capturing the 'Education' Moment?" *Education Week*, October 19, 1988.

Walker, Vanessa Siddle. "Ninth Annual Brown Lecture in Education Research: Black Educators as Educational Advocates in the Decades before *Brown v. Board of Education*." *Educational Researcher* 42, no. 4 (2013): 207–22.

Walker, Vanessa Siddle. *Their Highest Potential: An African American School Community in the Segregated South*. University of North Carolina Press, 1996.

Walker, Vanessa Siddle. "Tolerated Tokenism, or the Injustice in Justice: Black Teacher Associations and Their Forgotten Struggle for Educational Justice, 1921–1954." *Equity & Excellence in Education* 46, no. 1 (2013): 64–80.

Walker, Vanessa Siddle. "Valued Segregated Schools for African American Children in the South, 1935–1969: A Review of Common Themes and Characteristics." *Review of Educational Research* 70, no. 3 (2000): 253–85.

Walton Family Foundation. "2015 Walton Family Foundation Grants." Accessed December 7, 2023. https://www.waltonfamilyfoundation.org/about-us/reports-financials/2015-walton-family-foundation-grants.

Watts, Micaela. "D.C. Public Schools Officials Tour Memphis iZone." *Chalkbeat*, January 13, 2016. https://tn.chalkbeat.org/2016/1/13/21098227/d-c-public-schools-officials-tour-memphis-izone.

Wells, Ida B. *Crusade for Justice: The Autobiography of Ida B. Wells*. University of Chicago Press, 2020.

Wrenn, Lynette Boney. "The Politics of Memphis School Reform, 1883–1927." In *Southern Cities, Southern Schools: Public Education in the Urban South*, edited by David N. Plank and Rick Ginsberg. Bloomsbury Academic, 1990.

Zimmer, Ron, Gary T. Henry, and Adam Kho. "The Effects of School Turnaround in Tennessee's Achievement School District and Innovation Zones." *Educational Evaluation and Policy Analysis* 39, no. 4 (December 2017): 670–96.

Zubrzycki, Jaclyn. "Green Dot Prepares to 'Transform' First School in Memphis." *Chalkbeat*, January 14, 2014. https://www.chalkbeat.org/tennessee/2014/1/14/21100186/green-dot-prepares-to-transform-first-school-in-memphis/.

Index

Tables and figures are indicated by *t* and *f* following the page number.